NORMAN TEBBIT

Upwardly Mobile

NORMAN TEBBIT

Upwardly Mobile

Norman Tebbit

WEIDENFELD AND NICOLSON
LONDON

Contents

Illustration Acknowledgements		vi
Foreword		vii
1	Escape from Ponders End	1
2	Upward and Mobile	16
3	'Unsuitable for Management'	44
4	'First, Find Your Principles...'	68
5	Back Bencher	91
6	Ted Heath's Road to Disaster	114
7	The Gang of Four	135
8	Into the Cabinet	164
9	On to the Second Term	197
10	Trade and Industry	212
11	Brighton and After	225
12	Chairman of the Party	243
Index		270

Illustration Acknowledgements

The photographs in this book are reproduced by kind permission of:

courtesy of Garland 11 below; Michael Heath, courtesy the London Evening Standard 12 above; Johnston, courtesy the London Evening Standard 12 below; JAK, courtesy the London Evening Standard 8; courtesy of Ken Gill 5 below; London News Service 9 below; Press Association 10, 14; S & G Press Agency 13 above; Smith's Dock Ltd 5 above; Syndication International 7, 11 above, 13 below, 15, 16.

Foreword

Upwardly Mobile is a story of one man's life through almost sixty years of Britain's history. It is not a history of those years, nor even of the years I spent as a Cabinet Minister. All of that has been – and, no doubt, will be further – chronicled from many differing points of view. My account is unashamedly subjective. It is as much about how events affected me as about how I affected events and in general does not deal with events in which I played little or no part.

In short it is a biography. It has allowed me to say some things and tell of some events hitherto not well known, but it is not a 'kiss and tell' tale nor a plea of self-justification or for sympathy. It had no coded messages, nor is it written to 'even old scores'.

If it has a political message at all it is the message of the Thatcher revolution. It is a revolution that deserves the name, for, whatever contribution others may have made, the revolution of the last decade is Mrs Thatcher's. It might have happened without her – I doubt it – but it certainly would not have come so far, so quickly, so soon – nor have so far yet to go.

My thanks are due to an understanding publisher, to Michael Trend for his researches, to John Torode of the *Independent* who set out to write a biography of me and generously allowed me the use of a series of tapes of our conversations about his projected book, and above all to Beryl Goldsmith, my secretary, who transcribed every word of my handwritten story.

This book is dedicated to my wife. She has paid a high price for my life in politics. I hope that the story she has allowed me to tell of her courage will give courage and understanding to others.

I

Escape from Ponders End

Whatever control we may have over the time, place or manner of our departure from this world, we have no influence at all over our arrival.

The 29th of March 1931 was not the best time to be born. The great Depression had still not burned itself out and war was only eight years away. And Ponders End, a poor North London suburb in the Lea Valley, was hardly the best place either.

The fortunes of my family seemed modestly encouraging at the time of my birth. My father, Leonard, was assistant manager of a jeweller's and pawnbroker's, sufficiently well paid to be buying his house, to own a motorcycle and sidecar, and even to have domestic help for my mother.

The Tebbits were East Anglian farmers but, as a younger son, my grandfather saw little opportunity on the family farm. Perhaps in any case his talents were not agricultural as, when he came to Enfield, then still a small town in Middlesex, he set up in business as a sign-writer and supplier of oils, colours and paints. In a family photograph he appears as a slim good-looking young businessman, but sadly he died young. In 1901 he was tipped out of his pony trap in a London traffic accident, contracted pneumonia, which complicated his injuries, and died soon after. My grandmother was left to bring up my father, then aged five, his sister and five brothers. A determined and tough woman, who lived well into her nineties, she turned to retail trade running a sweet shop to keep her children until, in her old age, they cared for her.

As Europe erupted into the First World War in 1914 my father was eighteen years old and, together with his younger brother, Arthur, he joined the Middlesex Regiment and soon found himself in France. They both survived the war, being demobilised when still private soldiers in 1919. They remained close to each other until my father's death in 1975.

Arthur remained a bachelor until after the death of my grandmother, with whom he lived and for whom he cared until she died, but in 1926 my father, by then a young trainee jewellery and pawnbroking shop manager, married my mother Edith. She was a daughter of Sam Stagg, a local butcher who lived above the shop nearby.

The Staggs, like the Tebbits, were recent arrivals in London. Although my mother was born in Holloway, her family had its roots in Yeovil in the West Country, where they had been merchants and excisemen for many generations. Sam Stagg was short and thickset, a practical man of firm views. As a child, and indeed as a man, I had great affection for him and I loved to hear my mother recount stories of him in his young and impetuous days.

Marvellous tales they were too, often involving him in brawls, though always in a good cause! Before the First World War he led the local tradesmen of Ponders End in running out of town a group of atheists who had caused outrage by their preachings – not least on Sundays. I had the impression that it was love of a good fight, as much as piety or love of God, that led my grandfather to organise the barrage of bad eggs thrown by local shop boys which preceded the swift attack and the ducking in a nearby horse trough. He was a jaunty and fearless man. Like most butchers in those days he slaughtered his own animals, pole-axing cattle (a potentially hazardous business if bungled), and on occasions laid out obstreperous drunks who had misguidedly wandered into his shop to tease his wife or my mother.

When the lease of his shop expired he unwisely left the trade he knew and became a publican, running an inn in a small Hertfordshire village. It was not a successful venture and he eventually took a job in an abattoir in the new town of Letchworth, where he lived until his death in 1966.

Like so many families, mine was hit by the economic troubles of the late twenties and early thirties. My father lost his job soon after I was born and the motorbike, the house and most possessions of any value were soon gone. There followed a series of moves, always going down-market, looking for cheaper accommodation around Ponders End and Edmonton.

I particularly remember living in part of a huge old Victorian villa in Church Street, Edmonton, the remainder being ocupied by an extra-ordinary family, the Wartons. They turned their hands to almost any-thing but their basic trade was the manufacture of tennis rackets. To this day I can recollect the smell of glue, usually boiling in cans (or over the sides of cans) on gas stoves in the basement. The house was demolished long ago and, not inappropriately perhaps, the site is now occupied by a fire station.

From that house we moved on to live in the top half of a small three-bedroomed house in Bury Street, Edmonton. My mother cooked on a gas stove on the landing and we shared the bathroom with the family living downstairs. I am not sure whether that was the lowest ebb of our family fortunes or whether it was just that by then I was more aware of what was happening, but life was far from easy.

My father (with the help of his bike which became famous many years later!) set out each day looking for work. The building industry was leading the recovery from the 1931 slump and he found work as a house painter. As with most painters at that time he was a self-trained casual worker on piece-work. Often the work came through his brothers Sydney and Alfred, the latter a much loved uncle, hunchbacked from a malformed spine, but always full of fun and generosity.

At the best of times it was a precarious, bare living supplemented by my mother's small earnings from domestic work for a comfortably-off schoolteacher. The teacher treated me kindly and until starting school I loved going with my mother when she went to work. The garden round their house at Wellington Road – the smart part of Bush Hill Park – seemed huge. The dahlias, among the first flowers I knew by name, were taller than I was. The lawn, on which I once suffered the mishap of sitting on a bee, seemed vast, and even being stung had its good side, winning a great deal of sympathy and chocolate biscuits. The house was full of delights, even a train set with which I was allowed to play. It was well worth the walk, which these days would be deemed unacceptable for teenagers, let alone a four-year-old. In contrast starting school seemed rather dull; but things were soon to change.

As rising international tension increased the pace of rearmament my father found regular work as a clerical officer at the Royal Small Arms Factory at Enfield. My earliest jumbled recollections of events outside my own family stem from that time – of people talking about Hutton's record innings of 365 against Australia and Neville Chamberlain returning from his negotiations in Munich with Adolf Hitler. Even so the biggest event in my own life that year was the birth of my younger brother Peter. It came as a surprise to Arthur, my older brother, and me to be told that we were to have a younger brother or sister – as it did, too, I suspect, to my parents. Not only did it mean another mouth to feed and more overcrowding of the three small rooms in which we lived, but my mother was already thirty-seven years old and suffered from high blood pressure, necessitating an early and extended confinement in hospital which added to the dismay we felt.

However, the year had its successes for us too. I learned to ride a bicycle, taught by Arthur using a neighbour's bike, and rode up and down the alley which ran behind the gardens of the houses in Bury Street. Arthur, for his part, passed his eleven-plus examination and started at the Edmonton County Grammar School only a couple of hundred yards from home. I missed his company at the Raglan Road primary school. A friendly elder brother was a great comfort to a child as shy and unsure of himself as I then was. Not that school was unfriendly. Not even on the day which sticks in my mind when, having committed some misdemeanour (talking in class, I think), I was sent to collect the cane from the headmaster's study only to be redirected to my brother's classroom where it was already in use. I arrived there in time to be told to wait a moment until my brother had received his punishment. He and I agreed that this double punishment was not a matter about which we had to bother our parents.

Childhood memories are a jumble dominated for me by happier events, which in retrospect emphasise what these days would be seen as a life of material deprivation.

I remember so clearly one Guy Fawkes night in about 1937 or 1938. It started with Arthur and me being allowed to watch other people's fireworks soaring over the roofs into the night sky, whilst we bravely held a few sparklers and waved them out of our open bedroom window. Then it culminated in sheer delight when Uncle Syd arrived with a *box* of fireworks which we lit in the garden. Many people were very kind to us, our neighbours over the road, the Collins family, who once took me on a day-outing to the seaside at Southend. It is hard these days to think back to a time when a day at Southend was an incredible adventure from which a child would return proud and excited at having actually seen the sea!

Sweets or chocolates were real treats associated with visits from popular uncles, and a childhood marred first by my father's unemployment and then by war-time rationing is perhaps partly responsible for my keen interest in food today!

Happily my mother was a good traditional cook and even as a small child I learned how to shop, usually on Saturday night at Edmonton market just before the stalls were closing. Lacking refrigeration – let alone freezers – the stallholders were always anxious to clear their stocks of perishable goods, and the bargaining between hard-up customers and stallholders rose in a crescendo as the evening drew on.

By the summer of 1939 I became aware of the threat of war. My parents, and my elder brother, listened more intently to the news on the wireless. I listened to the talk of my elders and tried to fit it together and understand what it was all about. Although we hardly had a book in the house my reading already extended to newspaper headlines, comics, magazines and library books like *Biggles* from which I had gained an impression of the First World War. I knew who Hitler and Chamberlain were and was held by the same tension which gripped the whole country during that fateful weekend over which our ultimatum to Germany expired. We had a wireless set and listened together to Neville Chamberlain's sombre broadcast telling the world that our ultimatum had been ignored and in consequence Britain and Germany were at war. I went at once to the window, peering out to see in what way Bury Street and the Cambridge Road had changed, coming away puzzled and perhaps disappointed that it looked just the same as it had in peacetime.

I did not have long to wait before the war began to change our lives. The sequence of events is muddled in my memory into a whirl of collecting gas masks (including a sort of gasproof tent for the baby), ration books and identity cards, sticking glued brown paper strips on the windows and putting up black-out curtains. Suddenly the streets were dark at night and sandbag walls began to appear protecting vulnerable doors at school. Even more worrying and mysterious was the talk of evacuation. There was great fear of devastating air raids, and the evacuation of children was being swiftly organised. Every effort was made to keep brothers and sisters together and before long I found myself attached to Arthur, as his younger brother, when his grammar school organised its evacuation to Wales. We assembled early in the day in the school playground. Arthur in school uniform and I in my suit and open-necked shirt, identity labels firmly tied to us. Our gas masks in their cardboard boxes were strung around our necks, and on our backs we carried canvas knapsacks containing our changes of clothing, flannels, toothbrushes, and a few precious toys. In our hands we clutched packets of sandwiches for the long journey ahead.

I cannot remember saying goodbye to my parents – I suppose we must have done but we were an unemotional family and I doubt if there were any tears. I suspect Arthur was none too pleased at having his 'kid' brother attached to him and I was determined not to make things worse by letting him down and blubbing in front of his friends. Anyway, what was there to blub about – our life in Edmonton was not so great and things in Wales might be better!

Paddington Station was full of noise and bustle. I had never been on a train and the smoke and steam from the great locomotives was even more exciting than I had expected. The journey itself, although it became boring as hour followed hour, was illuminated with such moments of adventure as the passage through the Severn Tunnel bringing us into Wales.

At last we stood on the platform. Great queues of evacuees were confronted by great queues of prospective foster-parents, eyeing each other up and down across a few feet of pavement and great gulfs of class, culture and geography. Somehow we all found billets though by what process I have never known. Arthur and I seemed to have fallen on our feet being assigned to, or chosen by, an older couple (to us they seemed *very* old) whose son had already left to serve in the Royal Navy. They were retired, and obviously well off, living in a pleasant part of the Cardiff suburb of Llandaff and employing a maid-cook. The latter soon became the victim of our blackmail as we discovered that she had a horror of snakes. London proles that we were, we soon discovered the differences between grass snakes, slow worms and adders and, by passing off as vipers the harmless varieties, gained excessive influence in the kitchen. We were fascinated by such exotica as the framed and illustrated certificate that bore witness to our foster-father having held the bardic chair at an eisteddfod, and we were entranced by the Welsh which they often spoke. Since that was clearly a device to avoid us understanding what was being said we rapidly began to pick up a few words ourselves.

However, we did not stay long with them. Whether it was that they found us too noisy, or that the maid could not stand the snakes, or that my habit of climbing on to the chair in which our foster-father enjoyed his post-lunch nap in order to raid the top shelves of his bookcase was too much to bear, I do not know. In any event we were transferred to the care of the Greenaways, a much more modest household not far away in Llandaff. They too were kindly folk, much younger with children even younger than us. Mr Greenaway was, I think, either medically unfit or in a reserved occupation but he took his duties in Civil Defence most seriously and it was not long before they became all too real. We were in Cardiff during the Battle of Britain – a fact that I as a Londoner have always regretted – and we saw only a few of the daylight air battles over Cardiff. However, that winter saw some more serious night raids. Children adapt to almost anything and I soon learned to sleep through guns and bombs, waking only to enquire if there was any nearby damage worth going to see. I recollect walking one morning to see the smouldering ruin of Llandaff Cathedral, its outer walls festooned in ice from the hoses still being played on the smouldering timbers of the collapsed roof. Only a few nights later a sea mine dropped by parachute landed, not as intended in the approach to Cardiff Harbour, but in my school playing-field a few moments walk from our house. For us and our neighbours that meant midnight evacuation and a temporary billet in a church hall. That was a great adventure, made even more exciting by our skilful evasion of a police cordon, which allowed a quite close examination of the mine itself sitting menacingly half covered by its drab olive parachute before we were spotted by the bomb disposal crew and shooed away.

Such adventures did not impress our parents. If we were to be bombed then it seemed to them that we might as well be bombed as a family, so we returned first to stay for a while with our grandparents in Letchworth and then, not least to achieve stable schooling, back home to Enfield. By then, I had attended five different schools, a record qualifying children today for 'deprived' status. I sometimes reflect that it was possible in those days for a teacher to achieve a hundred per cent literacy amongst classes of forty to fifty children, often with two schools sharing one set of school buildings on a shift system, whereas today a class of thirty is too much to manage and literacy may take second place to learning 'life skills' or racial awareness.

In 1941 back in London, life resumed almost as normal. Whilst we had been away our parents had moved to a house a few doors from that of my father's mother and his brother Arthur, in the street next to that in which I had been born. It was a small terraced house, originally three-bedroomed but one bedroom had been turned into a bathroom with a huge smelly, noisy and inefficient gas-fired geyser, and its only w.c. was across the yard outside. However, at least we no longer shared with any other family. The rubble of the bombed houses opposite to ours had been cleared away and we took over their gardens 'digging for victory' and growing vegetables to supplement scarce supplies from the shops. Like my class mates I eagerly collected the spent cartridge cases from the guns of our fighters, and fragments of anti-aircraft shells which fell into the streets. From time to time I picked my way to school through the porridge of broken glass, debris and water from fire hoses or shattered water pipes in the aftermath of air-raids.

Perhaps it was partly having fallen in love with the countryside or just the effects of being away from home, but neither Arthur nor I found an easy relationship with our parents – or, more particularly, with our father. Our horizons were broadening rapidly and his seemed narrow and dull. My first escape was into books – books often totally unsuitable.

I think I had read all Leslie Charteris's 'Saint' books by the time I was eleven, as well as P. G. Wodehouse, much of H. G. Wells and a lot of natural history. My other escape was simply to get out of our drab house and its drab street. It was drab indoors, the bricks were grey, the slate roofs dark grey – even the gardens seemed grey. I could see the sun neither rise nor set – or indeed any horizon beyond the lines of houses behind or in front of ours.

Walking had its limitations – I often walked either on my own or with my brother to Chingford where, at the end of Station Road at the edge of Epping Forest (just about where my constituency Conservative Association now has its offices), there was a wonderful model shop. I spent many hours indoors model making, mostly Second World War aircraft. Another escape was provided by my Uncle Arthur, who from time to time invited me to go with him for the day in his ballast lorry. That was a real adventure, often going into central London to load up with bomb debris, dumping that and bringing back sand and ballast from the Hertfordshire quarries and pits. The lorry was noisy, dirty and hot, grinding its way slowly up the hills, banging, bouncing and thumping down. But there was always something new around the next corner or over the next hill. The shared sandwiches and the strong sweet tea from my uncle's thermos flask or even a snack in the lorry drivers' cafés were a peep into an adult world.

School too was a welcome escape from home, and after a year of regular schooling at Bush Hill Park elementary school in 1942 I passed the eleven-plus examination. I did well enough to be offered a choice of local grammar schools, including the élite Enfield Grammar, but out of perversity, shyness or insecurity opted to follow my brother to Edmonton.

Grammar school stimulated my desire to discover how the world worked. I lapped up all that my teachers could offer, and was forever torn between the attractions of history and English on the one hand and science, particularly biology, on the other. In retrospect I fancy that it was the quality and personality of my teachers as much as my natural talents that guided and developed my interests. Most teachers were in the armed services at that time but, as my school was for both girls and boys, the female teaching staff was quite strong and the men, although lacking youth – other than those who were unfit for armed service – had experience and remarkable enthusiasm. They will live forever in my mind: Mr Comber who kindled my love of biology, Miss Emery, Miss Henderson and George 'Gussy' Locke who recognised in me a wordsmith and encouraged me to write and to widen my reading, and the long-suffering Miss Staples who struggled to eliminate the mixture of London, Hertfordshire and Welsh accents which permeated my French. But perhaps it was Miss Rudwick who in teaching me the history of Europe from 1830 to 1914 most excited my mind and may have set me on the path to politics.

By 1942, when I started at grammar school, it was clear that Germany was unable to invade Britain and would not therefore win the war. But even with the Americans fighting alongside us there seemed no end to it in sight. Air-raids continued sporadically, and rationing, shortages and queues were part of life. We fattened chickens in a shed in the garden to eke out our meat ration, and in the winter walked the mile and a half to the local gas works with our younger brother's old pram, and waited in the long queue to buy a sack of coke to supplement our coal ration.

As the war approached its end with the invasion of France so Hitler's V weapons made their final assault on London. First the V1s – flying bombs, with the strange unmistakable note of the pulse jet engines and the sudden urgent menace of the silence as the engine stopped and the missile began its final plunge. At such moments the scramble for cover could be unseemly. Our own house was damaged by a nearby V1 and the miserable routine of broken nights dragged on. Then came the V2s. Being supersonic they had the virtue of arrival without warning, so making me somewhat fatalistic. There was a grim satisfaction to be had from the awful retribution of our bombing raids and particularly, during the approach to D-Day, in the streams of bombers heading towards Europe. Day after day we saw the Lancasters, the Halifaxes and Stirlings – the last often quite low – outbound in the evenings just before dusk, soon after the American B17s had returned. Then as the RAF returned so the Americans were on their way on the daylight raids. Despite news censorship we were aware of the terrible losses we sustained – all too rarely did 'all our aircraft return safely'.

I vividly remember cycling with my grandfather to Bassingbourne, a US Air Force base, to see the bombers return. Following the main formation there always came the stragglers, some on three engines, some on even fewer, others with huge holes in wings and fuselage or missing bits of tail, crunching on to the runway like great wounded animals.

The war was a fact of life with which we lived and throughout my childhood from eight or nine years of age I assumed that my turn would come to fight. Unattracted by the sea or the miseries of trench life which my father had experienced, I decided I would join the RAF to fly, and another part of my future life began to be shaped.

In the meantime my quest for escape from the dreary limitations of home continued.

I had to have my own transport and that meant a bicycle. There were few to be had during the war, and those in the shops were 'utility bikes', depressing black-enamelled sit-up-and-beg bikes which sold for fifteen or sixteen pounds – something like two hundred pounds today. There was only one answer. I had to earn money.

I followed the traditional route and got a job delivering newspapers. Soon I had a morning round, then the Thursday evening delivery of local papers, the *Radio Times* and weekly magazines, and in addition I collected the weekly bills on Sunday mornings.

Eventually, despite being called upon to make a contribution to our always depressed family finances, I saved enough to buy a good secondhand frame, some expensive chromium-plated handlebars and wheels, a saddle and other bits and pieces to assemble what became a very good bicycle.

During my early years of grammar school my older brother's three and a half years' seniority began to draw us apart and soon he was at work and a member of the Air Training Corps awaiting his call-up. I was more than ever a 'kid' brother still at school. Nor did I have much to do with my young brother Peter – the gulf of seven years was too wide to be bridged in my teens. My days were spent at school and whenever the weather allowed I used my bicycle as an escape. Together with my school friends I began to explore the Hertfordshire and Essex countryside, often covering sixty or seventy miles and sometimes a hundred in a day. Not only that but in the weekday evenings my social calendar began to include some of the girls from school too.

As the war ground towards its end the papers began to talk of the post-war reconstruction. I was an avid reader of the papers and news magazines like *Picture Post* and *The Sphere* and the *Illustrated London News*, spending a fair proportion of my earnings on them. What is more, my political views had begun to take shape. Mainly by intuition I came to believe in what we would now call Capitalist non-interventionist economic theories and to discard completely the fashionable paternalistic and socialist doctrines of the mid-1940s. So even at fourteen years of age I had conceived a distrust of Socialism and a sympathy with the liberal free-market views which, unknown to me, Professor Hayek was expressing in *The Road to Serfdom* – a book I was not to read for almost forty years.

Eventually VE day came, the blackout was ended and there was no more need to draw the light-proof curtains every evening. Street lights came on and shop windows were lit. At hundreds of thousands of street parties bonfires blazed, giving a glow to the night sky last seen during the blitz. I felt a profound sense of relief at the prospect of sleeping again without fear of the bombs or the rockets and thankfulness at having survived. The war against Japan was not forgotten but it was far away and the outcome was inevitable, and our minds turned towards peace and reconstruction – and that meant politics.

The great wartime coalition came to an end, Churchill forming the caretaker Government in preparation for the 1945 election. I attended every local meeting I could, firm in my support for Bartle-Bull in Enfield and Squadron Leader Sparrow in Edmonton. In the event, like the Churchill Government, both were defeated, as I was, in my first election standing at school as the Conservative candidate for form IIIS.

Shortly after this, the first nuclear weapon was exploded over Hiroshima on 6 August 1945. The news was accompanied in the papers with the shattering photographs of the huge mushroom cloud of smoke and debris. I found it hard to grasp the significance of the event but only three days later the second hammer blow fell on Nagasaki. Japanese resistance ended, the war was over and British politics really entered the post-war period.

My interest in politics was increasing, despite the shadow of school examinations to come, and as I saw the programme of the Labour Government unfold I became more fiercely convinced that Socialism was bound to fail and that in its failure it might well turn towards the authoritarianism which was spreading over East Europe. As I reached my fifteenth birthday I joined the newly formed Young Conservatives. The nearest branch, a couple of miles away at the upmarket end of Enfield, was often derided as The Ridgeway Social Club – The Ridgeway then being the most exclusive road in the town. I was not only from a different social background but I was much younger than most of the other members. The secretary of the branch, Colin Turner, was some ten years older than me and from a very different family background, and further distanced by his RAF war service as a navigator during which he had reached the rank of Squadron Leader and won his DFC. Yet it was he who made the effort to bridge the gap and bring the still shy and awkward schoolboy that I was into the mainstream of the activities of the branch. I was soon elected to the committee and sent as a representative to area and national YC meetings and political school weekends. Colin was not alone in his kindness but his later intervention, after I had completed my national service, was to change the course of my life.

I quickly gained confidence, and a few other stalwarts from the otherwise staunchly working-class Labour side of Enfield helped to establish a YC branch in Ponders End. My status as a branch officer gave me a role in the procedures to select a new prospective parliamentary candidate for Enfield. Inexperienced as I was, I recognised one outstanding applicant, a young, recently demobilised Army officer called Iain Macleod. Luckily the Conservative Association was of my view and Iain was adopted as prospective candidate for Enfield, and after the redistribution which split the constituency into Enfield East and West, he fought and won the Enfield West seat in 1950 to begin his remarkable parliamentary career. Sadly it overlapped mine by only a few months before his tragic death shortly after the 1970 General Election.

As I approached my General Schools and Matriculation examinations (broadly the equivalent of O levels or GCSE today) I decided that like my elder brother I should not go on into the sixth form but leave school at sixteen. I cannot recollect ever discussing it with my parents and although I had played with the idea of going to a university I was uncertain of what that entailed or what I would read. I was becoming less attracted to science and contemplated law but was well aware that my failure to have studied Latin was an obstacle. It was not the first nor the last time in my life that I felt the lack of advice of anyone whose experience extended beyond the restricted society of my family. I suppose that I drifted into leaving school more because of a lack of awareness of the alternatives than anything else.

My father's job at the Royal Small Arms Factory had ended with the war and he had returned to his original occupation as a retail salesman, this time managing a menswear shop in Wood Green. At his invitation I became an extra Saturday saleshand earning a useful ten shillings (around £5 or £6 in today's money). The finances of my family, however, were as precarious as usual and I was expected to contribute to, rather than continue to be supported by, our limited means.

Although my class mate Jack Pearce and I discussed our hopes and ambitions I hardly dared to admit to myself, let alone even to him as my closest friend, that I had aleady begun to think of a life in politics. To confess to such an unlikely ambition would have been to invite derision. The Conservative Party was far from exclusively 'top drawer' but there was then hardly a single Tory MP who had not been educated at public school. Although there had been a sprinkling of working-class Tory Members over the years they were certainly a rare breed indeed. Nonetheless I began to think of what sort of career might lead me to Westminster. The law was clearly one, but that route seemed barred.

Journalism was another. I knew I could write – indeed the only school prize I ever won was that for the year's best short story – and I realised that it was a dog-eat-dog world in which ability, luck and drive could outweigh the advantages of birth and education.

My teachers warned me I was up against long odds, especially as I had set my heart on a job in Fleet Street, not on a local paper. However, the long shot came up and within a week of leaving school in July 1947 I started work in the prices room at the *Financial Times* at a salary of two pounds two and sixpence a week. Like much of Britain in the 1940s the *FT* seemed intent on getting back first to prewar days before moving on into the next decade. The war had left great gaps, most tragically the loss of some of the best of the generation born immediately after the First World War. The fabric of London and many other cities had suffered severely, and on the roads the loss of six years' car production sharpened the distinction between car owners (themselves very much a minority group). You were either an owner of a pre-war vehicle (six years old or more) or a post-war car. Rationing continued and many socialists favoured permanent rationing to ensure a 'fair' allocation of food and clothing. Indeed it was extended after the war when bread and potatoes were rationed for the first time. As a result there was a thriving black market. Freed from the wartime odium of profiteering, it rapidly became acceptable to buy clothing or sweet coupons and 'points' coupons for luxuries such as tinned food. In mind-boggling detail, absurd restrictions laid down specifications for 'utility' clothing and furniture, and permits were needed to carry on almost every aspect of business life. All this convinced me more strongly than ever of the virtues of a market economy.

Nor was it to be long before I had my first personal encounter with the trades union movement.

My ambition was to become a journalist but the *FT* still held fast to the pre-war system of bringing in promising youngsters through the prices room or library and on through reporting and sub-editing to feature or leader writing.

In the prices room I became the most junior of a team of two pre-national service youngsters and one just returned from his two-year stint. We collated the closing stock market prices brought back each afternoon, then prepared and sent them down to the printers. Despite our inexperience and lack of formal training we also calculated the stock market indices. They were far fewer in those days – the Industrial Ordinary (the 30 share index), the Gilts and Gold Share indices – and without the benefit of computers we used logarithms and a wheezy clattering hand-powered adding machine.

I can only recollect one occasion when this rather basic system failed. It was a day of particularly heavy and hectic trading so it was no surprise that the index rose sharply. On the following day of quiet trading with hardly any movements we discovered to our horror the error of the previous day. The index should have been two points lower! We decided to say nothing and to ease the index down a fraction at a time as conditions permitted. With life's usual perversity we encountered more than a week of quiet trading with the market mostly firm, during which the FT Ordinary Share Index inched its way slowly down. Somehow we managed to fob off enquirers with technical gobbledegook until, to our great relief, the index was right again.

Whether in ignorance of our error and cover up, or perhaps because of it, I was then asked by the Markets Editor, Mr Shillady, to reconstitute the Gold Share index. This had not been done since before the war and over the years a number of its constituent companies had been taken over or simply gone out of business. The increasing number of 'dead' shares left the index unrepresentatively stable in a volatile market. I had no instructions, nor advice, beyond a list of the shares to make up the index and an injunction to ensure that the transition from the existing index to the revised one should be smooth and hopefully imperceptible even to those who followed it closely.

Starting from first principles and what advice and help I could get, I constructed the new logarithmatically based index which to my relief behaved itself perfectly during its trial period and was then substituted for the old index.

I have often wondered since how many graduate statisticians, market specialists and computers would be needed for a similar operation today!

Our hours of work set us apart from the humdrum world of clerks and other office workers. We started at 11 a.m. and worked until our part of the paper was complete and 'sent to bed'. We enjoyed ourselves, we were noisy and enthusiastic, particularly after lunchtime visits to the city pubs. Fortunately the news-tape machines outside our office were old and noisy, drowning our chatter and frequent bawdy or obscene shouts and even occasional songs. Our more senior members enjoyed the privilege, which I soon shared, of compiling short paragraphs on the more interesting share movements, and better still composing head-lines for them. The main aim in writing a heading was to achieve an obscene, or at least doubtful, meaning sufficiently ambiguous to get past the watchful eye of the sub-editors. The best examples from many years past covered the walls of the office but in an act of sheer corporate vandalism were destroyed by the office decorators over a bank holiday.

However, none of these functions qualified me as a journalist, and the *FT* operated a union closed shop so I became a reluctant and hostile conscript to the ranks of NATSOPA. I had no interest in the printing trades, and was being paid well over the NATSOPA negotiated pay scales. What is more, as I read the union rulebook I was outraged at the blatant unfairness of the rules which provided for the 'fining' or even expulsion (and thus loss of job) of those with the temerity to 'bring the union into disrepute' by such conduct as criticism of its officials. NATSOPA paid dearly for bullying a sixteen-year-old boy into its ranks. I swore then that I would break the power of the closed shop, an ambition I finally achieved thirty-five years later.

I spent only two years at the *FT* but almost every day had some element of fun as I grew up and widened my experience of life. In my city suit I looked older than my years and I began to enjoy drinking good bitter ale. I played a fuller part in the local Young Conservatives and, not least with the prospect of national service in mind, my interest in aviation deepened.

Even on my modest pay I had a great deal of fun. A new bicycle was well used. I enjoyed two holidays on the Norfolk Broads and will be forever thankful that I saw that lovely place before a surfeit of people destroyed so much of its unique character and charm. And my fascination with speed was gratified by seeing the first post-war British Grand Prix. Nostalgia it may be, but I think that those early post-war racing years were more exciting and interesting by far than today's.

Despite a long-standing friendship with one girl from my schooldays I preferred male to female company. My first Broads holiday, in fact my first real holiday, was with Jack Pearce and another schoolfriend. After many lunchtime visits to the office of 'Blakes Holidays Afloat' near the Law Courts in the Strand and hours of debate over their catalogue we hired a three-berth motor cruiser. Petrol was rationed so our range was limited but I can still recapture the memory of mooring for the night without another boat in sight and waking to the loveliness of the early morning sun breaking through the mist over the great reed beds.

2

Upward and Mobile

I approached national service with mixed feelings. I had no wish to interrupt my career at the *FT* but life at home was no easier than when I had been at school. My mother's health was not good. She had had a spell in hospital a few years earlier and arthritis, which had crippled her mother and was already badly afflicting her younger sister, began to attack her too. Her life was very narrow and my father, who frequently spent his evenings playing billiards and snooker, at which he was quite adept, almost never took her out. Money was always a problem as my father never earned very much and tended to fritter away what he did make leaving my mother struggling to make ends meet. On leaving school my elder brother had set out to become an industrial chemist, but national service in the RAF had interrupted that career and on his return he had joined the Anglo-Iranian Oil Company (later to become BP) and secured an overseas posting. By an odd coincidence we each left home, Arthur to Abadan and I to join the RAF, on the very same day, 20 June 1949. I was luckier than Arthur, who had been called up just after the end of the war when opportunities for national servicemen were very limited. By 1949 the Iron Curtain had fallen across Europe, the cold war had begun and suddenly the RAF was facing a potential shortage of both serving and active reservist aircrew. The Royal Auxiliary Air Force, created in the late twenties and early thirties and embodied into the RAF in 1939, was re-formed and pilot training offered for 200 national servicemen a year to feed the reserves. It seemed pretty long odds, but I felt that if I had to do national service I should try to gain something from it and so I volunteered for pilot training.

Like all other recruits I reported to RAF Padgate, to become 2435575 Aircraftsman 2nd Class Tebbit. We were issued with our kit and taught the rudiments of marching in a few days before being sent south again to RAF Hornchurch, the aircrew selection centre. I was glad to get away from Padgate. It was a pretty dismal place, wooden buildings and steel Nissen huts, drab and colourless even in summer. Happily it has long since been bulldozed to make way for a bright and cheerful industrial estate for Warrington new town. At Hornchurch we spent almost a week battling with every imaginable form of test of suitability, both physical and mental. For me it ended in partial failure. I was not acceptable for pilot training but the RAF would accept me as a navigator, flight engineer, radio operator or air gunner – provided I would sign on for eight years regular and four years reserve service. It did not take me too long to make up my mind. I did not want to fly that much, certainly not unless I could be a pilot. I had already begun to think of a life in politics and eight years seemed like a lifetime commitment to the RAF.

So that was that. I was to be some sort of penguin – flightless in a world made for aviators. My intake of recruits was divided into the eagles and penguins rather than sheep and goats; the eagles went on their way to pilot training and we began the drudgery of square-bashing and bull.

It did not come too hard to me. I had never had much in the way of home comforts so an iron bedstead and 'biscuit' mattress, a small locker and a few jealously guarded square feet of floor space in a hut holding twenty or thirty recruits was discomfort but not disaster. Happily I have always been tidy minded so the ritualistic precision-folding of blankets and laying out of kit caused me no problems. Not all of my colleagues were so fortunate either by background or temperament, but remembering my elder brother's dictum that in a recruit training camp success and anonymity were synonymous I simply tried to avoid criticism or praise from that demon father figure, the corporal. Each hut full of recruits was designated a squad and allocated to a corporal drill instructor who lived in a cubbyhole at one end of the hut. For the six-week term of initial training – really indoctrination into military mode of thought and life – the corporal mattered more than anything or anyone. His power to make life miserable or bearable was absolute but our corporal was not a bad example of his kind. Clearly a corporal drill instructor is unlikely to be an intellectual but he knew his job, which was to convert us from a 'shower of civvies' into a disciplined squad that would move together swiftly and cohesively without question or hesitation. What bullying there was – and I experienced no physical violence – was the monopoly of the corporal and it was not tolerated between recruits. I did not find it too difficult to achieve the physical obedience essential to a military force whilst simply separating my mind from the process and remaining emotionally and mentally quite untouched by it.

My protective mechanisms of personal detachment and anonymity suffered a sharp shock in the second or third week of square-bashing. We were on the parade ground, feet already tingling and shoulders stiffening as our boots crunched into the tarmac and heavy Lee Enfield rifles impacted time and time again on to our collarbones, when a messenger arrived on the square, spoke and handed a message to our corporal. The corporal seemed slightly put out, read a list of half a dozen names, mine amongst them, and instructed us to fall out and report at once to the squadron adjutant who had some news for us. Any break from the square and routine was welcome but we had some unease as we arrived at the adjutant's office and were ordered in. Brusque and business-like he checked us by name and number and broke the news to us. Aircrew selection centre wished him to ask us if we still wanted to volunteer for pilot training as national servicemen. I think we might have considered a posting to a kamikaze squadron to be out of Padgate a month early but this seemed too good to be true. There was, it seemed, no explanation for the change of mind and no-one ever told us whether our test scores had been wrongly added up or the next batch of volunteers had failed to provide sufficient candidates. Whatever the explanation we had no doubts about our response. Within twenty-four hours we were joyously on our way from Padgate to Wittering in the old county of Rutland (now long since swallowed up by Northamptonshire) to join No. 36 Pilot Training Course.

What a change! We were no longer just recruit aircraftsmen second class – the lowest form of life in the service – we were pilot cadets, our 'erk's' uniform adorned by white, not RAF blue, blancoed webbing belts, white shoulder flashes and white discs behind the RAF badge on our peaked caps. Wittering was a pre-war RAF station – a real airfield – with Bomber Command hangars built for Lancasters, Stirlings and Halifaxes, and brick-built barrack blocks. I had not completely escaped from square-bashing but it had now moved to the bottom of the training priorities. Our days were to be spent mainly in the classroom studying aerodynamics, the principles of flight, aero engines, basic navigation, meteorology, weapons and the like.

My fellow students on 36 Course were a mixed bunch. We were mostly grammar schoolboys, sixteen- and eighteen-year-old school leavers, of whom only a few were intending to go on to university. Most of us were national servicemen with some four former aircrew, engineers, navigators or radio operators re-mustering as pilots. The latter were older, war-experienced non-commissioned officers – vastly more experienced in every way than most of us who were hardly more than schoolboys. Our numbers were completed by Don Batt and Dick Richards, who had entered the RAF at fifteen as apprentices and become skilled tradesmen, both engine fitters if I remember rightly, and finally Alan Holbrow who was quite unique – a former Fleet Air Arm pilot trainee whose training had been cut short at the end of the war by demobilisation. Alan was making his second attempt at a service flying career, sadly to meet a tragic end before our training was completed.

The course soon shook down as we learned the routines and established the pecking order. Alan Holbrow was rightly designated course leader – he was older than most of us, had style, came from a better-off family and had been educated at public school. He was a leader by nature and upbringing with enough experience and sense not to push his luck in dealing with the elders of the course, the other aircrew and the street- or barrack-wise ex-apprentices.

Not only the pecking order but friendships soon became established, some of which have remained life-long.

My consecutive number in the RAF, Derek Yates, and I have remained friends to this day, keeping in touch with several others who were with us almost forty years ago.

I enjoyed the instruction, indeed I think we mostly all did so, not least because it was a path leading us towards flying training. The square-bashing became an almost automatic routine as I learned the technique of almost detaching my thinking mind from my body, leaving only that limited part of my brain needed to obey simple commands in gear. In any case the flavour had changed. We were being trained not just to obey but to command.

No such detachment was possible during our academic instruction. The instructors were experienced and good at their job. We were all desperately keen to learn and to survive the regular tests which led to our final examination.

Not that our lives revolved solely around work, despite lack of free time and being mainly confined to camp. Even our outings to the pubs of Stamford, only a few miles away along the Great North Road, were inhibited by our lack of civilian clothes. Being compelled to wear uniform made us all too obvious in a crowd, and we had no doubt that landing in any sort of scrape or escapade of the kind familiar in the pubs of university towns would see us back at Padgate in short order.

In any case we lacked not only civilian clothes but personal transport and indeed money. Our pay was four shillings a day – £1.60 a week, which even before the great inflation was not very much – about £18 or £20 in today's money. Best bitter ale was only a shilling (5 pence) a pint, which helped, but the long walk back to camp ensured reasonable sobriety before negotiating the hazard of the guard room at the gates.

On 12 December, with the final examinations behind us, the twenty-three survivors of the final stage of No. 36 pilot course were posted to No. 2 Flying Training School at South Cerney, near Cirencester deep in the Cotswolds.

As officer cadets we lived in the officers' mess – a comfortable pre-1939 building, sharing two to a room – luxury indeed compared to Padgate. The food was quite good and the mess life had a sort of club atmosphere which suited me and most of my fellow students very well. Our numbers had already been whittled down and we were all too well aware that we were approaching the real test – not just to learn about flying – but flying itself.

We were soon allocated to our instructors, Bob Ewing, Crawford Simpson – both Scots – and I to Flight Lieutenant Bob Ross. Curiously, the three of us shared the same birthday, although readers of newspaper astrology columns would have found it hard to believe. Jock Simpson was full of nervous energy, superficially over-confident. Bob, with whom I have remained friendly to this day, was a tall laid-back fellow with a slightly shambling gait. He was intellectually bright and had been educated at Herriots Grammar School. We could not have drawn a better instructor than Bob Ross. Highly intelligent, thoughtful, a meticulous pilot, but no simple airframe jockey, he went on in later years to win the McKenna Trophy for best graduate of his year at the British Empire Test Pilots School at Farnborough. Sadly he was killed not very long after while testing an early prototype Javelin fighter. His aircraft encountered control difficulties and Bob Ross, leaving it too late to bale out safely, was lost together with the plane in the Severn Estuary.

Our 'wings' course was scheduled to take a year, split equally into terms of six months and a hundred flying hours first on the Prentice and then the Harvard. Both were single piston-engined trainers, the Prentice being a surprisingly ugly post-war design from the Percival stable which had earlier produced such beauties as the Mew Gull and Proctor. The Harvard – familiar to tens of thousands of wartime pilots, both British and American – was perhaps the finest ever of its kind, ranking alongside the legendary Tiger Moth.

Although I was twelve or fourteen years removed from the excessively shy child whose voice disappeared approaching the counter even of a sweet shop, my self confidence was still not much more than bravado – and only skin deep at that – but I was in love with flying and badly wanted to succeed. The beginning of the consummation of that love affair came on 19 December. Flight Lieutenant Ross said the weather was good enough for a first familiarisation flight and I struggled into my heavy flying suit, leather helmet, with its goggles and oxygen mask, gloves and finally parachute harness.

South Cerney was a grass airfield, the only concession to modern ways being a tarmac perimeter track along which we rumbled our way to the take-off point.

'All ready?' asked Bob. I nodded back, my words sticking on a dry tongue and failing to compete with the roar of the engine as the throttle went fully forward, and we began to trundle, then rush, over the grass. At about 30 knots or so the tail came up and we were in a flying attitude but still bumping over the rough turf. 50 knots, 60 knots and, with a firm but gentle back pressure, the bumping suddenly stopped. I was airborne and at a steady 70 knots climbing out over the muddy fields with their stone walls, over the farm houses, orchards, roads and rivers of Gloucestershire. Of course almost everyone flies now, but to fly then was to be in a world known only to a few and in machines more like their First World War predecessors than the big jet airliners of today.

I could still hardly speak and my eyes must have been popping out of my head when Bob Ross said, 'Right, I want you to try the controls.' The plane, which in his hands was stable and well behaved, changed character at once and became quite unmanageable. 'Never mind – just relax – it's trimmed, let it fly itself' – and gradually it did. Our thirty-minute flight passed in a flash, South Cerney was back under our port wing as we flew the circuit round on to the final approach, over the Cirencester road, over the hedge and the rough turf of the undershoot area, across the perimeter track, then with the throttle closed and engine exhausts crackling, a back pressure on the stick and bump-bump-bump-bumpity-bump back on to the turf, and we were down.

I'd done it. I'd kept my head. I hadn't been sick or scared or done anything stupid. I'd flown. There was a second longer flight that day and three more before Christmas, and then ten days' leave.

Even on the train home to London at Christmas, on a bus or my faithful bike, I could already recapture the raspy cough of an aero engine starting from cold and the harsh sweet smell of hot metal and engine oil that has forever encapsulated memories of my early flying days.

The new year could hardly come too soon. I was eager to get away

from Ponders End with its drab grey streets and dirty privet hedges –
back to the Cotswolds, to the mess ante-room with log fires, club leather
armchairs and comfortable rooms, back to the fields, trees and open
skies – skies in which I was to live, using my wits to challenge the ever-
changing weather and winds. Ever-changing they were, and all too often
for the worse, and it was not until 18 January, after almost twelve hours
of instruction, that Bob Ross turned to me after landing and said, 'All
this flying is too dangerous for an old man like me. Would you like to
do the next one on your own?' Then without waiting for a reply, he
said, 'Stop here and let me out – do one circuit and pick me up here –
and don't kill yourself or I'll be in trouble.'

He was out, the hood slammed shut, he jumped down off the wing
and walked away without a backward glance. I took a long deep breath
and began to chant my check lists with the fervour and purposefulness
of a Benedictine monk at Mass, confessing sins, asking forgiveness and,
more particularly, protection against harm.

I was back at the caravan, the green light was on. Nose into wind,
pointing down the runway, the final checks once again, throttle forward,
the surge of power, speed building, forward pressure on the stick, tail
coming up, rudder ... more rudder, keep her straight ... don't overdo
it – how she accelerates without Ross's weight – bump-bump-bumpity
... ease back on the stick – she's off. We're airborne, watch the speed,
keep it straight – phew! With take off checks all complete, the tension
eased. Well, I was up, but the tricky bit was to come.

As I began the turn to take me back around the circuit I looked over
my shoulder to make sure my way was clear. There, busy spinning his
web on the crash pylon which supported the canopy roof, was a spider.
'Thank you for your confidence,' I said to him, then concentrated again
on keeping the speed, height and heading steady to position ready for
that last descending turn on to the final approach. Then, there it was,
the Cirencester road, the hedge, the undershoot, the peri-track, speed
right, height right, she's sinking on, power off, stick back, bump-bump-
bump – my first solo – I'd done it. I could fly.

I almost forgot to pick up my instructor who had been sitting on his
parachute – no doubt biting his knuckles. He gave me a grin. 'That's
enough for today – I can't stand the strain – taxi in please.'

My first solo completed I celebrated that evening. Not too wildly, as
I already strongly suspected that I was not a natural pilot and, lacking
the intuitive skills of some of my colleagues, I would have to use every
bit of brain I had to earn my wings. Time soon proved me right.

Flying, even without such escapades, was a demanding business and we were encouraged to unwind from the tensions and stress of the course by letting off steam on the sports field and, more to my liking, by some pretty 'lively' mess games and other pranks. Both my lack of enthusiasm for conventional games and liking for a good drink and pranks were to land me in trouble.

Life in the mess was convivial. Indeed our instructors and the other officers on the station were generous in their tolerance of our under-graduate style of revelry – perhaps because the hard drinking and wild parties, which were an anaesthetic or antidote to the carnage of war, were still commonplace events. Dining-in nights usually developed into riotous parties. The tying together of the diners' shoe laces on opposite sides of the long trestle tables always led to chaos as officers leapt to their feet to drink the loyal toast – though the risk of being caught crawling under the table to perform the deed and being thoroughly kicked was pretty high. Mess games, always including such favourites as High Cockalorum, mess rugby and 'around the room without touch-ing the floor' normally followed dinner, becoming progressively wilder, usually until the mess secretary or the president closed the bar. At such times we saw our seniors in a somewhat different light – and we all learned a lot about each other and even ourselves – *In vino veritas*! I heard at first hand the tragic yet inspiring stories of Poles and Czechs who had escaped from East Europe to continue their fight, from Britain in the RAF, to free their countries, only to see the short-lived flames of freedom snuffed out as ruthlessly by Communist Russia as by Nazi Germany. Some, like Flight Lieutenant Schermak, had briefly returned to serve in the Czech Air Force before escaping for a second time into exile in the RAF. Others had simply never returned home, but almost to a man they were amongst the most passionate lovers of freedom I had ever met.

A number of us, Derek Yates, Bob Ewing, Brian Reed and one of the ex-apprentices, Dick Richards, also enjoyed the local pubs, especially the Black Horse in Cirencester (now sadly degenerated into an estate agent's office), but quite often travelled further afield to the cider houses of villages as far as the Stroud Valley. Rough cider (tanglefoot) was cheap and good though it certainly lived up to its name. All manner of wild ideas were hatched in those pubs. Normally in the sober light of day they were ditched – but not always.

A good deal of our mischief arose during idle hours spent dodging any form of unnatural exercise such as team games on Wednesday afternoons, whilst the wing commander in charge of ground studies sought to make sure we would be kept fully occupied. I cannot remember quite how, but in a bizarre piece of miscasting I was appointed cadet in charge of sports. I soon realised the possibilities of such a post. It was not too difficult to fix games, either between units on the station and nearby RAF stations or with local schools and colleges. The away games provided us with a legitimate use of service transport – a valuable commodity indeed in those days – and I gradually became a dispenser of privilege to my friends and any others who preferred a less active Wednesday afternoon than could be found on the sports field. To these fortunate colleagues I allocated mythical fixtures, usually home games between cadets, but sometimes at places convenient for the cinema or other attractions. To keep up this steadily inflating pretence I invented the results of the games (like a one-man pools panel) and duly reported them on Thursday mornings. Whether out of pride in such healthy and keen cadets, or suspicion that he was being conned, the wing commander eventually decided to attend some of the activities on my impressive list. The game was up for me. I was relieved of my responsibilities and received a severe dressing down.

I had begun to reflect that I had forgotten my brother's good advice of the virtues of anonymity in service when I was unexpectedly promoted to Cadet Corporal – a fairly clear signal that if I gained my wings at the end of the course I would be commissioned too. Perhaps, I thought, this whole RAF class of gamekeepers is one of poachers at heart!

The weeks slipped by, my flying hours increased, and my skills of airmanship in using the aircraft, as opposed to just landing and taking off, were painstakingly built up under the guidance of Bob Ross. I never found it easy. I was a thinking, hard-working pilot, not a natural, and I worried as our numbers were steadily reduced by failures. I had a few more frights in the air, once suffering radio failure whilst above cloud on a night cross-country navigation exercise. There are few more lonely places than the cockpit of a plane below the vast canopy of stars and above a great white sea of moonlit clouds, without any sign of the existence of another human being in the universe – nor indeed any sign that the solid world of airfields, runways, hangars and warm comforting mess armchairs exist at all. Such moments are the tests of training. Will that flutter of concern turn to fear and panic – or will self-discipline assert itself? One way lies safety, the other disaster, and throughout my life I have had profound reason to be grateful to my early flying mentors who instilled airmanship and much more into my barely formed character.

By early June I had completed 100 hours of flying and passed the check of basic flying skills. We celebrated by taking our instructors to dinner.

Derek Yates and I had become firm friends and we spent our leave that year sailing on the Norfolk Broads.

Then it was back to South Cerney and the Harvard. It was an impressive aeroplane, far more like a fighter than the ponderous Prentice. Indeed the surviving examples of this fifty-year-old trainer often appear in Second World War films playing the part of American and Japanese fighters and dive bombers in the Pacific campaigns. Its Pratt and Whitney Wasp engine was more than twice as powerful as the Prentice's Gypsy Queen and the pupil and instructor sat in tandem in roomy cockpits. Unlike the Prentice it had a retractable undercarriage and it did not just look like a fighter, it flew like one too. With crisp, well-balanced positive controls, the Harvard handled well and could perform almost any aerobatic or normal manoeuvres with precision; but badly handled it would quickly bite back. Careless application of high 'g' forces would send the Harvard flicking suddenly into a spin, the right way up or inverted. A moment's lack of attention on take-off or landing and she would 'ground loop' – that is swing violently off the runway – even slithering backwards, as I discovered, or, worse still, collapsing the undercarriage.

Again I had to work hard, especially to cope without Bob Ross. My new instructor, Sergeant Forster, was nice enough but did not have the same breadth of interest in things outside flying. There were no more intermissions from the sweat of aerobatics or instrument flying to look at Roman remains or local churches from the air; it was sheer hard work. Instrument or 'blind' flying was simulated by hanging amber screens around the inside of the cockpit canopy whilst the student wore blue goggles, the combination blocking out the view outside.

Halfway through the Harvard stage I think I must have been only just above the failure level, still somewhat intimidated by the Harvard. Flight Lieutenant Byrne was assigned to see whether or not I would reach 'wings' standard. Byrne was an outstanding aerobatic pilot and set about pushing me into mastering the machine.

'There is nothing clever or difficult about it,' was his motto. 'Use the controls – make it do as you want.' He frequently proved his point by telling me to loop or roll the plane whilst flying blind in cloud. At first I hesitated. 'What's the worst mess you can get into if it goes wrong?' he asked.

'A spin or a spiral dive,' I would reply.

'Well, can you recover from those?'

'Yes, Sir.'

'OK then, let's go.'

And so we did – at first finishing inevitably in a spin or spiral dive!

His technique was successful and in October I cleared the penultimate hurdle at which one or two more cadets failed. I gained my instrument rating authorising me to fly in 'white card' (bad weather) conditions. I then passed my final handling test on 17 November 1950 and five days later flew the Harvard, sadly for the last time, in a great formation flight to celebrate the end of the course.

On 30 November, watched by my parents, I paraded proudly as Pilot Officer Tebbit to receive my wings, with 200 hours flying in my log book, and an assignment for training on Meteor jets as a fighter pilot.

Derek Yates failed to be commissioned and Bob Ewing was given early release to take up his place at university. Dick Richards and the ex-flight engineers and signallers went on to bomber and transport squadrons and the eighteen-month life of No. 36 Pilot course came to its conclusion. Only seventeen of us had survived – but we had suffered no loss of life, although that was to come.

Throughout December and January I was left at home impatiently awaiting posting to advanced flying school. I bought my officer's 'best blue' – the tunic and trousers still hang in my wardrobe today (the hat, having suffered many indignities at the hands of my children, was lost years ago) – and had my photograph taken in uniform before proudly visiting old schoolfriends such as Jack Pearce whose medical category had restricted him to ground duties. Such activities soon palled and it was with a great sense of relief that I once again left Ponders End – this time heading north to No. 205 Advanced Flying School at Middleton St George in Teesdale.

Middleton St George had a comfortable pre-war officers' mess, good hangars and runways, situated in North Yorkshire countryside not far from Darlington, on the edge of the North Yorkshire dales. The Tees, and the little village of Middleton One Row, with the The Davenport Arms (known as No. 2 Officers' Mess), was conveniently within walking distance across the airfield.

There was a fortnight of ground school and briefing before we made our first flights and we found our concentration frequently broken by the thunderous roar of jet engines and glimpses of Meteors thrusting upwards on near-vertical climbs. In 1951 jet airliners were still a novelty and the Meteor remained a formidable jet fighter. It was the only Allied jet to have seen war service and only five years earlier had broken the world's air speed record at a speed of 616 mph. Its jet engines apart it had more in common with pre-war and wartime fighters such as the Mosquito than modern aircraft like the Tornado. It was, of course, subsonic; it simply would not go faster than about Mach .84 or .85 (84 per cent or 85 percent of the speed of sound) even directly downwards on full power, and in any case became progressively less controllable beyond .81 until control was totally lost at around .83 or .84. Nor was the contrast with modern aircraft limited to sheer speed. The equipment on board could have been transferred from a Spitfire or Hurricane of a decade earlier!

Flying Officer Farley ran through the pre-take-off checks as we briskly approached the runway and, with no need for the engines to be warmed up or checked, swung on to the runway, opening the throttles fully, and in seconds I was into a breathtaking introduction to high speed flight. It was quite shattering! Thrusting up past 30,000 feet, a familiar experience today to millions of holiday-makers in the comfort of airliners bound for the Costa Brava or Majorca, was in those days at the very frontiers of flight. And it was somewhat different. The unpressurised cockpit of the Mk 7 trainer was cold and draughty. Even in fur-lined boots, silk inner and leather outer gloves and leather helmets (the modern 'bone domes' were not invented until much later) it could be uncomfortably chilly at times, and once beyond 35,000 feet even breathing pure oxygen left one progressively short of breath, risking incipient anoxia. That first forty-minute flight left me still breathless even back on the ground but somehow almost at once I felt more at home with the Meteor than the Harvard or Prentice.

The February weather was poor but, seven flights later, totalling less than five hours instruction, I soloed on the Mk 7 trainer and then a few days later flew the Meteor 4, my first operational single-seat fighter. The training was intense and thorough, even though most of our instructors were almost as new to jets as we pupils were, so we all approached the Meteor with wary respect. For me it was not just my first jet, but my first twin-engined aircraft and it was one that could be, and often was, vicious and lethal.

On one occasion I found myself getting low on fuel, above thick cloud, anxious for a 'fix' (in those days it meant a good reliable position) or a bearing to guide me home. Then as if in answer to a pilot's prayers, I spotted a hole in the clouds, at the bottom of which I could see the ground. With the throttles closed and the dive brakes out to avoid gathering unwanted speed I descended in a tight spiral down the hole – staying out of the thick cloud that could cloak the hard rocks of the moors and mountains. I emerged below cloud level and to my horror found myself only a few hundred feet above ground in a narrow valley with towering hills going up into the clouds on every side – and the hole down which I had descended rapidly closing behind me. Within the few moments it took to climb blind through cloud back above the level of high ground I was breathless and soaked with sweat. Another bit of luck, another lesson learned.

We were not all so lucky. Our course leader, Alan Holbrow, whom we had all come to love and admire, one day failed to return to base. The only clue to his fate was a slick of oil found by fishing boats whose crews had seen an aircraft emerge from thick cloud and plunge almost vertically into the sea. Alan was the first fatality, indeed the first serious accident on the course, and we mourned his loss.

I spent only just over three months at Middleton St George – months in which I think my character became more firmly formed. Not least due to my jet instructor, Flight Sergeant Howard, I began to gain confidence. The upper skies were still empty then and I was free to roam south over London or across the border to Scotland with no air traffic restrictions at all. I started to love flying, not just the idea of flying. My love of the countryside grew stronger. I began to discover the staggering beauty of Britain from the ground, scrambling over the rocks of Teesdale, lying on my back on a bank alongside the early spring flowers and bursting buds of hedgerow hawthorns, gazing up at the cirrus clouds sweeping in ahead of the rain; and from the air, muffled in flying kit, gazing down from 40,000 feet at England – laid out coast to coast, mountains, moors, valleys, villages, towns and cities.

I remained far more fond of the company of other males than of girls. Life was so full that I hardly had time for girls – anyway, lacking a car and being dependent on public transport meant it was all too much effort. I think we were mostly all of the same view. Alan Holbrow, like a good ex-Navy man, was a great pursuer of the other sex and his current love at the time of his death was a girl called Wendy Craig. She was naturally very upset, and her father picked on me – the Lord knows why as we had never met – to join them for dinner once or twice and take Wendy out. I don't think we had much in common; I was slightly bored with anyone who did not make flying, politics and the countryside their top priorities, and Wendy Craig put acting and the theatre top of hers. As a result, for the last thirty-five or forty years as we have each progressed in our chosen professions I have seen her only through the TV screen though with great admiration.

By the middle of May the survivors of No. 5 Jet Conversion Course had become reasonably proficient in handling the Meteor.

We were now ready for the final stage of our training before the national servicemen were released to the reserve and the regulars went on to operational squadrons. We were posted back to the south to No. 226 Operational Conversion Unit at Stradishall in Suffolk where we flew alongside the last of the Spitfire conversion courses for photographic reconnaissance pilots. In gently rolling Constable country the crispness of spring was already melting into the lush leafy greens of summer.

For eighteen months I had been taught how to avoid letting aeroplanes kill me. Now I faced not the generalised romance of being a fighter pilot but the reality of learning how to use a fighter to kill. The course lasted only six weeks and my mind had already begun to turn to civilian life, although that was over-shadowed by the escalating war in Korea. The United Nations forces – largely American – that had been committed to turn back the North Korean aggression against the South were being hard pressed. Britain and other countries were sending troops, too, and it began to look as though the RAF could find itself in action again. I began to realise that before long my new skills might be put to the ultimate test. Battle formation, the art of deploying numbers of fighters in formations which could readily manoeuvre, protect each other and bring the maximum of fire on an enemy, was our first lesson. I found it immensely demanding.

The training was tough and I sweated pints even in formations of six, but it prepared me for flying in the North Weald wing, which comprised three squadrons of ten aircraft each and on great occasions manoeuvred in a 'Balbo' of three such wings. At such moments the whole sky seemed filled with aircraft as 'number twos' crossed over with their leaders, pairs crossed over within squadrons, squadrons crossed within wings while wings themselves crossed over. Halfway through the turn the formation which had been miles wide when fully deployed became densely filled with aircraft stacked one above the other in an awesome ritual dance thousands of feet deep.

In practice the large formations always break up once rival forces are engaged and air combat becomes a series of individual battles. We practised for those, too, by tail chasing, taking it in turns to be pursued or pursuer trying our utmost to either hold on to, or shake off, one's partner during the wildest manoeuvres we could devise.

This was all very well but the object of keeping an opponent in one's sights was to destroy his aircraft as quickly and cleanly as possible. The Meteor carried four 20-mm cannon, two on either side of the pilot, with gun ports almost level with his feet and some six hundred rounds of ammunition – about a minute's supply – in a great bin immediately behind him and just forward of the main fuel tanks. Ten seconds was a very long burst of fire and a well-directed five seconds would be more than enough to destroy most aircraft. I found it a frustrating exercise and my shooting improved only slowly with much practice over the years.

Ground attack has always been part of the fighter's role and, almost as a treat at the end of our course, we tried our hands at air-to-ground firing. The technique was to dive at an angle of thirty degrees or more, firing at targets looking like large bill boards which were set up on the salt marshes beyond the sea wall at an east coast range. Firing at a ground target has the inherent advantage that you can see where your shells are hitting and correct aim if needs be, and the inherent danger of an almost intoxicating fascination, tempting the pilot to follow his own shells down to perilously low break-off heights.

Stuart Watson, like me a national serviceman, found the temptation irresistible. On his last sortie on his last day in the R A F the range safety officer warned him that he was leaving the break-off dangerously low and one more low pass would cause him to be sent home. On his next attack Stuart's aircraft struck the sea wall and disintegrated, killing him instantly.

We, the survivors of 36 Pilot Course, had now passed every test. Some of us were on bomber and transport squadrons, some on night fighters, but most of us were ready to go either to day fighter squadrons or back to civilian life.

I realised I had changed over the two years of service life. The shy, naive boy from Ponders End, although still young, had become a man, and a decidedly upwardly mobile one at that.

During my leave between Middleton St George and Stradishall I had gone back to the *Financial Times* to discuss my possible return to work. I found that much had changed there too. The *Financial Times* and *Financial News* had merged, the former editor Hargreaves-Parkinson had gone and a new man, Gordon Newton, had arrived. The old order had changed. Would-be financial journalists were no longer recruited from sixteen-year-old school leavers – it was to be a graduate's world. I had a legal right to my old job back, and the editor made it plain I would be welcome, but I told him I had heard things had changed and that following the merger the paper was heavily over-staffed which left little room for a non-graduate like me to gain promotion.

'You'll leave me to be the judge of whether we are over-staffed,' he told me.

I observed that perhaps his view from the top of the tree was different from mine at the bottom looking for a way up and I felt I would be better off in another job. Despite that difference of view he made it plain that if I changed my mind and wanted to return there would be a place for me. I thanked him and left – uncertain of what I wanted to do but certain I could not settle down to a junior office job.

In a rather similar quixotic way I refused an offer from an acquaintance of my father, Robert Silk. He owned several estate agents' offices around Wood Green and asked me to join him with a view to partnership and then taking over the business on his retirement since he had no children of his own. I had it in mind to join the Royal Auxiliary Air Force and Saturday working would clash with Saturday flying, and anyway I had no desire for the night school and correspondence studies to qualify as a surveyor or valuer. I have often wondered since if I would have just muddled along selling houses or become a property developer!

My companion during excursions from Middleton St George and Stradishall had often been John Picken, and on leaving the RAF we decided to take a holiday in Scotland, unknown country to both of us. John managed to persuade his father, a Methodist minister, to lend him his 1947 Standard Eight drop-head coupé. I joined him at Market Drayton and we set off with no plans except to see Scotland.

I am glad we saw the Highlands then before the new roads and tourist coaches changed so much of the landscape. At that time the main road from Kincardine to Ullapool was not just single-lane: there were just two strips of tarmac, one for the offside wheels, the other for the nearside with the grass growing in between. It was then that I fell in love with the west coast, with its hilltops draped with clouds and the sea lochs dappled with sunshine, and the winding lanes. I was immensely sad to return to London and job hunting, and have seldom since missed a chance to be in Scotland.

I knew I could not settle to a humdrum life and fancied a spell abroad but my application to become to Falkland Islands air ambulance pilot was unsuccessful. Then my eye was caught by an advertisement for young men to become tea planters in Assam. A far cry from the Falklands but a clear escape from Ponders End! The application form required the names of referees, and one who occurred to me was Colin Turner the ex-RAF Young Conservative local chairman. I wrote asking if he would be kind enough to give me a personal reference, and was more than surprised when a couple of days later he arrived on our doorstep asking for me.

His message was quite clear. No, he would not do anything to help me to do such a daft thing as to go tea planting but he would like to offer me a job in his family firm. I was to work with them for two years. The job was not too well defined but Colin was clear he needed more help – not least because he was intent on entering Parliament. The firm was quite small: Colin; his father; a delightful eccentric and elderly Scotsman; and an equally delightfully eccentric accountant, Potter Irwin – 'PI'. The main business of the firm was selling advertising space in overseas newspapers, mostly Far Eastern and Australian and Scandinavian, which the firm represented in the United Kingdom, and a bit of publishing – a magazine on golf and a couple of trade publications. I can still recall the names of some of the papers today – the *Nanyung Siang Pau*, the *Kin Kwok Daily News*, as well as the *Singapore and Hong Kong Standard*. Selling advertising space in Chinese language newspapers had its funny side – not least convincing people that the front page advertisement for which they had paid a premium price naturally appeared on what we would regard as the back page!

Much as I liked Colin, and indeed his father with whom I got on exceptionally well, the job was not for me. When the owner of one of the small periodicals we represented, the *North Borneo News*, told Turners that he wanted to retire and offered to sell the business to them if they could find someone to run it, there was even a thought that I might go out to do so. I was attracted to the idea – but not to the commitment of spending a lifetime there as had the owner. I certainly knew that a life spent commuting from Ponders End to the Turners' office in Shaftesbury Avenue was not for me, but my mind had begun to turn to flying for a living, rather than publishing in North Borneo.

Flying had already begun to take over my life again after only a short spell during which I had put it into second or third place. My uncertainty about my career had held me back from making the major commitment to join a Royal Auxiliary Air Force squadron, and I had entered the Royal Air Force Volunteer Reserve. The difference was considerable, the VR flew single piston-engined basic trainers – Chipmunks – and expected pilots to fly about thirty-five hours a year to keep in practice, ready if need be, for re-training to an operational role. The Auxiliary squadrons flew front-line fighters and were regarded as fully operational, the pilots flying a minimum 100 hours a year, including the intensive two-week 'summer camp' exercise.

Whilst I enjoyed flying the Chipmunk as a 'fun' aeroplane it was small beer after the Meteor and I soon became bored with the VR and its nannyish attitude to pilots like myself.

In the meantime I had kept in touch with Derek Yates who, being possessed of a more orderly mind than I, had returned to his old job in an insurance office and had joined No. 604 County of Middlesex Squadron, Royal Auxiliary Air Force, at North Weald, flying at weekends as a reserve pilot.

Talking things over with Derek at one of our lunchtime pub meetings I became convinced that I should follow his example, and in February 1952 I was accepted, on probation, as a week-end flying member of 604 Squadron. On probation meant just that. There were three requirements which the probationer had to meet. Technical competence as a fighter pilot; the willingness to devote enough time – most weekends and two full weeks a year; and personal compatibility with the other members of the squadron. 604 Squadron had a proud history as a Second World War night fighter unit led by Group Captain 'Cat's Eyes' Cunningham flying Beaufighters, and had re-formed after the war under his command as a day fighter squadron with Spitfires. By the time I joined, the Spitfires had been replaced with Vampires, De Havilland-built single-engined fighters so small and agile that they earned the nickname 'kiddy cars'. In the meantime John Cunningham had become so involved in his work at De Havilands, testing and proving the Comet airliner, that he had handed over to Keith Lofts. Tragically, Keith was killed soon after whilst flying his Vampire in an air race, and command of the squadron had fallen to Russian-born Andrew Deytritch.

I began with refresher flying on the Squadron's familiar two-seat Meteor 7 trainer and by early April, having renewed my instrument rating, I was ready to fly the Vampire. Although a two-seat trainer version was developed later, at that time it was a matter of reading pilots' notes, listening carefully to the advice of the other pilots, getting in and flying the machine. I was still very inexperienced with less than 300 hours in the air and I gained an immense thrill from flying a new type without any instruction. With only half the power of the Meteor, the Vampire accelerated less quickly, was slower in the climb and slightly more so in level flight but it was the more manoeuvrable aircraft and a smaller target to hit. It had its bad habits – pushed to the limits in a tight turn the Meteor would groan, shudder and judder, and if one persisted it would eventually flop semi-stalled out of the turn; but the Vampire, with little warning, would flick quite viciously on to its back. That was how Keith Lofts had died, turning too tightly at low level around a pylon marking the course of the race.

I soon integrated with the squadron – the life suited me very well indeed. About half of the pilots and other officers were post-war trained, the others mostly had combat experience. They were a delightful lot, mostly bachelors too much in love with flying, cars and parties to contemplate jilting the squadron for marriage; and the wives of the minority who were married realised that the squadron was the first love and their husbands' mistress.

Ian Ponsford, my flight commander, was a solicitor by profession (he has acted for me for over thirty years). Tough, funny, kind, belligerent, but not bellicose, with a character as bristly as his moustache, he was a very masculine man, full of 'press on', yet underneath immensely sensitive, and above all a born leader. I was totally convinced that if I could hang on in tight formation with Ian I would always emerge unscathed – and neither as a pilot nor solicitor has he ever let me down. Tom Turnbull, Ian's brother-in-law, half French, with a relaxed air that concealed an ability to move swiftly, was a Lloyds underwriter and farmer whose Aston Martin cars were the envy of us all. When Andy Deytritch was tempted back into the RAF to use his skills in the Russian language, he was wealthy enough to accept the not inexpensive post of squadron commander. Another pilot, Derek Dempster, was a journalist, an air correspondent on a daily paper – a rare example of knowledge of flying in the press – and our intelligence officer was ex-pilot Tom Russell, president of the Squadron mess and bank manager to almost all of us. The latter role, a bed of nails to any bank manager, was cushioned by Charlie Zorab – our equipment officer – who had joined the squadron when it was formed in 1931, served through the war and rejoined as soon as it was reformed in 1947. Charlie inhabited a different world to the rest of us – he was a friend of Nubar Gulbenkian the oil millionaire – and as Tom Russell explained to his Barclays bosses, the squadron's business came to him as a package in which Charlie Zorab's account more than balanced the financial shortcomings of the rest of us.

An account of squadron life, personalities and adventures would justify a book on its own. Such sagas as how Jimmy Phillips' Vampire collided with a railway train (the latter suffered a lot less damage), why the Oxford's undercarriage collapsed when the engines were started, how the illiteracy of Wee Georgie – one of our most loyal ground-staff airmen – was concealed from authority, how Joe Hoare coped with a very weak bladder on very long-range ferry flights, and a hundred other incidents were all part of a life full of the comradeship of shared fun, 'blacks', dangers and disasters – the *joie de vivre* of the squadron.

It was a life I entered into fully, enjoying the Summer Camp in June – the first post-war Royal Auxiliary Air Force overseas expedition. We spent our two weeks in Malta, based on the Royal Naval Air Station at Takali. It was my first trip overseas and as the most junior member I flew out on one of the two York transports which took our airmen and kit – a long and noisy trip, whilst the more senior members ferried the Vampires via the French Air Force base at Istres, near Marseilles.

Britain was still struggling to emerge from its dreary, socialist, post-war era of shortages, rationing, utility goods and stifling regulation. Malta was an eye opener. No regulations, no utility, no rationing. Huge steaks, fresh fruit, beer, spirits, wine and the typical sleazy clip-joints found in every big port city were all there. Like the notorious Gut – a street of such places in Valetta – it was a world I had never before encountered. We flew hard and played hard – not just enjoying ourselves in town but exploring the island from its beaches to its old city of Medina, by way of innumerable restaurants and bars.

I flew as much as I could, both because the main activity was live air firing at which I was not particularly good, and because I knew we were soon to lose the Vampires and be re-equipped with the new Meteor 8s – the latest version of that type. Back home again my log book records that I flew on every weekend in July and four out of five in August.

By then my probationary period was well over and I had firmly established myself in the squadron. Derek Yates had failed to secure a commission at the end of our flying training and had joined 604 as a sergeant pilot, but RAF policy had changed by then and required all pilots to be commissioned. Along with our other sergeants he was therefore soon to join us in the officers' mess. We were lucky because North Weald had a very good mess building and only one regular squadron (72 Squadron at that time) on the station, so there was plenty of accommodation for us auxiliaries. I shared a room with Bob Staton who was at university in Bristol and therefore not such a regular weekend attender. We also shared with many others a rather lugubrious civilian batman who I think found us somewhat of a trial.

Enjoying mess life and disliking home life, I often went directly from work to North Weald on Friday evenings and in to London on Monday mornings, so North Weald soon became like home.

Squadron life was about parties and flying. The parties took a regular pattern but there was a good deal more variety in the flying: formation work, both close and battle, had a high priority as did instrument flying – especially let-down and approach procedures to return to base in bad weather. I enjoyed the practice interceptions in which the ground controllers guided us to intercept aircraft playing the role of intruders into British airspace. The intruders comprised a variety of aircraft. Sometimes they were other RAF fighters, although it was more fun if they were bombers, usually USAF B29s or B50s – big four-piston-engined aircraft, or RAF Lincolns, both Second World War types, or the huge B36 with its ten engines. Gradually the RAF's newest bombers, the Canberras, were sent to plague us – I say plague because they were faster than Vampires, more manoeuvrable than Meteors and could fly higher than either. Intercepting and attacking aircraft of such superior performance required a mixture of skill (on the part of both controllers and pilots) and a degree of bravado and cunning too.

The clash of a whole wing of three fighter squadrons meeting a large formation of bombers was a spectacular sight, a vast airborne replay of the headlong clash of opposing cavalry charges of earlier years. Usually the aircraft of each squadron would be in line abreast formation with pairs of fighters separated by about 200 yards, and the squadrons in line astern separated by about half a mile. On rare occasions when the incoming bombers came in real strength then the squadrons were ranged in line abreast, hopefully with another wing of fighters to follow.

The effect of two great formations hurtling towards, and then through, each other was dramatic. Of course it was only practice – not for real – and the rules of engagement were intended to prevent collision, but the adrenalin ran fast in the veins with no one willing to chicken out by breaking away a fraction of a second earlier than necessary. I can still recapture that mounting tension and the sudden action – the blurred vision of aircraft passing within feet of each other as Vampires or Meteors jostled through the tight formations of bombers, in a contest of nerves and brinkmanship in which, inevitably, some bomber pilots would flinch and their formation would begin to crumble.

All those actions took place high above the North Sea but the air war tacticians were well aware, especially in a nuclear age, of the danger of low-level raiders, flying below the height at which 1950s radar could detect them. In contrast to the 'bandits' intruding at higher levels, these were the 'rats'. From time to time we played the role of rats and ratters. I loved every minute (bar the nasty frights) of flying either role. The rats were normally solitary or in pairs although a whole pack of them might be launched against a number of targets in the same area. Usually for us the action took place over East Anglia with the rats going out thirty or fifty miles over the North Sea, then dropping down to about 200 feet to head inland to the target. The ratters might be aloft at high altitude to conserve fuel, or on the ground ready to be scrambled, either from dispersal areas or on the readiness areas alongside the end of the runway. The height of ignominy was to be caught there by an undetected rat, swooping down on his simulated bombing or strafing attack. Humiliation could be piled upon humiliation if the rat was equipped with those most devastating of peacetime weapons, toilet rolls to be strewn over the sitting duck fighters.

Once airborne the ratters listened in to a ratting controller giving constant updates of rat sightings, leaving the ratter to make his own interception since at 300 feet (or even less) rats and ratters were not within constant radar coverage. It is very difficult to spot a low-flying aircraft, especially from above, so whatever the risks of prosecution for low flying below the limits laid down (normally 500 feet but in some areas 200 feet), the temptation was for the rat to fly as low as possble and the ratter to get lower still, hoping that his quarry would show silhouetted against the sky. I know of no more exciting sense of the chase than those low-level flights – always accompanied by the tingling of nerves acknowledging incipient dangers at every second.

I habitually flew lower than most, taking advantage of every rise and fall in the ground, ever watchful for the danger of high-tension cables – especially in hazy weather. We flew at high speed – 480 knots was normal, 500 or just over at a pinch.

Even with its belly tank of extra fuel, the Meteor 8 flown at very high speed and low level had an endurance of little over 30 minutes – but what a 30 minutes! It was nearly 300 miles of sheer animal thrill, the physical exertion of handling the last RAF fighter without powered controls, the numbing bruising ride on a bumpy day, the sweat of excitement and the heat of the atmospheric friction as the two jets smashed the aircraft through the resisting air, all combined with the spur of competition and the thrill of danger. I have never fox hunted but I cannot believe that even that thrill can compare with airborne ratting in the style of the 1950s.

By the early spring of 1953 I was not only head over heels in love with flying again – but I was more and more at odds with my working life commuting to the West End. The crisis point came one day when I found myself running down an escalator which was taking me down to the Piccadilly Line tube at Turnpike Lane. 'This is bloody insane,' I thought, and instead of struggling to force myself into the crowded rush-hour train I sat waiting on the platform until a train with room to sit down arrived. By then my decision was taken. I would resign my job and follow Derek Yates' example once again by joining British Overseas Airways.

Half afraid I might change my mind if I hesitated, I told Colin Turner and his father of my decision as soon as I arrived at the office. They were sad but not altogether surprised, and I agreed to stay on for a couple of months whilst they found a replacement for me. During those months I bought a correspondence course to study for the commercial pilot's licence, studying on the tube on my way to and from work. BOAC did not require any more pilots until the winter of 1953 so I decided to spend the summer flying as much as I could with 604 Squadron. Auxiliary pilots were allowed to be paid for three days a week and for four full weeks a year – enough, together with some small savings, to live on for the summer.

By this time I had acquired a 125 cc two-stroke BSA Bantam motorcycle, which provided cheap transport. In a fit of madness my brother Arthur borrowed a similar machine from a friend and we decided to ride to the South of France, with Nice and Cannes as our objectives.

The whole of our trip was marred by bad weather across France and through the Alps but it was a trip not to have been missed. France was just recovering from the war but the scars still showed. The roads were almost empty and we buzzed along flat out at 55 mph for hour after hour, pausing only to refuel the bikes and ourselves as we pressed on towards the south. Stiff backs, legs, and arms and sore backsides were all worth it to have seen the Côte d'Azure, Nice, Cannes, Monte Carlo, the Promenade des Anglais, the Casino and the glorious backdrop of the Alps. They were still as they had been before the war and before the ugly sprawl of high-rise developments and the rising tide of housing spread up the foothills, and the South of France became a package holiday destination.

Although it had its difficulties, 1953 was a good year for me. I passed the written examination for my commercial pilot's licence without difficulty but BOAC required me to have a civil instrument rating too. That examination proved more troublesome. Foolishly I did not prepare myself sufficiently for the flying test, which was undertaken in the civilian version of the Airspeed Oxford. The Oxford was the standard twin-engined trainer used by the RAF to prepare pilots for heavy transport and bomber aircraft and I had never flown it or anything like it. It was slow, old-fashioned, propeller-driven and quirky. I was too hard up to afford any proper instruction in civil flying techniques, such as airways flying and ILS (the civil bad weather landing system), and I simply read the theory and tried my best in an unfamiliar aircraft.

Not surprisingly, I made a monumental hash of the test – a severe blow to my pride but a lesson learned. BOAC proved quite understanding and stood by their offer of a job commencing in November but as a cadet at £500 a year rather than a second officer at £950. The test was not an easy one and a good many pilots failed, but having managed to scrounge a couple of flights in an RAF Oxford I achieved an almost complete pass on my next attempt. To my great relief I finished the job in a final attempt early in 1954 – with an understanding examiner!

My social life revolved more and more around the squadron and the Herts and Essex Flying Club where my brother Arthur was learning to fly. To keep him company I too joined the club, both to enjoy an occasional flight in light aircraft and, of course, the inevitable parties. Like North Weald, Broxbourne attracted a rich variety of characters but where at North Weald we flew fast aircraft and mostly drove old and slow cars the mix at Broxbourne was of slow aircraft and fast cars. A local farmer who flew a Miles Messenger and drove an Aston Martin was well matched by Eric, a local dentist, whose new Jaguar XK 120 was faster than his Piper Cub aircraft. Eric's Jaguar was the first car in which I exceeded 100 mph on the road, following a dispute over his claim to 'change down at ninety'. My brother and I were appointed referees and were despatched successively as Eric's passengers on hair-raising demonstrations of the Jaguar's performance along a twisting country road over a hump-backed bridge, into the local station yard and back to the bar.

We acknowledged that alcohol and aeroplanes were a lethal combination but like most people at that time had a relaxed attitude to drinking and driving. That was mainly because the roads held far less traffic and the majority of cars on the road were of pre-war manufacture. Neither they nor many early post-war designs were capable of speeds much above 60 mph and needed a long straight to achieve that, so accidents were less likely and less horrific than the motorway carnage of today. However, amongst members of both the flying club and the squadron, driving accidents and car write-offs were almost a part of life!

One popular late night pastime was car racing around the mess. The drive was too narrow for true racing so the contest was for the fastest lap but a complication arose because the back straight of the course was the main road from Epping to Ongar. We resolved this by stationing marshals with red lanterns to stop local traffic, mercifully normally very light at the times of our events. Mishaps were not uncommon. My unfortunate lapse of judgement which led me to borrow the station commander's official car and equally unfortunate lapse of concentration which led to an encounter with an air raid shelter, rather put me off the contest. Fortunately no damage was done, the car and the shelter were disengaged by a good deal of lifting and shoving so I received no more than a warning against over-enthusiasm for the sport.

Another craze was indoor motorcycling. My BSA Bantam, being light and manoeuvrable, was quite popular for this game. It was, however, a mistake, when I realised that it had sufficient ground clearance, to ride it upstairs. This act was sufficiently popular to call for an encore which I willingly set out to perform. However, I did not know that my friends had loosened the carpet clips, and as I approached the landing I heard a cry of 'Now – Pull'. The carpet was hauled back down the stairs, both the bike and I following it in an almighty crash. Remarkably, injuries in such escapades were few and little damage was caused. The injuries received scant sympathy, and the damage had to be paid for – a code of ethics well understood and decently honoured.

Our 1953 Summer Camp was again in Malta but by now, as an established member of a squadron, I flew out in a Meteor 8 rather than as a passenger in the York freighter. It was even more successful than my first camp as I had gathered a good deal of confidence and was in far better flying practice.

The 1954 annual defence of the United Kingdom air exercise code-named 'Dividend' was held in July, and to add to the realism a new rule was introduced. Weather was not to be taken into account in scrambling the defending fighters.

On Saturday afternoon we had been prevented from landing at North Weald by bad weather and after a somewhat difficult time had arrived at Waterbeach near Cambridge. We were in bed quite early having agreed that we would be the first squadron to be scrambled on Sunday morning. Getting up was a quick business. We had slept in our flying kit and had no shaving tackle. By six o'clock on another gloomy and miserable wet morning we were in our Meteors on the readiness platform, ready to be scrambled. It was not too long a wait. 'Scramble – steer 060° make angels two five zero' (25,000 feet), came the instruction.

My memory of that day is still vivid. I reacted like a hunting dog let off the leash. A stab down on to the port starter button, high pressure fuel cock on, the 'woof' of the light up, keep easing the cock fully open, stab the starboard starter button, revs rising, cock on, light up, wave the trolley away, both fuel cocks fully open. Keep one eye on the leader, the other on my number two, brakes off, roll on to the runway, complete the checks turning to line up behind the leading pair. Check thumbs up from my number two – then my usual nervous twitch – checking my harness tight, seat locked. The first pair accelerating away in a cloud of spray – keep counting . . . eight, nine, ten. Then swinging my right hand down to warn my number two, brakes off, throttles fully open, by now the leading pair are out of sight over the hump in the runway. Then back in view, they are airborne turning on to heading 060° and climbing.

We are splashing along in their wake – on and on and on.

Something isn't right – something isn't right. Suddenly we are over the hump in the runway and the end of the concrete is looming up. My aircraft won't fly, it won't come off, the nose wheel seems stuck to the ground, I get it a foot or so off and it wants to go back.

My number two is beside me, still in tight formation. 'Hey,' he calls, 'what goes on?' Split seconds count. I slam the throttles shut, jamming on the brakes – I know I can't stop in time.

'I'm ploughing in,' I shout, and as he pulls away airborne I pull up the landing gear and my aircraft smashes down on to its belly tank of 175 gallons of fuel. The tank is ablaze as we toboggan across the grass, smash through the boundary fence, ricochet over the deep wide ditch in which others had met their death, over the road, through the next hedge. At full tilt we are a blazing torch of flame crashing along the line of approach lights, cutting down the heavy wooden poles like a scythe. The screeching noise of tearing metal fills my whole brain, driving out any thought. It is punctuated with colossal bangs as the plane breaks apart. The port wing is severed and finally the appalling, pummelling smashing progression stops. My eyeballs stop bouncing and through a haze of pain I begin to focus again.

My oxygen mask is full of blood, and looking down at my left leg I see my flying suit reddening as pain throbs out all over my body. There is not just a smell of burning, I can hear and see the flames licking up from the belly tank, and feel the heat of the blaze.

'Out' – the word wells up into my still-stunned brain. I hit the quick-release button of my harness and press the switch to open the cockpit canopy. There is no comforting whir of machinery, and no movement of the canopy. 'Fool,' I think – 'the electrics must be done for,' and I declutch the motor and try to slide the canopy back. It does not move. 'Ah, the quick-release canopy jettison,' – I pull the handle and push at the canopy. It does not move.

The flames are fiercer and I know that there are another 360 gallons of fuel only a few feet behind me. I push again at the canopy but still it does not move.

It is drizzling outside. The wreck of Meteor 8 WL132 is burning in a field of wet corn. It is Sunday, still only 6.30 in the morning, and I am trapped in a funeral pyre.

'Bloody fool! You're hardly injured, just a few cuts and bashes, everything still works. You can't just sit and die. Think, man. Think.'

I think. The crowbar – there it sits in its clip – designed for this very moment. I try to lever the canopy back with the crowbar but still it does not move. Out of breath and with pain singeing through my whole body I flop back into my seat.

'Well I'm damned if I'll burn to death. Perhaps the fire crew will get here in time – if not then I'll strap back in and fire the ejector seat. If I keep my head well down the head rest should smash the canopy before I do. It will throw me sixty feet but on to soft earth. I might survive with broken legs – if not it's better than burning.'

Then I think again. 'You fool – try to *force* that hood'. Somehow I half stand in the cockpit, head bowed, shoulders against the canopy, and straightening my legs I force my back upwards. There is a sudden cracking, splintering, tearing noise and it moves – the canopy lifts at the front and standing erect I push it aside. The heat of the flames mixed with the cold air of the morning seems to fill my lungs and I half fall, half jump, out into the corn and stagger away to a safe distance from the blazing wreck.

When the first rescue crew arrived on the Land Rover emergency vehicle they found me sitting in the wet corn – dishevelled, stinking of smoke and blood. They were youngsters with only a corporal in charge so I took control. 'I think you'd better take me to sick quarters,' I said, and took the front passenger seat. Events began to take a surreal air. I was conscious of the vehicle moving but now hardly aware of pain.

'Are you all right, Sir?' asked the corporal.

'Yes I think so,' I said, and feeling I should make conversation I asked, 'Do you mind if I ring your bell?' – it was a splendid red handbell on a bracket by my seat, and I gave it a couple of lusty dings.

I was still buoyed by adrenalin as the duty medical officer began to examine me in the sick quarters. Then suddenly I felt safe and the adrenalin supply was cut off. I had done all I could to survive. I felt cold and began to shake – things began to blur and I lost consciousness. I was out for only a few moments but I was left as weak as a kitten when the medical officer stitched up the gash in my leg and the medical orderly began to tidy me up.

By the time we arrived back at North Weald at lunchtime I was feeling empty and slightly sick, and I convinced myself that I desperately needed a drink and a meal in that order. A friend drove me to the bar and I walked in through the french doors. The weather was still filthy, the air exercise was over, flying had ended for the day and the bar was full. Mine was not the only accident of the weekend. There had been two fatalities and half a dozen aircraft lost, and a number of pilots were expressing some pithy comments to the air officer commanding our fighter group who was standing at the bar with his back to me. I heard him saying in self defence, 'You have simply got to understand that in this context fighter aircraft are expendable.' It was too good to resist. I tapped him on the shoulder and he turned around to see what must have been a pretty ghastly apparition. I stank of smoke and blood. I was unshaven and my flying overalls were torn, muddy and blood-stained.

'May I quote you, Sir,' I asked, 'at my court of enquiry?'

There was a long pause as the air commodore looked at me.

'Would you like a drink?' he asked.

The court of inquiry could no more reach a conclusion on the cause of my crash than I. The aircraft was totally destroyed – the only clue being that the trim was set at fully nose down. That might well have been caused by the break up of the aircraft and I was convinced that having checked the trimmer through its full travel I had set it for take off, so the verdict was listed as 'cause unknown'.

I was flying again within a month but it was not until a year later that during a regular licence medical a doctor noticed my spine had a curvature not recorded in earlier medical records. An X-ray examination revealed that I had compression fractures of two vertebrae which by then had fused leaving me with a twisted spine. It had been a lucky escape.

I suppose I had experienced in peacetime a small part of what many had experienced in the war. Like all experiences I found a positive side to it. My crash at Waterbeach was a close brush with death, not an experience to be welcomed. I believe it has given me a great strength at times. Ever since that July Sunday in 1954 I have regarded each day of my life, however hard or disagreeable, as a bonus. After all, I might by now have been dead for almost thirty-five years – instead, I have been, as it were, playing with the casino's money, having all but cashed in my own chips.

BOAC took the Waterbeach incident surprisingly well. The natural bureaucratic system had drawn such a distinct line between civil and military flying that it really did not have any way of noticing my mishap except through my request for a week or so of sick leave.

3

'Unsuitable for Management'

By November 1953 when I had joined BOAC, I was an established Royal Auxilliary Air Force officer, a member of the squadron with almost two years service and had been promoted to flying officer. BOAC was different. There I was the lowest form of life – a cadet pilot. Like most entrants at that time I was assigned to a navigation course. BOAC policy was to work towards a single type of multi-skilled flight deck officer, and the training of pilots to be fully qualified navigators was part of that programme. The technical examination for the navigation licence was of a very high academic standard.

All told, it was twenty weeks of intensive instruction and many hours of homework swotting.

To my great relief I fluffed only one paper – the signals practical. The requirement was to send and read Morse code at six words a minute – difficult enough for me – but, worse still, to read Morse sent by Aldis lamp or as flashed by airfield beacons. Even worse I failed my retake. Understandably I was nervous when I went for my second retake. We sat, about forty of us, in a great room with the examiner at a desk at the front. To my surprise he called me out and with a worried and sympathetic air said, 'You know the rules, don't you? If you fail any subject three times, even this practical test, you have to retake the complete examination.'

'Yes,' I said, 'I do.'

'Then you mustn't fail,' he said.

'I know,' I replied – 'but I'm not much good at this.'

'I know that, so if you miss anything give me a nod and I'll repeat it – oh, and if all else fails I've put you next to an RAF signaller!'

I passed! Once again someone had steered me around a difficult course in my life.

The next tricky bend was not long in coming. Having passed the Ministry of Aviation's technical examinations we had progressed to instruction in practical chart work before our first attempts actually to navigate an aircraft. Meanwhile I was still spending every weekend flying at North Weald, luxuriating in the pleasure of not having to swot for examinations, and enjoying life.

My airborne navigation training began that September with a series of trips mostly to Shannon in southern Ireland in a small Dove aircraft of BOAC's training fleet.

Before long I progressed to flying on an old Avro York freighter converted to navigation training. Known as Nan Sugar from its registration letters it flew a regular training route to Kano in Northern Nigeria.

We flew by way of Rome, a flight of over four hours, skirting the Alps over Marseilles, then across the Mediterranean to Tripoli. Libya, then ruled by King Idris, was a sleepy kingdom, and Tripoli a peaceful town.

We used to stroll along the seafront with its dazzling white traditional buildings to the cool sanctuary of the Elizabethan Club where the expatriate British sat on leather-covered stools sipping gin and tonic at the bar. Across the desert at Kano a herald, riding a camel, welcomed the safe arrival of each aircraft (usually one a day) by joyous blasts on a three-foot long trumpet. One could walk in the huge open-air market in the old walled city for half an hour and see scarcely another European. There the Muslim Hausa traders held sway, confiding in Europeans their contempt for the Ibos, 'mission boys' – not men, they told us. Kano lacked any hotel fit to use and we stayed in the BOAC rest house in wooden chalets raised well above the ground to minimise the wild life content of the cubbyhole rooms. We usually arrived there around first light in time for the standard BOAC West African breakfast of kippers and Carlsberg before retiring to bed until lunchtime and a stroll down to the Kano Club, another bastion of colonial expatriate life. The lifestyle was still modelled on the pre-war era, and good colonial administration ensured order, justice and a modestly growing prosperity for the native population.

It was a world as distant from today as the navigation of the old York was from the push-button systems of a modern airliner. In those days, standing up in the astrodome with a sextant, one would navigate by the stars. At first it was intimidating but before long I was confident enough to have time to eat a meal at the navigation table.

Once I had qualified as a navigator, as well as a commercial pilot, I was posted to the Argonaut Fleet. The Argonauts, a Rolls-Royce Merlin powered version of the American Skymaster transport, flew BOAC's African and Far Eastern routes. Having been promoted to Second Officer I began to feel more financially secure so the BSA Bantam went and I bought my first car, a 1948 Humber Hawk. It was a splendid car, rather heavy for its 14 hp engine but very comfortable with leather seats and walnut trim. Home life at Ponders End was no better than for years past and I began to look for a home of my own. My brother Arthur had rejoined Anglo-Iranian after a spell with another firm and was based at the Isle of Grain in Kent, too far from Heathrow for us to share a house or flat. One of my BOAC contemporaries, Mike Bull, faced a similar problem and we decided to look for better accommodation together. Our next decision was I think open to question. We decided to put an advertisement in the *Morning Advertiser* – the daily paper of the public house trade!

Looking back, I can see that squadron and BOAC life might have benefited from rather more contrast than a home in a pub, but it seemed a good idea at the time.

We settled upon The Red Lion at Betchworth in Surrey, a quiet pub, slightly run down because of the serious illness and impending death of the landlord whose wife was running the business aided only by one barman. It was a lovely spot and Mike and I soon settled in, often taking over the running of the pub, but I think it was just as well that it did not become my permanent home.

1955 was generally a good year for me, apart from one somewhat ridiculous incident in my political career. Whilst working for Colin Turner I had rejoined the Young Conservatives, becoming treasurer of the Home Counties North Area with Peter Walker as my chairman. The post was really a sinecure as we had no funds nor accounts of our own, our office and full-time organiser, Lyn Latrobe, being provided by Area Office which also financed our general expenditure. In return we raised a reasonable sum by way of the Area YC Ball whose profits were set against a nominal charge for the services we received. The main point of being treasurer was to use the post as a stepping stone to the chairmanship. But this had no interest for me at the time, for my increasing preoccupation with flying, and my absences abroad persuaded me to wind down my political activities, much as I had enjoyed YC conferences and events such as the political leaders' courses at the Conservative College at Swinton which were attended by almost every leading Conservative of that generation.

I managed to arrange my trips so as to return in good time for my last Area AGM but as usual Murphy's Law operated with a delayed flight and I arrived home only the night before. Fortunately, as I expected, Lyn had already produced the accounts for the year – actually a nominal extract of figures from the Area accounts – and handed them to me with a lovely smile (she was a most attractive girl) as I arrived for the meeting. Foolishly I had forgotten that Lyn's undoubted skills did not include numeracy and cheerfully presented the accounts. All was well until a numerically orientated member of the committee said, 'The figures on the right-hand side don't add up to the bottom figure.' Even worse, a moment later someone else said, 'Nor on the left-hand side.'

It was my responsibility and I could hardly blame Lyn, so I said the only thing that came into my head at the time. 'It's a bloody good job that I'm not standing for re-election.'

It was a good lesson to learn at an early age and the tale will no doubt reassure many civil servants and business colleagues that I neither unworthily mistrust them, nor question their competence – it's just that once bitten I am more than twice shy!

Having stood back from politics at the age of twenty-four I took no part in the great Conservative victory of 1955 except to cast my unavailing vote in the safe Labour seat of Enfield East – now of course the Conservative Enfield North, and to help undermine the morale of the Liberal candidate for Epping, John Arlott.

As a keen cricket follower I greatly admired Arlott's superb radio commentaries and I was delighted to find him with his wife and election agent in the bar of the officers' mess at North Weald canvassing for votes. Too convivial a man to be a good candidate, John Arlott allowed himself to be drawn into a game of liar dice at the bar. Needless to say, playing with half a dozen of us – all friends and ruthless dice players – he was soon set on a losing streak. The stakes went up from rounds of drinks to bottles of Champagne, and trying not to run foul of electoral law Arlott kept turning to his agent to finance his losses. I suspect that compounded the offence of 'treating', but whilst he kept losing and the Champagne kept flowing, who cared! Mrs Arlott clearly knew her husband well and could see a disastrous evening in the making. It was well after midnight before her suggestions that it was time to leave ceased to be met with the response of 'Don't niggle, woman,' in that lovely west counry accent which made Arlott's comments all the richer. Far too late for his own good he took his wife's advice, leaving all the poorer – except in experience and in the friends he had made even if he had gained no votes. As I gently weaved my way to bed I had no thought that fifteen years later I too would be canvassing for votes at North Weald.

Perhaps it was just the pressure of a very hard working period in BOAC – I flew over 800 hours in 1955 – perhaps I had some instinct that it was time for another break in the pattern of my life, but the end of my time with 604 Squadron finally came as a result of a party and my rather bad driving habits.

My beloved Humber had been declared a total write-off by my insurers and it was clear that they were less than anxious to keep my business. I had replaced it with a new Austin A30 saloon, which was not quite my style but new cars were still at a premium with long waiting lists so I had grabbed the chance to buy it at list price. It was still quite new when in November 1955 another pilot on the squadron, 'Buster' Browne, was asked by his girlfriend, a nurse at Westminster Hospital, if he could bring along some chaps to her flat-warming party and I volunteered to be the duty sober driver for the night.

The party was going particularly well, but without the benefit of a drink I found myself slightly detached and bored until a young nurse arrived late, just off duty and similarly not quite with the mood of the party. Nothing was more natural than that we should find ourselves sitting away from the noise and frenzy, drinking coffee and talking. Before the party broke up we had exchanged addresses and agreed to meet again when I came back from my next trip.

Our friendship developed apace from what we later discovered had been intended on both sides as a temporary 'fill in' whilst our respective boy- and girlfriends were not in London, and early in the New Year I asked Margaret Daines if she would marry me. We became formally engaged on my twenty-fifth birthday, 31 March 1956, and set the date of our wedding to be Michaelmas Day, 29 September that year. Most people who knew me were surprised and none too sure that we had made the right decision. Indeed at our engagement party in the mess at North Weald (where else!) our adjutant Johnnie Bishop – a regular RAF officer, slightly older than most of us – took Margaret aside in a fatherly way to explain that, nice chap that I was, I led a feckless and irresponsible life, was unlikely to change and was not really the marrying kind.

I had some worries of the same sort myself. Indeed I had to confess to Margaret that the date of our engagement was set not just because my birthday was on the twenty-ninth of the month but because my pay was not credited to the bank until the twenty-sixth, and until then I would not have enough money to buy the ring!

However, I was determined to change my life and half sadly I said goodbye to The Red Lion at Betchworth. Living in a pub had not been the best idea in the world but I had learned quite a lot about people, particularly whilst working behind the bar. Certainly I had learned that running a pub is a pretty hard life and crossed it off my list of potential post-retirement jobs! I was still at odds with my parents, or, to be more correct, without anything in common with them, but having nowhere else to go I returned home which was at least cheaper than living at The Red Lion.

Apart from that, my lifestyle had hardly changed before Margaret and I were married on 29 September 1956. My move from The Red Lion to live at home had been a concession to financial responsibility – but not a large one. As a second officer my pay was just about £1,000 a year – equivalent to £10,000 today – but it all seemed to go all too easily. We decided on a London wedding and Margaret's hospital connections led to a ceremony at Westminster Congregationalist Chapel. The squadron provided my best man, Alec Patmore, and its town headquarters at Notting Hill for the reception, with catering organised by the squadron mess.

It was a happy day. The triple streams of guests from the Daines family, the Tebbits and the squadron rapidly blended and the reception became a family party. Indeed I recollect making the first tactless remark of my marriage by observing that it was a pity Margaret and I had to leave! We spent the first night of our married life at the White Hart in Windsor having survived the embarrassment of insisting on a change of room on discovering that we had been booked into a twin, not a double room. We spent the next few days of our married life at our new flat in Sunningdale and then enjoyed a short honeymoon in Wales, touring in our faithful little Austin A30.

By the time we returned, the familiar envelope containing the notification of my next trip was on the mat. It was a long one leaving on 16 October – three weeks to Tokyo and back – hardly an ideal wedding present but at least it would give me a chance to save a little money, I thought. That was certainly needed as our wedding and honeymoon, modest as they were, had seriously depleted my resources. Margaret claims I left her with little more than the money for a phone call, and a cheque book which I emphasised should not be used before the end of the month when my pay would be credited to the bank.

On arrival at Heathrow I met the other members of my crew, to be captained by 'Corpus' Deadman – a long-suffering man at the hands of the crew roster office which often took delight in crewing him with First

Officer Mort and Stewardess De'Ath. We set out on our first day's work to Rome, a sector on which we still navigated in traditional style but I had time enough to read the papers which were full of the Suez crisis. I was firmly on the Eden side of the controversy, although wishing that the man would get on with it and act decisively, little thinking that twenty-five years later I would be in a Cabinet facing similar hard choices.

Our trip had been eventful enough with a typhoon at Hong Kong, riots in Singapore and a passenger who went mad in Colombo, and we were left uneasy by the news that the Israelis had attacked Egypt on a pre-emptive strike. We wondered if British forces might become involved but were still somewhat surprised to be recalled as we taxied out at Karachi ready to depart for Bahrain. No clear explanation was given and without a telephone land line to London I found the HF radio link was too overloaded to get a call home, leaving us to speculate on what rumours and facts we could collect during 30 and 31 October.

Eventually we left Karachi for Bahrain on 1 November. Soon after passing our point of no return to Karachi our radio officer leapt to his feet and with a flow of colourful expressions told us the news that the RAF had bombed Cairo. We had no choice but to continue to Bahrain.

In those days the airfield at Muharraq, a smaller island, was connected to Bahrain island by a causeway. It was controlled by the RAF and garrisoned by the British Army, a comforting thought since gangs of marauding youths were out in the town stoning British premises. Despite honeyed (and complacent) words of reassurance from the local BOAC staff we declined to go into town and accepted the offer of hospitality in the officers' mess on the airfield. It was a wise decision. The families of BOAC staff were evacuated that night not long before the mob set fire to their block of flats. It was a far from restful twenty-four hours before we left for Basra which remained a safe haven until the murder of the Iraqi King, Crown Prince and Nuri Pasha, the veteran statesman and premier, in July 1958.

The trip had a last challenge for us. Unsurprisingly we were to be re-routed away from the war zones of Egypt, Israel and Jordan to Istanbul, on a route that took us over Lake Van, not far from Mount Ararat and the Russian border. We carried no approach charts for Istanbul nor maps for that route but, happily, during the stop at Karachi I had pooled knowledge of possible routes around the Suez conflict with the crew of another airline. To the great relief of Captain Deadman, I had made carbon copies of their approach charts for Istanbul and then, armed with latitudes and longitudes of the check points *en route* for Istanbul,

I thought back to my navigational training courses and constructed the chart on which I then navigated!

Despite the Suez War we arrived home on our original schedule and it all seemed rather an anti-climax. Then I opened my mail to find that my opposition to the management's rules on the training required to graduate from second officer to co-pilot had earned me not only a further rebuke but three months notice of dismissal unless my behaviour improved. Phone calls to my colleagues rapidly uncovered that, despite many assurances that we would all stick together on the issue, only a handful of us had done so – and we were all under notice. It was another unwelcome wedding present but I had learned a lesson which I have never forgotten. I have never since imagined that easily given pledges of support will last once the going gets rough.

My ten- or twelve-day stand-off went by all too quickly before I set off again, this time to East Africa. The pattern of our early married life was being set and already we began to wonder if we had been wise to move to Sunningdale or whether it would have been better to have stayed in London and for Margaret to have continued nursing. Our little flat was nice enough but we knew no one in Sunningdale and my expected conversion course seemed likely to be long delayed.

We soon fell to planning a move but it was no easier then than now to find an unfurnished flat. However, about eighteen months earlier I had applied to rent a bachelor flat at Hemel Hempstead new town, and as a Londoner seeking to move out of London had been put on the waiting list: in the bureaucrats' jargon I was a 'decantee'. I discovered now, however, that by being married I had qualified for immediate re-housing in the small non-subsidised housing sector, so our unfurnished flat was suddenly in sight.

At that time Hemel Hempstead was very much a new town in the making, and for the first six months we lived on a building site. Wellington boots were *de rigueur* for shopping as our neighbourhood of Warners End grew up around us. As is the way of new towns, Hemel Hempstead terminated with a knife-edge division between high density housing and rural Hertfordshire, and our flat in the little cul-de-sac of Elm Green was right at the edge of the town. It was a happy community and we still exchange Christmas cards with one of our former neighbours who has remained there to this day. We were better off than most, owning a car and qualifying, by reason of sometimes being 'on call' for work, for that prized and still rationed device, a telephone. Because of this we became virtually a communication centre and occasional emergency taxi service. My work had a sort of *cachet* about it, too, at a time when few except the rich ever went abroad except on war service, and, with Margaret's nursing experience, that made us an informal local citizens' advice bureau! In turn our neighbours rallied round to support Margaret when I was away. In fact we were our own social services department, our own social workers, meals on wheels, community advisers, dial-a-bus service – indeed, we provided mutual support of a kind now clumsily and expensively run by local authorities.

It was not long before we benefited from that support network. Margaret was some eight weeks pregnant by the time we moved but within another month she had miscarried and lost the child. As seemed usual in BOAC family life she was alone at the time and it was our neighbours and friends who took over. A message to phone home awaited me on my arrival in Karachi and I eventually achieved a call to be told of this setback to our hopes. The mishap brought us closer to our local GP – an extraordinary man, Bob Sutton, and his wife, Pat. Bob was the son of a doctor who had practised in the East End, moving only once in life when his home was bombed and then only a few yards to set up home and practice again. Like his father, Bob lived for his work, and for seven years we became the closest of friends.

With the advice and support of Bob and Pat (a former nurse), Margaret successfully gave birth to our first son, John, in April of the following year. The birth was at home and for once so was I. Directed by Bob and Pat, who acted as midwife, I rushed around with hot water and cups of tea in traditional style. It was thought very modern in those days for a father to be present at the birth (and I had some doubts beforehand) but in the event I believe it brought us closer together.

We were doting parents but quite strict with ourselves as we were determined not to let John become a spoiled brat of the kind we heartily detested. I was now a little better off so we began to afford a few luxuries – a refrigerator came first (television and clothes washers were still years away) and we rather went over the top in buying John a magnificent traditional pram. I think it was the pram that really prompted me to buy a larger car, as the relative sizes of our tiny Austin A30 and the large pram became too much of a joke with our friends, and even when dismantled the latter would not go into the boot of the former.

My old friend Len Walters produced what looked to be just the thing – a two-year-old Standard Vanguard for £670.

Our delight in John, and our belief that it is very much more difficult to bring up a happy single child than two or three, was soon marked by Margaret becoming pregnant again. Our joy was short lived when once again at about three months she lost the child. With two miscarriages we began to wonder if John would be an only child – indeed we seriously thought about adopting a child; but Bob Sutton counselled a policy of wait and see coupled with heavy doses of vitamin E for Margaret. His advice was good and before Christmas 1959 she had survived the critical three-month mark and was looking forward to the birth of our second child in the summer of 1960.

The flat at Elm Green, with no garden and only two bedrooms, was hardly adequate for the swiftly growing young John, and with another child in the offing we had decided to move. At first, having as usual no money, we thought of renting a house in Hemel Hempstead. Fortunately Margaret was more willing to be adventurous than I and she sought the advice of Tom Russell. Although the Royal Auxiliary Air Force flying units had all been disbanded in 1956, Tom had remained banker and father figure to many of us and he invited me to lunch to discuss my affairs.

'Find a house that you can easily re-sell and come back to me. I'll see you can find the money,' was Tom's advice. Within weeks I had signed a contract to buy a new house on an estate being built at Berkhamsted, only five miles from our home in Hemel Hempstead. It was quite large though poorly fitted, but with a decent garden. The sole heating was an open fire at one end of the large living room and its dormer bedrooms were badly insulated and bitterly cold. The ice not only formed on the windows but during one harsh winter over the water in the glass at our bedside! Nonetheless at just over £3500 it was a good buy for a four-bedroomed detached house, even in those days.

We moved in during the autumn of 1959 with a ninety per cent mortgage from the Abbey National and a bank loan of about fifteen per cent of the price too, but at least we had entered the property market. I was free to indulge in my love of gardening, and Margaret to buy another dog to replace our mongrel 'Pooch' whose wayward habits had sadly led to her being run over by a car. Thus Biddy – our faithful and much-loved dachshund – joined the family, and with a wife, child, dog and mortgage, I began to feel almost middle-aged.

In the meantime I had settled my differences with BOAC for the time being at least and as a result had undertaken a conversion course on to the Britannia 102 aircraft, moving from the navigation table to the co-pilot's seat. I enjoyed my time on the Argonaut, and the challenge of navigation, often with no more aids than earlier generations of pre-war aviators. However, my promotion to first officer required an airline transport pilot's licence, and for that I needed more pilot flying time.

I was always looking for new challenges, or at least when they presented themselves I was unable to resist them, and after an initial refusal to join the pilots' union BALPA, based on my experience of the print union NATSOPA, I had succumbed to the pleas of my friends and not only joined but became a working member. At first I had confined myself to the technical side of the union becoming a member of the Technical Liaison Committee between BALPA and BOAC. The Committee did a good deal of useful work dealing with technical problems, especially relating to new aircraft coming into service. It later spawned the Supersonic Committee on which I also served. There we were thinking about the operational and safety standards, and requirements for supersonic transports well before the Concorde design was completed, let alone flown. Gradually, however, bit by bit, mainly in response to management stupidities, I was dragged into the mainstream of union activity becoming something of a spokesman for my generation of pilots. This led to our long friendship with a contemporary in BOAC, Roy Hutchings, and his wife, Sally. Roy became even more involved than I, eventually becoming chairman of BALPA and taking it through several years of difficult industrial relations with considerable skill and success. However, Margaret was not always too pleased about my BALPA work which intruded unreasonably into my all too short off-duty time and seemed singularly unrewarding too.

I suppose it has always been one of my faults as a husband that I am something of a workaholic – in fact obsessive about whatever activities I take up. Certainly flying and politics have both taken enough of my time away from Margaret to have tested our relationship thoroughly. I had established myself as a co-pilot and flying the Britannia had taken me even further afield, not least to Australia for the first time. A combination of long trips (away three weeks or more), my BALPA politicking and my demonic attack on the rough ground – which we called the garden – of our house in South Park Gardens all took more than enough of my time, leaving all too little for my family.

I enjoyed flying the Britannia which apart from a few minor bad habits was a docile and forgiving machine – just as well since it saw into safe retirement some very, very senior pre-war pilots who had the right to continue flying to the age of sixty-five.

Some of those old hands were larger than life and I never saw such skill and judgement so well concealed until I joined Willie Whitelaw in the Cabinet more than twenty years later.

Sadly, development delays left the Britannia too late in entering service to gain the commercial success it deserved. The Boeing 707 was too close on its heels and about to set amazing new standards of speed, reliability, comfort and range.

British Airways had placed an order for the new Boeing to be delivered in 1960 and well in advance began to select crews for the new fleet. I volunteered straight away whilst some of my more senior colleagues were debating whether to do so or not. As a result, although very junior and still only a second officer, I was accepted as a co-pilot on an early conversion course. However, as the 707 was to start on the blue riband route to New York, and I had never flown the Atlantic route, I was posted to the DC7c fleet in May 1959 to gain Atlantic and North American experience.

My time on the DC7c was also a time of political reawakening as I realised the scale of immigration from the Caribbean. Night after night charter flights brought immigrants into Britain. There was no doubt in my mind that this tide of immigration was sponsored by the Government and I came to the conclusion that it arose from a totally wrong analysis of our economic problems. With unemployment at about two per cent there were acute shortages of labour, shortages which not only led to excessive union power and strong upward pressures on pay without improvements in productivity, but shortages which literally prevented expansion or new ventures from going ahead – one of the famous bottle necks of the stop-go era. In fact we had a vast concealed surplus of labour locked up in the grotesque over-manning and feather-bedding that stretched from the shop floor to the boardroom. I believed that the Macmillan government, unwilling to tackle at its roots the problem of the legal immunities which gave unions their excessive powers and (with the exception of Ted Heath's brave stand on the abolition of resale price maintenance) the anti-competitive and complacent management in business, saw the use of cheap labour as the easy answer to our problems. The belief seemed to be that the new supply of labour for dirty and low-paid jobs would release indigenous labour on to the labour market. Thus the shortage of labour would be eased and the bargaining power of the trades unions undermined.

How, I wondered, could senior politicians not see the risks of de-stabilising our society, the risks of creating a new social and economic under-class like that I was now seeing for myself in America?

However, for a while my unease was pushed into the background by work and my family.

We were looking forward to the birth of our second child, Alison, who arrived slightly late in early June. Once again I was at home with Margaret for the birth. We were both delighted to have a daughter, especially since female children are rare in the Tebbit line. Life seemed to be treating us more kindly and I had settled down to my civil flying career with my posting to the 707 fleet in May 1960.

The entry of the Boeing 707 into passenger service established the jet age which had begun with the Comet. Bigger, slightly faster and with much longer range, the 707, more than any other aircraft, was the bedrock of the explosive growth of air travel which began in the 1960s and continues today.

At the time, however, there were still those unconvinced that such an expensive and advanced vehicle could successfully be operated in a civil environment – let alone that it would bring fares crashing down and long-haul travel into the reach of millions of families most of whom had never flown before. As always with new aircraft it was held at first that the 707 required a breed of super-pilots to cope with its handling characteristics. As usual, it soon became clear that quite normal people could fly it quite adequately. However, when I started my conversion course in June 1960, within days of the birth of our daughter Alison, there was a false aura of élitism and a needless concern at the great technical difficulties supposed to stand in the way of mastery of the super-jet.

Whether it was the stimulus of the third conversion course in two years or the delight of flying jets once more, I rapidly felt more at home with the 707 than the DC7c or the Britannia and within eight flying sessions I had been cleared as a 707 co-pilot. Not that the course had been a pushover. Lacking modern simulators we had to push ourselves and the aircraft into what are today regarded as unacceptable situations as we learned to cope with extreme emergencies, but for me it was a return to real flying.

My first passenger carrying flight was completed by the end of August, and I looked forward to an enjoyable spell of flying on the best routes flown by BOAC – the North American, Caribbean and Pacific.

I soon settled into a steady routine of flying with several Atlantic crossings a month to New York and Toronto – often via Boston, Montreal, Manchester or Prestwick. New York in particular became almost a second home, and the *New York Times* as familiar as *The Times* of London. Although I found it easy indeed to resist American football and baseball I followed American politics (not to mention such American TV families as the Flintstones) as closely as their British equivalents – not least because in America I had little else to do.

The 707 pilots were the best paid in BOAC and a combination of increasing financial security, and an infuriating engine defect in my Standard Vanguard, soon led me to buy a new car. Childproof locks had hardly arrived by then so, as John was too big for a child's car seat, we looked to a two-door car, eventually settling for a Triumph Herald. As one of the first popular cars to adopt all independent suspension and one of the last to use a separate chassis it was a very individual and, to my mind, much underestimated car. For a while we settled down to a very quiet family life – improving our home, seeing friends, visiting family – but change was not far away.

BOAC was steadily widening the route structure of the 707 fleet and had scheduled the first trans-Pacific service for December. The Corporation's attempt to operate the route across the Atlantic and North America to Tokyo and Hong Kong with Britannias which would have outclassed Pan America's DC7c's had been delayed by the American Government. Protectionist as ever, and ever open to political lobbying, the American authorities had invented one reason after another to prevent BOAC operating the Britannia until Pan America put its 707s on the route. The only gainers on our side were some BOAC Britannia crews who had been posted to Honolulu to operate the trans-Pacific sectors and spent three months there without flying at all!

There were some tricky negotiations between BOAC and its 707 pilots over the Honolulu postings, as the management sought to worsen the conditions previously enjoyed by the Britannia crews. Attitudes hardened and it looked as though the service would be delayed when suddenly, just in time, an agreement was reached.

I was not a member of the negotiating team so it came as a considerable surprise to be telephoned just before lunch on a late November Wednesday to be told of the agreement and invited to go, together with my family, on a three-month posting to Honolulu. I was baby-sitting whilst Margaret made an early start to our Christmas shopping, but feeling that this was no time for family debate I agreed – and agreed to depart on Saturday afternoon. Margaret was not surprised that I had accepted the posting – but the prospect of leaving on Saturday did cause a raised eyebrow.

We all enjoyed life in Honolulu. Most people there still went barefoot except at work and adopting the local custom made life easy. Getting dressed was a matter of finding shorts and a shirt, and we spent most days with the children on the uncrowded beach splashing in and out of the water for hours on end. Of course we missed some things – our garden, friends and family and above all decent bread, biscuits and beer. Happily the latter could be brought back from Hong Kong so life was close to idyllic – and a well-paid idyll too – so we were sad to return to Britain early in March.

It took a little while to settle down back in England and somehow we seemed more aware of the shortcomings of our house in Berkhamsted. After a while we began to look around in the same area but found nothing we liked which we could afford. Roy and Sally were also looking with similar lack of success for another house and for a while we looked at large houses that we might split into two. Eventually, however, Margaret and I decided to buy a plot of land and build a house to suit ourselves. By good fortune we found an excellent site in the little village of Potten End, between Hemel Hempstead and Berkhamsted and persuaded an old friend Tom Lilley to design a house for us. We liked Tom's style as an architect and felt our friendship could even survive the trauma of building a house. That judgement proved right and although the work was delayed at the end by the appalling winter of 1962–3, we moved in March 1963 to our new house – Fryth View – the house we believed we could happily live in until our retirement. Certainly we had some very happy days there and the house proved to have been exceptionally well designed and built, but unforeseen events were soon to take a hand once again in my life.

The incompetence of management in BOAC steadily pushed me into a more active role in BALPA and at the same time the lack of purpose or direction (except that of staying in office) of Mr Macmillan reawakened my interest in politics. And in America my political hackles were raised as I watched the creation of the myth of John Kennedy.

It is all too easy now to forget the almost incredible bungling attempted invasion of Cuba at the Bay of Pigs. How anyone could have backed such a hare-brained adventure I could not conceive; and then, even with the lessons of the French colonial war freshly printed on the pages of history, Kennedy allowed himself to be dragged bit by bit into the Vietnam war. There were only 2,000 American troops in Vietnam at the beginning of his term and 16,000 at its end. It was Vietnam which did so much to undermine United States foreign policy throughout the world and Kennedy has quite wrongly escaped his share of the blame.

The truth about Kennedy is well recorded by Schlesinger in revealing passages in his book *A Thousand Days*. He describes him very well: 'Kennedy, with his own fondness for the British political style liked Macmillan's patrician approach to politics. . .'

Like Macmillan, Kennedy had no real principles – except a belief in being in government. His economic policies were a sad echo of the 1960s British consensus. Schlesinger quotes him saying, 'You know I like spending money. What I want are good programmes by which money can be spent effectively.' Later he tells us that Kennedy, 'lacking doctrinaire belief in balanced budgets,' found the French style of indicative planning attractive and thought that 'an incomes policy, perhaps new institutions assuring a greater public role in wage price settlements, might be a desirable step.'

Understandably I worried about the path on which America seemed set – a worry which shaped my growing belief that Britain should not rely absolutely on even such a powerful ally but should also strengthen its European links. The sad history of the Blue Streak and Skybolt added to my unease and the possibility of American economic and foreign policy dictated by the naivety and cynicism of the Kennedy group profoundly depressed me. America's fate, it seemed to me, was to duplicate the errors of the European powers – the Bay of Pigs was all too reminiscent of Suez; Vietnam of the French failure with its horrific climax at Dien Bien Phu; and the 'pragmatic' approach to the economy was becoming all too familiar under the Macmillan Government.

I had to readjust my view to a considerable extent as a result of the Cuban missiles crisis. It is hard now to recapture the sense of crisis – the fear that the world was on the edge of an abyss as America and Russia confronted each other whilst the Russian convoy carried reinforcements of nuclear missiles towards Cuba and the American fleet which blocked its path. I can remember discussions on what our airborne crews would do if a nuclear exchange were to take place whilst they were airborne over the Atlantic or Pacific. A great blanket of anxiety, even fear, enveloped the world. Perhaps it was a *Punch* cartoon which summed it up by showing two schoolboys in conversation, one saying, 'What do you want to be if you grow up?'

I found myself deeply concerned for the future of my own family as I headed across the Atlantic to New York as the crisis approached its climax. A few days later, seemingly like every other person in America, I was glued to my television set watching the dramatic confrontation at the United Nations whilst Adlai Stevenson was roused to passion as he produced the photographic evidence of the presence of Russian missiles in Cuba. Had Kennedy backed down – or had Khrushchev not – the history of the world might have been different indeed. It was Kennedy's finest hour – one which wiped away the failure of the rest of his presidency.

I was due to fly home from Chicago on the day that Kennedy was assassinated, and heard the news in the restaurant where I was having a snack before packing my bag. Even now I can recapture the sense of shock and incredulity that spread like a wave through the room as the news was passed from table to table. Perhaps nowadays we have become more accustomed to living in a violent age but the shock of that afternoon came into what seems in retrospect a rather innocent age. Even so, I am one of those who believe that the longer the Kennedy presidency had lasted, the more likely it was that it would have ended with America not only in a foreign policy mess, but a domestic mess, too, as the failing economic policies of Britain and France were applied to the USA.

At home my BALPA activities still took priority over any political activity and I became increasingly involved in the technical committee as well as the 707 pilots' council. In both of those forums I saw BOAC management pretty near to its worst. That is not a sweeping criticism of all the people involved – most were capable of being adequate, if not inspiring, managers; it was an inevitable consequence of ownership in the hands of politicians and civil servants and a board appointed to do their bidding rather than to run a business.

Membership of the technical committee was a privileged peephole into that system which all but destroyed the British civil aircraft manufacturing industry. Apart from our routine work, working with management to overcome the technical problems which inevitably arise in the operation of complex aircraft, and trying to avoid these becoming caught up in industrial relations negotiations, we also tried to feed practical experience of aircraft in operation back to those working on design and development of succeeding generations. During my time as a member the VC10 and Super VC10 were coming into service and I saw how those aircraft were damaged by the customer, BOAC, and how the manufacturer, Vickers, reacted – often as unreasonably as the customer. Whether BOAC would have bought the aircraft without political pressure is a matter for debate. What is undeniable is that because of political pressure they were bought with ill grace and BOAC exploited its position as virtually the sole purchaser to force often ill-considered changes, often too late to be made without excessive costs and delays. The manufacturers never forgave BOAC for its rejection of their earlier design for a transatlantic aircraft with performance much like the 707 on the specious argument that the inadequate runways and hot weather along the African and Eastern routes demanded an aircraft able to cope with relatively short runways and high temperatures. Those requirements had to be paid for and in the case of the VC10 they were paid for primarily in a poorer cruise performance than the 707. Exactly as the manufacturers had forecast, however, it was the North Atlantic route where the big jets made their greatest initial impact and the dominance of the 707 and, to a lesser extent, its American contemporary the DC8 brought about the lengthening of runways throughout the third world by the time the delayed VC10 entered service.

My opinion of BOAC management style was further lowered by the attitude of the secretariat (supplied by management) to the recording of the minutes of our meetings with them. It irritated me that the lists of those present were headed Employers and Employees. I regularly insisted that the correct designation was Management Employees and Pilot Employees since neither group owned the business and we were all merely different categories of employee. Of more consequence, and therefore the cause of even greater irritation, was the management habit of producing minutes which reflected what they thought ought to have taken place rather than what had taken place. After one particularly blatant rewriting of the record I objected in very strong terms, only to be told that after the meeting the flight manager had realised that the information he had given had been incorrect so had corrected it in the minutes. I invented on the spur of the moment the dictum to which I have held ever since, 'The minutes of the meeting should record the lies that were actually told, not the lies one subsequently wished one had told.'

It is an inherent problem of state-controlled businesses that objectives and responsibilities are inevitably unclear from the very top down, so management at all levels tends to be averse to taking risks and to seek self-preservation by irresponsibility in the literal sense of that word. My refusal to fudge won me few friends – indeed I later found out that I had been marked down as 'unsuitable for management'. I suppose that was quite correct in the sense that my ideas of managing were quite incompatible with those of nationalised industry management.

My search for clarity was not a high-minded act of purity – it sprang from my realisation that the seeds of most disputes were sown in the fertile soil of agreements designed to allow each side's negotiators to assure their people that they had achieved what were in fact mutually exclusive objectives. Such fudging did not arise only between the unions and the management. Time and time again in our internal meetings in BALPA I insisted that at the end of discussions we wrote down and agreed then and there our conclusions before moving to the next business. It was not always a popular move – all too often it exposed differences which had until then been slurred over by sloppy verbiage which then had to be either resolved or recognised and lived with. For my part I gained a reputation both as an abrasive committee member and a ruthless chairman – and lost a friend or two now and again.

As in my later life in politics, I enjoyed the challenge of problem solving in my trades union days and both my obsessive and competitive streaks showed in the amount of time I devoted to BALPA. My motivation too was the same as in politics – self protection, in that I felt I could not stand aside seeing my interests prejudiced by poor judgement, wrong policies or even lack of will of those in leadership posts.

Bad planning, narrow mindedness and lack of creative thought within management almost led to disaster in 1963. A failure to have sufficient 707 crews trained in time for the summer season and an inability to plan crew schedules efficiently led to an excessive work load, hand-to-mouth rostering of crews and too short rest times at home between trips. Before long the strains began to show in escalating sickness rates, further increasing the load on the remaining pilots, leading to a vicious spiral of sickness causing overwork and overwork causing sickness. An ex-navigator turned pilot, Chester Kirkpatrick, and I met the management's pleas of, 'It's all right for you to criticise but you don't understand the problems,' with a bold offer to produce crew schedules and a rostering system which would meet the management's requirements whilst giving pilots a more stable and less tiring life.

To the surprise of management and most of our colleagues, our system worked. Its guarantee to meet operational needs solved the management's problems whilst its guarantee of a predictable seven consecutive days at home in every twenty-nine worked near miracles for the family life of pilots, and gave Chester and me immense satisfaction in showing that in our spare time we could out think the full-time planners in BOAC headquarters. Eventually our system was replaced by a BOAC version of an American system giving pilots a right to pick trips on a basis of seniority, which I never really liked. In the meantime, however, it had provided a safe route out of a potential threat to safety as well as to the health and marriages of a good many colleagues.

By about this time my attention had already begun to turn away from BALPA and back towards politics as I saw the progressive disintegration of the Macmillan Government. The awful spectre of a Socialist Government again was enough to bring me actively into politics and I rejoined the Conservative Party through membership of the village branch at Potten End. Not long after the 1964 defeat I became its chairman, to the relief of my neighbour Jimmy Cree, a delightful but not very political retired lieutenant-colonel, who had nobly done the job for some years. The chairmanship made me a member of the executive of the Hemel

Hempstead Conservative Association where I met Cecil Parkinson who had come into politics for similar reasons to my own. I had no idea then that our political careers would be intertwined for the next twenty or more years. The executive committee comprised a remarkable number of energetic and able people – a fair sprinkling of whom were politically ambitious. Indeed a number of us, strongly encouraged by James Allason, our Member of Parliament, sought to enter Parliament and three of us, Cecil, Peter Rost and I succeeded. That, however, was in the future. At the time, Cecil was more concerned with his business career and despite my growing disenchantment with BOAC and the prospect of spending the rest of my life simply flying aeroplanes, I had not finally decided to attempt a political career.

Quite how to escape from a very well-paid career I had not worked out but I knew I needed a new challenge, and that if I was to make a break into a new career I ought to do it by the time I was forty in 1971.

One possible way was through politics but the years had slipped by and I was well out of touch. What I needed was some good advice, so in July 1964 I decided to draw on an old friendship and wrote to Peter Walker – by then an up-and-coming MP. He replied on 8 July suggesting that I should see him at the House of Commons for a drink, saying, 'I will certainly do all I can to assist.' We met one fine evening, enjoying a drink on the Terrace by the river, reminiscing for a while before I came to the point. What should I do to prepare myself for an attempt to enter Parliament? Peter's advice was practical and to the point. Relearn your politics, take office in your local Conservative Association, offer yourself as a speaker on the Party's list. We agreed it would not be practical for me to go into local government, but that I should seek every other way of supporting the Party. I remained still uncertain that politics was to be my next career but it began to look more likely than anything else.

In the meantime I flung myself into creating another new garden – a recreation I shared with my wife. We planned things together – just as well because her visual imagination made up for my word- not picture-dominated mind. My enthusiasm for what she called civil engineering in the garden supplemented her love of plants and we often worked together until dark during the long summer evenings. Feeling very settled in our marriage and home our thoughts turned towards our family. John and Alison were growing up fast and giving us so much happiness that we decided a third child would add even more to our family.

So much for my plans to buy a Jaguar XK150! The lack of space for prams and carry-cots ruled out that dream, but it was one I felt could wait whilst a third child could not. Margaret's pregnancy was straightforward and all of us, including John and Alison, looked forward to the new baby due at Christmas 1964. Both Christmas and New Year came and went and Margaret became concerned as the days went by. Eventually, Bob Sutton decided to induce the birth, a process which did not go well. In the end after a long and exhausting labour William was born at home on 8 January. Initially Margaret seemed to be recovering well but I had a deep unease as I left home on 11 January for a trip to Peru.

My unease became alarm on my return on the seventeenth. Margaret was far from well. Her behaviour was increasingly irrational and she began to suffer alternatively manic and depressive phases, outbursts of irrational fears and aggression. I turned to Bob Sutton who at first seemed to me not to appreciate that Margaret was really unwell. It was not long, however, before he recognised that she was acutely ill and a potential danger both to herself and the baby. Even now the memory of seeing her personality disintegrating is more painful than any other experience I have undergone. It is hard to describe one's emotions at seeing the person with whom one has been so close becoming a stranger.

There was no option but to persuade Margaret to go into hospital. I accompanied her in the ambulance on a thirty- or forty-minute journey during which her moods swung from depression to aggression – total confusion then brief moments of clarity in which she recognised her own illness. Her admission to hospital and my talk to the doctor in charge of her case seemed to go on for hours, and then at last I found myself wandering along a long nightmarish corridor back to the reception desk. The word misery is often misused but that day I experienced the very depth of misery. The bold front I had maintained to the doctor was gone. Perceptively he had identified the stress I was carrying and asked if I needed any medication to help. I brushed aside his offer, 'I'm indestructible,' I assured him, regretting the words as I saw the light in his eye. But as I stumbled along the corridor unable to stem the flood of tears I felt far from indestructible. I realised I had no car and telephoned home where Roy and Sally Hutchings were holding the fort. By the time Roy arrived I had regained control and, desperately tired, I slept on the way home where I found Sally in command organising children, food and drink.

Once the Hutchings had left I began to assess my situation. I had been assured that the prospects of a complete recovery for Margaret were good, but the time scale was uncertain. I decided that my only course was to take over my wife's role, staying at home to care for the children.

Hopelessly inconsiderate over minor matters, BOAC proved highly supportive in a major family crisis. Alan Sibald, the aircrew doctor, was free of any doubts. 'Norman, you are hardly fit to drive a car, let alone fly a plane. I've put you on indefinite sick leave – let me know how things progress.'

At first they progressed badly. For days Margaret was unable to recognise anyone, her depression so deep that the will to live seemed almost to have died. Her recovery when it came was slow but gradually the spells of lucidity lengthened and deepened. In the meantime I managed to combine the father and mother roles. Not without difficulty. Indeed I think that I began to understand how a mother, stressed beyond reason, could batter a child, as I uttered that sweetest goodnight when I laid William in his cot – 'Now go to bloody sleep you miserable child before I'm tempted to do something awful!'

Eventually Margaret returned home, slowly regaining confidence and overcoming her fear that she might sink back into her illness. By the second week of March I felt sufficient confidence to return to work although confining myself to short trips for some time. As the months went by the emotional scars began to heal and by the end of the year life seemed quite normal again. I had long believed that no experience is totally bad so long as one survives, and so it was with Margaret's illness. Of course I gained some understanding of mental illness but above all I had discovered the strength of Margaret's character.

We all admire those who seem able to stride without even a stumble over the most dangerous and difficult stretches of their paths through life but since that black winter of 1965 I have had a special regard for those who trip and fall into some terrible abyss but clamber back up on to the path. I began to see that just as courage is not simply an absence of fear but an ability to overcome fear, so the ultimate test of character comes not during the climb back from the first fall but at the bottom of the second or third descent into the pit.

Whilst Margaret was still in hospital I kept my first political engagement outside my own constituency since my Young Conservative days, and, not long after, we decided that I would work towards entering the House of Commons. I was thirty-four years old at that time and we agreed that if I had not succeeded by 1976 when I would be forty-five, I would soldier on until retirement from BOAC in my early fifties.

Flying had lost few of its attractions and I loved handling the 707. As a co-pilot I never flew the aircraft as much as I would have wished, and like all my colleagues I rated captains not least according to how often they were willing to play the co-pilot's role to their first officers. Naturally that depended also on how captains rated the ability of each co-pilot. Happily I managed not to cause too many extra grey hairs on the flight deck and I devoted a good deal of thought to giving passengers the smoothest possible ride. So long as air traffic control could offer an uninterrupted descent (not uncommon at that time outside the busy North American and European areas) my target was to arrive at the right place, height and speed on the final approach without having altered the power setting from the beginning of the descent. I set myself similar targets of smoothness and accuracy as a navigator and took pride in being able to enjoy a meal and to read both *Punch* and *The Economist* during an Atlantic crossing. Needless to say, things did not always work out according to plan but I was determined to avoid the bitterness and air of *maleesh* which infected some of my colleagues, frustrated at the years of snail-like progress through the seniority list towards their captaincy.

By the mid sixties the early post-war pioneering attitudes had been replaced by far greater uniformity and professionalism. There were fewer wild parties along the routes and although we enjoyed ourselves, often a drink too, attitudes to alcohol had become far more responsible and excessive drinking was recognised as a danger, not a joke. The other hazards of operating the early big jets in air-traffic control environments, which in some areas, particularly New York, were grossly overloaded and, in some third world areas, almost bereft of equipment or competent personnel, were quite enough without the needless aggravation of alcohol or fatigue.

Following Margaret's illness, and as I pursued my political interest, I began to play a less prominent part in BALPA. I had been vice-chairman of the 707 Pilots' Council and the Technical Committee and felt I had done my bit in what was a thankless task. It was the first time, but not the last, that I decided to let some of those who had offered so much advice to try doing the job themselves.

My political views – including a belief that BOAC and BEA should be de-nationalised – no more endeared me to BOAC management than my trades union activities. Not that I worried too much as I had decided that my long-term career was unlikely to be in the airline, but I was hurt by one irritating rebuff. After Margaret's illness and wanting to spend less time overseas I applied for a post as a navigation instructor. I had been qualified to supervise novice navigators for some time but instruction would have involved both the regular competence checks on experienced navigators and teaching novices the art *ab initio*. On returning from my interview I told my wife that I was sure I would be rejected – and I was right. A pilot cynic had told me years earlier that those with ambition in BOAC should regard the Corporation as a crowded ladder. To get to the top, he said, one needed to hold tight to a rung, place one's feet firmly on the fingers of the man below, one's head firmly on the backside of the man above and then push. That was not my style nor have I ever thought that loyalty or support need be synonymous with sycophancy. The comment 'unsuitable for management' – which a friend later told me had been marked on my file – was, however, one which came back into my mind in 1979 when with John Nott I had the task of preparing British Airways for life in the world of the private sector!

My latter years in BOAC were marked by increasing discontent amongst the skilled staff, ground engineers and aircrew alike. During that period I took part in a bruising 'withdrawal of co-operation' – a better description than work-to-rule for the tactics we employed – as well as a full-blown strike. Later I refused to join a further strike when I thought the union demands were neither reasonable nor of a kind that a good management should concede. I doubt if any other Conservative Cabinet minister has had any similar experience. It was unpleasant at the time but invaluable when I came to shaping legislation and dealing with industrial disputes.

·4

'First, Find Your Principles ...'

By the autumn of 1966 I felt I had done enough in my political activities to see Peter Walker again to report progress and ask for some more advice. We met at the Party Conference where Peter agreed to sponsor my application to go on the list of would-be Conservative parliamentary candidates. I needed three sponsors – a member of Parliament, a chairman of a Conservative Association and one other. By this time Cecil Parkinson had become Chairman of the Hemel Hempstead Association and I had succeeded him as Chairman of the Political Committee.

Cecil became my second sponsor. My third was to have been our neighbour Norman Lake, a very distinguished retired surgeon, but sadly he died, and his widow, also a doctor, acted in his place. By December 1966 I had completed my interviews and was 'on the list'. All I had to do was to find a seat. In the meantime my post as Chairman of the Political Committee increasingly brought me into contact with politicians who were to become major figures over the next decade or two. One of my duties was to maintain a regular flow of speakers for our political supper club which met monthly from late Autumn to Spring. As I was away so much it was really Margaret who did most of the organising – although from time to time I managed to disorganise things for her. The evening that I managed to get Nigel Lawson on a train which did not stop at Harpenden (where I had his audience waiting) still lives in my mind – and probably Nigel's too. However, a frantic car drive to the next station successfully retrieved him and the evening was saved. It was hard grass-roots work, fund raising, canvassing, producing leaflets, opinion surveying – all the voluntary work on which our democratic system depends. The word 'activist' is sometimes used in a pejorative sense, as though democracy depends on those whose commitment is no more than to vote every four years or so in a general election and is eternally under threat from the activists. But these are the people who ensure that candidates are fielded and supported. Without them the system would simply not function.

In our talk at Blackpool Peter Walker had told me that I would be wise to seek a difficult seat to fight for the forthcoming general election and in the summer of 1968 what seemed the right one turned up.

South West Islington was not the best constituency for a would-be Conservative parliamentary candidate, although in the late sixties the hard left had not yet made its takeover. A normal, incompetent, old-fashioned Labour council had held office for many years until the extraordinary election of 1968 which gave power to a coalition of Conservatives and a local residents' group. Nonetheless the election result in 1966 was dispiriting and that of 1959 in the year of the great Tory triumph not much better. It was hardly a strong and active association but they had a track record of selecting some bright young men as candidates. On the other hand I saw that the competition would hardly include any household names and realised it was unlikely that I would have the extraordinary good fortune to be selected for a safe or even a winnable seat at my first attempt. I wrote to Central Office to express my interest and next drove into Islington, bought the local papers and began a reconnaissance of the constituency. Even after the briefest look around, I concluded that to fight South West Islington would fit the next stage of my plan for a parliamentary career. I was almost at the top of the co-pilot's seniority list, looking forward to achieving my command and serving a few years on a captain's salary which would greatly enhance my future pension.

In that sense it was almost ideal, far better than a marginal seat that I might win in 1970 or 1971 and lose four or five years later, to find myself an unemployed ex-MP of little standing and former airline co-pilot at the age of forty-five. I convinced myself that Islington was made-to-measure for me. A spirited – but unsuccessful – campaign in 1970 or '71, only two years or so away, and then a good seat next time in 1975 taking me into parliament at forty-four – a little late for a ministerial career but fine for an active back bencher.

Margaret reminded that perhaps I should wait just a little before counting my chickens – I had after all only just applied to be considered as a candidate – I had not been adopted. However, she too began to eye the estate agents' advertisements for houses in central London, not least Islington itself. We were both sad to contemplate leaving Potten End, our house, garden and friends but agreed that I could never hope to reconcile the demands of my job, a constituency, our family and a large garden in Hertfordshire. So she was well prepared for the consequences when I telephoned her from a call box at Highbury and Islington station to tell her that the Executive Committee had recommended me to be adopted as their prospective parliamentary candidate. The final decision still lay with a general meeting of all members of the South West Islington Conservative Association but that was little more than a formality.

I had not faced too much competition in the selection procedure – but equally I realised that I could not expect too much of the local party organisation. The members were thin on the ground – and mostly thin on top too! At least they had a headquarters, an ugly old church hall in Furlong Road, a street of mostly attractive late eighteenth- and early nineteenth-century houses, many of them neglected and shabby, within a few yards of Highbury roundabout. The headquarters, Leeson Hall, was as shabby as most of the houses, but very much less attractive. Frank Pike, the Party's agent for a group of about a dozen north-east London seats – all Labour held – had his headquarters there and provided a framework of good order and organisation where otherwise there would have been almost nothing. Frank was the epitome of the good-natured, devoted Party professional, imbued with a love of the Party (and of East London) and a great sense of realism or cynicism which saved me from making a fool of myself more than once. I think he had a role in pointing the executive in my direction but if so, like an old warrant officer dealing with a young subaltern, he soon evened the score, reminding me that his most successful campaign had been fought in the absence of the candidate who was in hospital. 'The candidate, Norman, is an unfortunate legal necessity.'

A fortnight later Margaret came with me to the general meeting, which was not exactly packed out, to hear me make a speech, which was followed by a vote on a motion to adopt me as prospective candidate.

My speech was not too difficult. Mr Wilson's Government was in great difficulties and since I had last met the Association Executive it had lost two by-elections, Walthamstow West and Cambridge. Naturally I had a gloat about that and gave them a brief account of my background and career. The substance of my speech was that people, not Government directives, produce wealth and cause an economy to succeed or fail.

... politics is concerned with more than the price of marbles, or whether the *Daily Mirror* should cost 4d. or 5d., or even the price of butter. The present Government has illustrated this truth. It was elected on the claim above all others that 'it would run the economy', as George Brown put it in a lucid moment, 'like it had never been run before'. Since then it seems its great preoccupation has been whether a pound note offered for sale in New York or Zurich will fetch $2.78 and a half cent or $2.78 and seven thirty-seconds of a cent, and whether the index of production, provisional and seasonally adjusted, has made a great leap forward from 132 to 133, or slumped to the reactionary level of 131. Don't think these things are unimportant. They are very important, but not in their own right – only in that they affect people, and politics is about people and principles. It is not about units of personnel, nor expedients to botch through the next crisis at the next Labour Conference.

The people are real people with names. They are not bits of paper to be chucked from the in-tray to the out-tray of one of the 45,000 new civil servants in one of the new ministries with which we have been so sorely afflicted in the past three years. They have hopes – they have fears. They have ambitions and they have abilities.

They seek opportunities and rewards. They have standards of living and of behaviour and of ethics and each and every one is different. It is the work, the attitude towards work of these millions of separate individuals that move the index of production, that raises or lowers the prices. The decline in the economy of our country has come about largely because the government has preferred to believe that it, and particularly the Prime Minister, alone has the power to move the index of production up and down and thereby affect the lives of the people by plan, by exhortation, by decree and by law. And it will not admit that it is proven wrong. Even at Walthamstow George Brown said, 'it is you the people of Britain who are on trial, not we the Government.' In successive and unending crises the Prime Minister has blamed the Tories, the Gnomes of Zurich, the seamen's strike, the Arab–Israeli war, Mr Ian Smith, the lack of growth in the German and American economies, and now with startling foresight and planning he has produced a scapegoat for this winter's crisis before it has happened ... now it is to be the Communists. At this rate the only new scapegoat left for the General Election will be the Salvation Army.

Where does all this get us? It comes to this. You cannot base a political philosophy, a way of organising society, on the current favourite theory of some economist or another on how to achieve economic growth without inflation. That is putting the cart before the horse.

First, find your principles, your aims and objectives and then devise the methods. Then all becomes clear. My beliefs, what I hold to be the principles of Conservatism, are simple.

First of all that people come before the State.

That a man's first loyalty is to his own principles and to his family.

That Conservatives should stand for the individual, for freedom, responsibility, opportunity and free choice.

Socialism seems to me to rate the State above the people, to stand for restriction, state dependency, direction and allocation and drab uniformity.

If you start from these ideas economic policy makes sense. People will work for themselves and their families, they will not work for the tax collector. People will save for their future or to buy their own homes, they will not save to be robbed by inflation, by taxes or for the privilege of becoming a state tenant.

Tinkering with the bank rate, giving Mrs Castle power to run tea-shops, taxis and all that, can do nothing to increase the will of ordinary men and women to get to work, do a good day's work and do it well. And the cruel burden of tax can only do the reverse.

Socialism in action has, and always will, mean a loss of freedom in law as restriction is piled upon restriction and a loss of economic freedom as tax is piled upon tax.

The Conservative answer must be to lower taxes and to give the right to make one's own choices on one's own responsibility and judgement.

It has been said that there is no difference between the two Parties. I believe that there is and always has been a great gulf, the gulf of which I have spoken . . .

I ended with a call to my audience to come out with me and campaign, and expressed a personal view of how to campaign for which I was later to become well known.

I do not accept that in politics the meek shall inherit the Earth.

In campaigning I believe in being noisy and aggressive and that one should do all in one's power to take advantage of your adversaries' embarrassment, failures and discomfiture.

Neither my political beliefs nor my tactics have changed greatly over the years. It was the sort of speech I wanted to make and my audience wanted to hear and when the Chairman, Mr Taft, proposd my adoption it was carried unanimously.

My wife and I drove home in a warm afterglow of achievement. I had started on my political career and in five or seven years time I thought, given some luck, I would be in the House of Commons. In the meantime we discussed practicalities. I would resign my offices in the Hemel Hempstead Conservative Association. We had already put our house on the market and were looking for a suitable place in London. I wondered if Cecil Parkinson would think I had stolen a march on him, or that I was foolish to commit myself to a safe Labour seat. We agreed that Cecil, as a constituency chairman, was far enough ahead of me in the game to set his sights on a better seat than South West Islington and so it turned out. Not long after my adoption Cecil was adopted to fight Reggie Paget, the eccentric millionaire Labour MP for Northampton – a marginal seat he could well expect to win.

Before the end of November we had sold Fryth View for £10,450 – curiously enough to another airline pilot – and bought 58 Canonbury Park North for £12,200. No. 58 was an attractive 1830 semi-detached villa with only the tiniest of gardens, but in one of the nicest parts of Islington, at one end of a wide tree-lined street. Even where houses had been destroyed during the war they had been replaced by reasonably attractive buildings, and nearby Canonbury Square, though ravaged by traffic, was (and indeed still is) a near perfectly complete Georgian square of large and imposing houses.

The purchase of No. 58 had stretched my resources and it needed a good deal of work.

I managed to convince myself that living in London was a very good thing, but I do not think our children, certainly not the elder two, were ever convinced. They felt they had just been uprooted from their house and garden in the country, taken away from their school and their friends, gaining very little or nothing in return. In later years they told me they hated going to bed up at the top of this five-storey house whilst Margaret and I were right down in the semi-basement kitchen and dining room. Nor were local parks any substitute for our garden. Young William, only four years old, adapted most easily, soon becoming one of the 'thugs' of his nursery class at Highbury Infants School. At that time the Inner London Education Authority, although Labour controlled, was still concerned with education. Its descent into rabid left-wing politics, racism and campaigns for homosexuality was still to come, and our local schools were well run on traditional lines. Alas it was not long before the nasties came out of the woodwork and the destruction of education in London began.

John and Alison adapted pretty well at the Junior School under the care of its stalwart headmistress and her excellent young deputy. Indeed John did well enough to win a place in 1969 at the City of London School. Had he not done so he would have gone to Highbury Grammar School, whose headmaster, Dr Rhodes Boyson (later to be one of my constituents in Chingford), was already cutting a controversial figure. Sadly, although we were to live in Islington for only two years, we were to witness the beginning of the slide of standards which became an avalanche into an abyss of educational failure. The extreme left had already begun to infiltrate and I remember the sadness of a young deputy headmaster when he told me that he was leaving ILEA having realised that there was little chance of promotion for anyone but Marxists. Even then, as such good teachers and first-class professional apolitical officers, whom I met in ILEA's Islington operations, retired or left, they were being replaced by the hard left. The cancer that had taken root in ILEA in the early or mid sixties was beginning to grow; but at that time I had no idea that eighteen years later Michael Heseltine and I would lead the campaign for its abolition.

Settling in as residents of Islington was one thing. Making a local political impact another. Few people thought that it mattered who the Conservative candidate was and we had all too few activists working for the party. Our fund-raising was amateurish and we relied quite heavily on the centrally funded work of Frank Pike and his team. There were coffee mornings, raffles and, of course, jumble sales. Our jumble sales were popular with a good local following and the queue of mainly elderly ladies began to form outside Leeson Hall half an hour or more before opening time. The bargain hunters of South West Islington made the first day of the Harrods sale look calm and demure by comparison. Within an hour or two almost everything remotely useful had gone – mostly sold, but a good deal simply stolen.

My biggest political coup in Islington was in March 1969 when I persuaded Iain Macleod, the Shadow Chancellor, to come to speak in support of myself and the prospective candidates for the other Islington seats. I had the privilege of taking the chair, hoping to shine with a little reflected glory from that master of political oratory. He was on good form, declaiming in favour of cuts in income tax, the end of compulsory incomes policy, trades union reform and reform of the system of social security. The *Islington Gazette* reported him as saying the social services did not answer the needs of the day and as opposing indiscriminate subsidies regardless of need. Although Enoch Powell had by then left the Shadow Cabinet following the row over his so called 'rivers of blood' speech, Iain made it obvious he hoped for his return. On the social security issue he emphasised that his proposals for selective social services, not blanket coverage, had been pioneered by Enoch Powell and himself some years earlier when they had been regarded as heretical. As I hear some Conservatives today invoke Iain's memory against proposals to end the absurdity of paying child benefit to well-off parents I allow my mind to go back to that speech in Islington almost twenty years ago.

I had admired Macleod since first meeting him in Enfield in the late forties and was familiar with his prodigious memory. Such a memory is a great gift for a politician. Lacking it, I have often held back from a swift and effective riposte by that tingling fear that my memory of fact or quotation might not be correct. To be liberated from that fear must be a politician's golden gift. What is more, few of us are immune to the flattery of being remembered by prominent or important people. That evening I saw Iain using his gift to win friends (often more important than winning arguments, at which he was also adept).

Amongst those who spoke to Iain over a drink after the meeting was a retired actor of no great national fame who was a member of the local Party. I introduced him by name, a name which I have long forgotten, and mentioned his profession. 'Ah,' said Iain, 'but I don't remember you by that name,' and to my astonishment and the delight of the actor recollected not only his stage name but several plays in which he had appeared before the Second World War. It was a *tour de force*, a masterful display of an ability which I have never enjoyed.

It was in April 1969 that, unknown to me at the time, fate – in the shape of Jim Callaghan – took a hand in my political career. After the collapse of his economic policy and his gross mishandling of the devaluation of sterling, Chancellor Callaghan had been moved from the Treasury to the Home Office. It was therefore to him that the Boundary Commission for England presented its report, the first since 1954, on 21 August 1969. In those fifteen years the distribution of population had changed radically, leaving some constituencies with far too few electors and some far too many. The average number was around 50,000 but at one end there were constituencies like Birmingham Ladywood with only 18,000 and at the other Billericay with over 120,000 and Epping with 115,000. Callaghan's problem was that the existing pattern favoured Labour and the consensus of opinion was that the Boundary Commission's report, if implemented, would be worth fifteen or twenty seats to the Conservative Party. Because the Commission takes evidence in public, and discusses its provisional views with interested parties, the likely shape of its report was the subject of much well-informed speculation. Initially it was assumed that Mr Callaghan, unhappy as he might be at the loss of Labour's unfair advantage, would do as his predecessors had done – and, as we thought, the law required him to do – and lay the orders to implement the Commission's report in its entirety, except perhaps where a parliamentary consensus agreed on minor changes. After all, the system of the independent review of constituency boundaries to ensure, within reason, that each member of Parliament represented a roughly equal number of constituents and that constituency boundaries should follow natural or administrative boundaries was well established, well honoured and widely regarded as one of the pillars of parliamentary democracy.

As days and weeks ticked by, doubts and suspicions arose that Jim Callaghan was proposing the most outrageous piece of gerrymandering since the time when Mr Elbridge Gerry gave his name to the system of arranging constituency boundaries for partisan advantage. Gradually it became clear that Callaghan had no intention of playing the game by the spirit of the rules of the Representation of the People Act. Using as his excuse the Redcliffe Maud report proposing major reforms of local government, the Home Secretary was preparing to argue that almost all the changes in parliamentary constituency boundaries should await changes in local government administrative areas proposed by Redcliffe Maud. It was an argument breathtaking in its impertinence.

The only parts of the Commission's report which Jim Callaghan was prepared to accept were those relating to London (not affected by the Redcliffe Maud report) and a few constituencies with more than 100,000 electors. The Commissions's report was published on 19 June when the Opposition forced a debate and the following day Callaghan published a Bill to legalise his gerrymandering.

In Islington we realised that whether the Boundary Commission's report or the Callaghan proposals were implemented, there would be one seat less with the three constituencies in the south of the Borough being telescoped into two. Nor did it take long to see that it would simplify matters and save a lot of heartache if one of the three prospective candidates found another seat to fight, therefore avoiding a difficult choice for the Islington local parties.

Quite unknown to me Peter Temple-Morris, now Member for Leominster but at that time prospective candidate for Epping, was facing a tricky decision. Epping had the second largest electorate (115,000) in Britain and it straddled the boundary of Essex and Greater London. It included the Labour stronghold of Harlow new town in the north and the Conservative stronghold of Chingford in the south. As Harlow had grown, the balance had increasingly favoured Labour's Stan Newens who won the seat in 1964 and increased his majority to 7500 in 1966. The Callaghan proposals would have cut off Tory Chingford to form the major part of a new London constituency and left Stan Newens pretty confident of holding on despite any likely swing against Labour.

Peter Temple-Morris promptly – perhaps precipitately – told the officers of the Epping Conservative Association that he wished to put forward his name for the new Chingford seat. They wished him luck, but explained that they had to have a candidate who would fight Epping on its old or new boundaries as the case may be and that they would therefore have to ask for his resignation if he was not willing to stay on those terms. Honourably, but too quickly for his own good, Peter Temple-Morris resigned and, just as I was looking for a new constituency, Epping was looking for a new candidate.

I was one of more than 250 applicants for the nomination at Epping and might well have never been given much consideration at all but for two slices of good luck. First, as it looked as though I was to have my constituency shot away from beneath me I had a certain amount of sympathy going for me. Second, the Selection Committee, and particularly the Chairman, 'Bunny' Morgan, felt they had had a run of bad luck in choosing candidates – five since 1945 when Churchill's old Epping seat had been split into two and he took and won the Woodford half and Labour took the other half, still called Epping. Of them, only Graeme Finlay fought more than one election. As a result many members had formed strong views on what sort of candidate they wanted and even stronger ones on what sort they did not want. In short, they did not want a lawyer, a public schoolboy, nor anyone with a double-barrelled name. He had to be married with children, in a classless occupation, between thirty-five and forty-five years of age and, ideally, to have had political experience in a new town like Harlow. The description was virtually an Identikit picture of me, and a slice of luck which I am sure secured me an invitation to put forward my name to the Selection Committee.

My reply needed no time for thought and within a fortnight I received a second letter asking me to attend at The Thatched House Hotel at 9.00 on Friday 26 September to speak for ten minutes on 'My Policy for the Election'. The Thatched House! The very scene of so many rowdy 604 Squadron parties. A selection committee held within a couple of miles of my old base at North Weald and within ten miles of my birthplace. I knew almost every inch of the area. It was on my ground and I felt I had to have a good chance. A few drives around the area refreshed my memory of the geography, and allowed me to buy all the local papers. After that a little research into Stan Newens showed he was almost my ideal opponent. A left-wing schoolteacher who had refused military national service could not have a stronger contrast than a right-wing ex-North Weald fighter pilot and now an airline pilot!

I returned home on 17 September from an exhausting trip – a series of transatlantic crossings, six in all, from London to Toronto, back to Manchester, to Toronto again, Manchester again, Toronto again before returning to London with stops on each crossing at Prestwick and Montreal. It took a day or two to get over the jet lag and my speech was written so late that I arrived at the Selection Committee with it still untyped in manuscript form.

Like my speech at Islington, my first speech to the Selection Committee at Epping expressed the heart of my political beliefs. It was by far the best of the three speeches I made to gain the nomination and I would willingly make it again with one exception. I used then the words, 'sooner or later I believe we will become part of a great European state'. Today I do not think that is desirable nor likely within any political, as opposed to historical or even geological time scale.

No Party with serious pretensions to power can afford, as the Liberals can, to have candidates all pointing in different directions.

I am a Party candidate, part of a team pledged to form a government if elected and the voter expects that a Party candidate accepts the Party policy, and should see to it that if his Party is elected to government that policy will be enacted.

But the voter also expects that if a man stands as a Tory the Party policy on which he stands will be a Tory policy.

That does not make it necessary to be a Party Hack, or to stand on polling day as unprocessed lobby fodder. There is ample scope for personality, enthusiasm and reservations.

And outside partisan matters there are issues such as those of censorship, permissiveness, drugs and gambling and the local issues of airports, motorways and hospitals.

But before specific policies a candidate must get over the basic background of his beliefs.

Not just 'Wot's yer policy?' but 'Why are you standing as a Tory?'

I belong to and work for our Party because it is the National Party. It is for people who love Britain, her people and their ways, and wish to work along the grain of her fabric, not across it.

The people have withstood all manner of crises, all manner of bad government, puritanical dictators, mad monarchs, sloths, dotards and charlatans. They would not be destroyed by Prime Minister Wilson and his apprentices.

This is the starting point of my policy. That Britain is not bankrupt because our greatest asset is our people.

Sadly it has been misused. Its strong and vigorous growth stunted to encourage the pappy suckers that consume without giving first.

We must use, nurture, feed and protect that priceless asset.

At present it is stifled, strangled, corrupted and over-shadowed by government.

We need a touch of the Marxist maxim of the withering away of the State.

State-owned industries must be sold back to the public, especially workers in the industries.

Then away with the parasitic growths in government, N B P I, Land Commission and the like.

A real cutback in numbers of staff in departments, such as those managing our relations with Commonwealth countries, whose staff has increased as their responsibilities have decreased.

And let private provision replace State welfare wherever it can.

Secondly, as the size of government is reduced so can taxation be cut. And simplified and re-directed on to spending not earning.

As a consequence of this, and the abolition of subsidies on consumption, lower wage rates will rise.

Such a rise will require and impel more automation, the more efficient use of skilled labour. No bad thing to be parsimonious in our use of that asset. and it will militate against the import of unskilled immigrant labour.

That links to the third and fourth aspects of my policy.

The third is the overwhelming need of industrial law reform and the vital need to extend the law of contract to the supply of labour.

The control of immigration is my fourth aspect. The continuing high level of immigration compounding every social problem is a threat to our social stability. And that level must be further cut.

Fifthly, as we become richer so we can together provide for ourselves against the ordinary hazards of life.

Private provision in pensions, medical care and education should be encouraged, in order to provide a choice other than Hobson's, a standard for comparison and to bring more money into these services.

The subsidy on houses should be abolished, and market rents

allowed to operate. Subsidy should go to the families who cannot afford what they need. I emphasise 'need', not 'happen to occupy'. And that subsidy to combat a national problem should be national not a local one.

My sixth point is on Law and Order and the so-called permissive society.

Some parts of this permissiveness – I suspect those of sexual morals, particularly – are part of a cycle of fashion, and will turn back before long. Pornography will I think become a bore. Exhibitionist and erotic shows will become as *passé* as *The Dancing Years* – and Shakespeare will still fill the theatres.

But the preaching, as I heard on the BBC on Sunday, of the doctrine that if one disaproves strongly of a law one can break it – indeed one has a moral right and obligation to do so – is another matter.

I happen to believe that if a thug, who is planning a robbery, deliberately chooses to buy or steal a gun, to load and take it with him and use it to kill in the course of his crime, he should die.

I have the right to try to change the law on that matter. Whatever the permissives say I have no right to kill that criminal myself.

The law must be enforced. And whilst there is no place for revenge we must protect the lawful citizen against the criminal not the criminal against society.

Finally, Foreign Policy and Defence.

The object of foreign and defence policies is the security of the Realm.

If those policies fail, all else is dust.

Their object is not to overthrow the governments of China or Russia or South Africa, nor of Rhodesia.

Their object is to protect this Island.

Like all of Western Europe we have relied increasingly for that protection for over twenty years on the USA.

That cannot and will not go on.

Whilst speaking of economic affairs I did not mention Europe or the Common Market. For me the question of Europe is not the price of butter or even the size of the market for motor cars. It is a matter of national security. We need a Europe prosperous enough, strong enough to defend itself against all comers.

That is it.

Freedom not Equality.

Opportunity not Welfare.

Help for the needy not handouts for the greedy.

Above all Pride – not that goeth before a fall, but to get up from where we have fallen.

The speech went well. The questions even better. And I extracted not just smiles but some good laughs from the Committee.

To my great relief I was invited back, this time as one of six, to address the Executive, a far larger committee of some forty or fifty people on the theme of 'Current Politics'. It does not read as good a speech twenty years later.

I made the most of my role as personal assistant to Andrew Pearce, our candidate in the Islington North by-election the previous week, and concentrated on the need to bring out the government's record of failure, and the Prime Minister's drift from one expedient to another, a drift taking us nearer to a Socialist State. I put our lack of greater success in the by-elections to the success of the Government in blurring the policy differences between the parties whilst smearing on the immigration issue, and called for Conservatives to 'speak out loudly and clearly as Tories, proclaiming proudly what we believe.'

Although it was not a great speech it seemed to hit the right note, and questions went well. Margaret had been invited, perhaps required is the better word, to come with me although not to speak nor answer questions and we drove back to Islington assessing my chances of surviving to the next and final stage.

I could not bear to wait for a letter to hear of my fate and telephoned the Epping Agent, John Newell, the next morning. He gave me the good news. I was one of two candidates to be recommended to a special general meeting of the whole Association which would make the final selection on Monday 17 November.

By then Jim Callaghan's gerrymandering bill had fallen, having been defeated in the House of Lords. Still unwilling to implement the report and facing humiliation in the courts at the hands of Ross McWhirter, he played a last desperate, successful card. He complied with the law by laying the orders to implement the report – but spat in the face of parliamentary democracy by whipping the Labour Party to vote them down. As a result Epping would be fought on the existing boundaries. It was a tough but, may be, winnable contest.

Once again crew rosters were obliging, and a quick trip to New York and another to Toronto brought me back to London on Saturday morning with a half-completed speech in my briefcase.

For this final test I had fifteen minutes (earlier speeches having been ten minutes) and a free choice of subject. I began lightly with a little humour about the selection process and then, determined not to overrun my fifteen minutes, reflected on the wisdom of Ecclesiastes: 'Be not rash with thy mouth. A fool's voice is known by multitude of words.'

That made a good entry point for a brisk attack on the Labour government and again that call for what eighteen years later in the election of 1987 I was to describe as 'clear water' between Conservative and Labour policy.

I am not, never have been, nor do I ever intend to be an apologist for the Conservative Party.

I have no intention of slurring over the differences we have with socialism, nor concealing my belief that we are the National Party of Great Britain, representing not narrow class interest, nor the bigotry of the left wing intellectuals, but all those who reject the alien dogma of socialism and who support the British tradition of democracy, of personal freedom, of personal responsibility for one's own affairs and those of one's family, with the least possible interference from the State.

This is not the sterile doctrine of arrogant socialism, nor even of benevolent but stifling bureaucracy that would take away from ordinary men and women the right to buy their own homes, to choose their children's schools, the right to save in their own way for their own pensions in retirement.

Socialism, I told the Epping Conservatives, was not only economically inefficient but incompatible with personal freedom.

The economic and political facts of life entwine. If you give responsibility and freedom to a man, if you cut his taxes, increase his freedom of choice, then you give him the incentive to work and to save, which can lift us from the bottom row of economic sluggards to the top of the growing economies of the West.

I took a tough line on immigration.

We as a nation depend economically on the skill and industry of our people and we cannot afford to import ill-educated unskilled labour with a high ratio of dependants per wage earner whether they be black, white, brown or purple striped.

We do need to attract immigrants – who are well educated and highly skilled – again regardless of race.

Nor as a small densely populated island with a closely integrated population living cheek by jowl sharing common ethics, ambitions and standards – and prejudices too – can we afford to import large numbers of immigrants who neither share nor care for those ethics, ambitions or standards – and with prejudices of their own – nor can we allow them to set up foreign enclaves in our country.

The special status of these would-be immigrants as Commonwealth citizens has no reality when their countries are independent republics often at pains to reject all our political and cultural influence.

That is their right – but it makes them aliens without right to come here except by invitation.

That is Party policy and I support it.

Again, too, I emphasised the dangers for Europe in relying upon America for our defence.

I do not believe that we can continue to rely, as we have increasingly done for twenty-five years, on America to do it [defend Britain] for us.

We see today her lack of resolve to support her allies when the going is tough and vocal opposition at home is organised.

We cannot let our security be jeopardised by riots of students on American campuses or a march of demonstrators on Washington.

We must turn to Europe. We share a common danger with the countries of Western Europe.

And we must go into Europe not looking for a soft ride in the Common Market but determined to weld together and lead the great power of Western Europe.

Those speeches of twenty years ago set out my political beliefs which had changed little over the previous twenty years and even less since. They expressed my support for the Selsdon Ted Heath of 1969 and foreshadowed both my breach with the corporatist Ted Heath of 1973 and my part in the Thatcher revolution of the eighties.

But all that was to come. That night, drawn as the second speaker in the contest, I sat with Margaret in the waiting-room behind the packed Epping Hall, tense and dry-mouthed, listening to the applause which spattered the speech of my opponent Gordon Nixon. He had previously stood in Lewisham and outgunned me in experience but I correctly divined that I outgunned him in oratory, particularly platform passion and humour. As usual on such occasions the proceedings were running late because a few members of the Association either thought they, rather than the Selection Committee, should have sifted the candidates or because of unhappiness at the way in which Peter Temple-Morris, who had been a popular candidate, had left the constituency. As a result Gordon Nixon and his wife were still in the scruffy waiting-room when Margaret and I arrived. I strained every nerve to seem relaxed and to radiate confidence, cheerfully chattering at Gordon who looked as tense and worried as I felt; and it was not until he was called up to the platform that I was able to allow my limbs to tremble with the suppressed excitement and tension with which I was possessed.

After my speech Margaret and I returned to join Gordon Nixon and his wife in the waiting-room. We could hear only the buzz of voices, tread of feet and scraping of chairs. At last a long burst of applause signalled the declaration of the ballot and moments later John Newell, the agent, entered the room. The vote had been 159 for me against 82 for Nixon. I cannot remember how he imparted the news of my success to me and Gordon's disappointment to him. I think, indeed I hope, I said the right things to Gordon and I know that even as I walked up the stairs to the hall to be proclaimed as prospective parliamentary candidate for Epping I had time to think of him and his wife driving home, feeling so dejected to have been so near to winning and then to have lost. All that was forgotten once on the platform. All was applause, congratulations and handshakes. Then, a little later, Margaret and I were alone in our faithful old Vauxhall on our way back to Islington, thinking how strangely fate works. Thanks to Jim Callaghan, poor Peter Temple-Morris was left in the lurch and I was to fight Epping in his place, to win it from Labour, and, after redistribution in 1972, to win the new Chingford seat on which Peter had set his heart. Once again luck had played a part in my life – although some of our socialist Bishops might conclude that God does indeed move in a mysterious way His wonders to perform!

The following afternoon I looked down at Epping from the flight deck of a Boeing 707 on my way to Stansted airport on a regular check flight. I had a week at home before leaving for Tokyo. In that time I began the first round of engagements in an intensive programme to visit every branch in the huge spreading Epping constituency. In the speech which had won the nomination I had said, '. . . the road from Epping to Westminster, despite geography, goes through Harlow,' and although the new town was our weakest area and Labour's stronghold I determined to make an impact there as early as possible. I was lucky to have an excellent Conservative Association. Bunny Morgan, the chairman, was, and indeed still is, a considerable figure and he was backed by a formidable array of voluntary workers and Party members. Harlow new town with 47,500 voters was the challenge but I knew that I would not carry a majority there. I knew that most of the 35,000 Chingford votes would break my way, as would the 8400 in Epping town, whilst Waltham Abbey's 10,000 would split more evenly. The smaller centres such as Theydon Bois and the villages would be overwhelmingly Conservative and, although in penny packets, they totalled almost 14,500 votes. Harlow, however, would be the key.

The political context of my campaign was decided by my own instincts and the character and style of my opponent Stan Newens. I decided to target his left-wing sympathies (although by today's standards Newens is a moderate), support of CND, and his refusal to undergo national service in the armed forces which I paraphrased as pacifist. To his eternal credit, when Argentina invaded the Falklands, Stan Newens supported the use of force to liberate the islanders from fascist control. But that was unforeseeable in 1969. My theme was to be 'Stan Newens always votes the Labour line – unless he supports the Communist line instead.' Stan Newens also did me a favour by seeing the Arabs as underdogs in the Middle East and identifying with them. I never quite discovered why, perhaps it was the Suez adventure, perhaps it was the American support of Israel, but it posed him some difficult issues of conscience as the PLO became committed to terrorism. In contrast, holding a balanced position on the question of the rights of Jews and Arabs, of Israel and the Palestinians, opposing terrorism from whatever quarter, I gained the support of Chingford's not insubstantial Jewish population, many of whom as migrants from inner East London had a history of voting Labour.

In retrospect I suppose my campaign was as personal as it could decently have been without going over the top and it was many years before either Stan Newens or I could bring ourselves to acknowledge the other, but in Epping there was little room for giving quarter in a knife-edged campaign.

In that week after my selection I attended my first meeting of the Epping Executive Committee, and functions in three other branches. Then it was off to Tokyo.

Fortunately I was at home from 10 December until I left for South America on New Year's Eve and in that time managed to eat more Christmas lunches and dinners than I had ever managed before!

My cuttings from the constituency local press underline my 'high profile'.

I was determined that in the few months before a likely election I would ensure that all the voters would be aware that I existed. The local press was very active with no fewer than four main papers and two with several localised pages circulating in the constituency, and I reckoned they would give me most coverage whilst I was still fresh news and whilst I tackled controversial issues boldly. In late January the Waltham Abbey local paper was stunned by my views on housing, reported quite fairly under the headline 'Leave housing to private landlords – Tory candidate.' To hold such a view in 1970 was not just controversial, it was regarded as eccentric. The paper quoted me as saying, 'Ideally I would like to see councils out of the business of housing completely. After all, if you can rent a TV set or a car, what is immoral about renting a house?' Such radicalism drove the local Labour Party near to frenzy, especially in Harlow, and kept me in the local headlines.

It was none too easy to combine such a whirlwind campaign with the profession of a long-haul airline pilot. In general the roster clerks were helpful and we had an understanding that I would accept reduced time off between trips in return for their co-operation in scheduling me to be in England on key dates. Even so, it imposed quite a strain on my wife who stood in for me whilst I was abroad. A further complication arose in February 1970 when after sixteen years in BOAC, having finally reached the top of the co-pilots' seniority list, I began my command course. The first two or three weeks of ground study and flight simulator details at London Airport gave me extra time at home, even if it was hard work swotting for my old profession and for what I hoped would be my new one too. Then early in March I was sent to Prestwick for intensive advanced flying training concentrating on handling the 707 in extreme emergencies – such as failure of two engines, and in bad weather. Perversely, Prestwick, normally famed for its strong winds, experienced a series of lovely calm days and I was left cooling my heels waiting for strong enough winds to blow across the runway to demonstrate my ability to handle the 707 in such conditions. Indeed at one stage seeing the weather set fair for days I caught the train back to London to continue my campaign in Epping. Knowing that if I had asked for permission it would not have been given, I countered the wrath of the management by showing sweetly reasonable surprise that they should object to me taking a few days in London and by offering to return as soon as I was needed.

The course at Prestwick finally completed, I began a series of trips, still a first officer, but carrying out the whole of the captain's duties under the watchful eye of senior captains playing the role of co-pilot. I prayed that the election would be delayed long enough to complete all the requirements for my promotion to captain. It was, but BOAC, true to form, re-calculated its figures and decided that although I and most of my colleagues on the same course had successfully completed all the requirements our promotions would be delayed until the Autumn.

Before then, misled by a few favourable polls and fearful of troubles to come, Harold Wilson cut and ran, calling an election for 18 June. The announcement came on 18 May and I heard it that evening in New York. I arrived back in London from a five-day trip to Jamaica. Captain Eric Brown allowed me to land the 707, flight 508, from New York at Heathrow on Wednesday 20 May. It was to be the last time I would land a 707.

On Friday 22 May the *Epping Express and Independent* published on its front page a photograph of a smiling and confident Stan Newens below the headline: 'MP: I can't see how I can lose.' I was reported to be 'confident'. Outwardly I was, but inwardly rather less so although I believed I could and would just pull it off.

Once again I enjoyed good luck. After quite a good showing in the fifties, when John Arlott had been their candidate, the Liberals had fallen on hard times. In 1966 they had come close to losing their deposit and after a long and difficult meeting the reportedly hard-up local Party decided not to contest Epping. Their decision suited my tactics. With 10,000 Liberal votes going begging, the more I could depict Stan Newens as an extreme left winger the more of them I would collect. Even so I knew it would be a tight election and that I had to go for every vote.

We produced three main pieces of literature. An introductory leaflet, election address (each in two versions, one for Chingford the other for the Essex part of the constituency), and the final appeal leaflet. The address itself enjoyed the free-delivery facility of the Post Office, the others were distributed by hand. The introductory leaflet was a very personal appeal. Printed in neither red nor blue, just black and white, it made no mention of the Conservative Party. One side carried a picture of me, in uniform at the controls of a 707 with the caption: 'Why is a man with one of the best paid jobs looking for another?'

On the reverse a list of public meetings gave the only clue to my politics in the names of my supporting speakers, Conservative MPs, a Conservative peer, the party's Area Chairman, David Sells, the national Young Conservative chairman, and two local councillors. With a total of fourteen public meetings – two in Harlow, to keep Stan Newens on the hop – I spoke in every part of the constituency, including six of the larger villages – four on one night alone.

The leaflet had exactly the effect I wanted. The Labour party protested it was unfair to issue literature which did not identify me as the Conservative candidate, thereby giving extra publicity to what was a simple publicity scheme. It also had the merits of intriguing people sufficiently to persuade them to read on, and of interesting them in me as a real person, not just a cardboard cut-out candidate. Partly as a result of that leaflet my fourteen public meetings were very well attended. Central Office did not regard Epping as a marginal seat so I had no priority call on the Party's big-name speakers. Instead local MPs like John Biggs-Davison, Bernard Braine and Derek Walker-Smith came as support speakers, as did James Allason from Hemel Hempstead, and the ever cheerful and bouncy (but soon to be disgraced) Lord Jellicoe made a flying visit, joining me in speaking from the roof of my campaign Land Rover. It was only at my final eve of poll rally in Chingford that I had a member of the Shadow Cabinet to speak when the biggest hall in Chingford was packed to the very doors to hear Quintin Hogg – now Lord Hailsham.

Margaret and I had little time to think about anything beyond polling day. We slogged our hearts out canvassing, speaking, appearing, rallying and encouraging our supporters. The weather was glorious with a succession of long sunny days, and our Party workers worked as they had never worked before, but the polls were none too encouraging and towards the end most observers fancied Wilson to just hold on to a majority. Yet somehow, in that last vital week, I sensed a change of mood back in favour of us. I suppose more than anything else it was my reception in Harlow new town, where on walkabout of the shopping centre I looked into Woolworth's to find many of the young girl assistants wearing Tebbit stickers. 'If they vote for me – then I'll win,' I told Margaret.

Although it was immensely hard work, I was buoyed up throughout the campaign by a feeling that I had nothing to lose. As Epping was not on the Central Office list of marginal seats I was not expected to win it, so if I failed having fought a good campaign then, with no shame or regrets, I could return to the flight deck, looking forward to promotion and financial security – at least until a by-election in a Conservative seat or selection for the next general election. On the other hand, if I won then I would have embarked on my new career, although in a very risky way since redistribution might leave me without a winnable seat – or any seat to fight at all.

I fought the campaign to the very last day. I canvassed on hundreds of doorsteps, shook hundreds of hands during dozens of walkabouts in shopping centres and made speeches on the least provocation – or none at all – at any time of day and in almost any place. My speeches were all on the themes which I had set out in the contest to gain the nomination – spiced with lines that emerged from the issues in the national campaign. I still have the notebook which I used for the campaign, containing the outlines of two campaign speeches, covered with notes and additions, and a sheet of paper on which I calculated from canvass returns, national polls and the local election results my forecast of the result in Epping. I showed it to no one except my wife – I wanted no one else to know that it forecast that on an 85 per cent poll I would secure 49,900 votes with 47,850 for Newens – a paper-thin two-per-cent majority of 2,050.

It was a fine month with only a few thundery days to interfere with electioneering, and our Land Rover (borrowed from Jocelyn Hambro who lived in the constituency), pounded the roads and lanes, covered with posters and adorned with loudspeakers, stopping wherever we could find voters to address. The children thought it rather good fun, although John, who at that time suffered from hay fever, spent most of the time with streaming nose and eyes semi-prostrate in the back of the car.

At the beginning of the campaign, polling day had seemed ages away but it came at last and with a great sense of relief I made my tour of polling stations and committee rooms. There was nothing more that I could do. The die was cast and I had won or lost.

My parents had come to stay at our home in Islington to look after the children on election day, and Margaret and I had a room to stay overnight at the Tree Tops Hotel in Epping. A party had been organised there for our key workers, starting after the polling stations were closed to while away the hours whilst they waited for the result. We joined the party at about 11 p.m. tense and nervous, as I waited for John Newell, my agent, to phone and report progress from the count.

From the beginning of the campaign I knew that I had been in the driving seat. Newens had fought a defensive campaign complaining of 'smears' and had been complacent throughout. The local paper headline of 22 May, 'I can't see how I can lose,' was ironically true. His complacency blinded him to how he was losing and the last local papers' headlines said it all: 'There'll be a recount, but we'll win – Tories.' 'A 10,000 majority – Labour,' proclaimed the Epping paper; whilst the Harlow paper headlined 'Labour agent forecasts 12,000 majority.' It was hardly the way to get out every last Labour supporter from Newens' new-town stronghold.

The figures I had calculated kept going round in my mind as I pretended to listen to what people were saying to me and stole quick glances at my watch. That seemed to slow to an agonising crawl towards

1 a.m. which was the appointed time to go to the count. Margaret had gone to our room to rest but the very idea of rest was laughable to me. Indeed I was shaking with excitement and nervousness when I went to tell her it was time to leave. We received a cheer from the small crowd waiting outside the hall and as I walked in I could see the count was almost complete. The bundles of votes were laid out in two lines – almost exactly equal in length. There was a buzz of excitement and I was told there was a problem. The percentage poll was lower than I had expected at 73 per cent, some 84,650 votes having been cast. The count showed 41,040 for Newens and 42,615 for me – a majority of 1575 – but the two tallies totalled only 83,650. Somewhere a bundle of 1000 votes had gone adrift. If they turned out to be mine I would have been home and dry with majority of 2575 – if they were Newens' then my majority would be only 575. That would mean a recount with the possibility that Newens might yet scrape back by the skin of his teeth.

I could feel the contents of my stomach rhythmically revolving and I exerted every ounce of willpower to keep my face a mask to conceal my feelings. I caught sight of the faces of my supporters outside climbing up to peer over the windows into the hall and pretended I did not know they were there. I tried not to catch anyone's eye for fear that my expression would show that I believed I had won. The returning officer came towards me – I guessed what he would say from the face of my agent and that of Newens. I had won – by 2,575 – he was ready to declare the result. My memory of the declaration is hazy. I know I embraced my wife and made the traditional speech of thanks (both are recorded in the press), but I cannot remember in which order they took place. I remember, too, catching sight of a senior local police officer also embracing my wife – whether before or after me, once again I cannot recollect.

I'd done it. I'd won – and what's more it was becoming clear that the Labour Government was defeated. We struggled through our supporters within and outside the hall and back to the Tree Tops Hotel where the news had preceded us. It was dawn before I got to bed and fell into a deep sleep from which I was awakened by a waiter with a tray of tea and the morning papers. It was 19 June.

5

Back Bencher

I was a Member of Parliament. We were in Epping. I had a new insecure £3250-a-year job. I would have to leave the security of my £5000-a-year job with BOAC. I was thirty-nine years old. I had no money, a wife, three children, a mortgage I could no longer afford and I had taken a gigantic leap in the dark – a huge gamble in a game in which I had little idea of the stakes and even less of the rules. We still had no car of our own since I had not had time to replace the faithful Vauxhall, which had been written off in an accident a week before the campaign.

I turned to Margaret. 'What have I done?' I asked. Practical as ever she said, 'If you don't know by now you best begin to find out.' Later that day someone drove us to Len Walters' garage at Ponders End from where I had bought my cars in the past and I threw myself into Len's hands. 'I need a car – I don't know yet how I'll afford it but what can you provide?' Provide he did – a rather awful but quite serviceable MG-badged Austin Cambridge saloon and in that we continued home. There I found my parents were still ecstatic – our children perhaps less so. John, despite keeping a brave face, disliked and resented the change in my life that had dragged him from the village home and school he loved into the noisy dirty city but he was full of how my father, in pyjamas and minus his false teeth, had awakened him and his brother and sister exulting, 'He's won, he's won!'

We packed my parents off home and began to cope with a flood of phone calls and an avalanche of telegrams.

The whole country was taken aback by Ted Heath's victory and over the weekend after polling day I searched the results listed in the election newspaper supplements assessing that victory in detail. It was an impressive upset. Mr Wilson's 1966 majority of ninety-seven had been reversed to a Conservative majority of thirty.

I was also concerned to see what had happened to my friends. James Allason, despite the problem of an increasing Labour vote from the growing Hemel Hempstead new town, turned in a majority of over 12,000. My good friend, John Szemery, who had fought South West Islington in my place, had gone down by over 6000. Sadly I found that Cecil Parkinson had failed to unseat Reggie Paget at Northampton. Later he was to tell me he had been immensely confident until quite late in the campaign when his chairman had said, 'Cecil, if you win do you think Reggie Paget would still let us have his place for the Hunt Ball?'

Eventually, amongst all my mail, I found a letter from BOAC. It was a crew duty warning notice telling me that I was to be standby crew on one-and-a-half-hours' call from noon on Sunday. It began to concentrate my mind. I rang the 707 Fleet Manager and told him that I did not quite see how I could comply with that request and suggested he might let me know what arrangements BOAC would like to suggest. As I expected he said that he would have to consider that matter, which gave me a little time to play with. More than a little, I thought, if I knew anything about the BOAC system facing the challenge of a new situation with no precedent to rely upon.

It was not long before things began to fall into place. The Whips' Office rang to tell me the first bare essentials I needed to know. The Fees Office wrote to tell me about pay and I began my new life – an ex-airline pilot who had to make his way in politics.

Within a few days I decided I could no longer afford my mortgage, and honouring the rather more than half promise I had given to live in the constituency I put our London home on the market. We had already identified a couple of houses that might be suitable in Epping and I felt that the sooner we moved the better. That would not all be honey and poor John would a loser again as it would have been just too unsettling to have moved him from the City of London Boys' School at that stage of his education. He would now have a wretched journey every day. But the financial drain had to stop and buying a cheaper house was the first step.

Selling the house in Islington was not too difficult although it almost went wrong at the last moment. The flat roof over the extension which housed the bathroom was none too good and, to my horror, during a heavy rainstorm an hour and a half before our intending purchaser called to discuss some final arrangements, water began to pour through the ceiling. Frantically working on the roof to staunch the flow, I was soon soaked to the skin. Fortunately I managed to dry up the bathroom floor and myself in the very nick of time before he arrived and the deal went through!

After a couple of false attempts we found just the right house. Just at the edge of Epping town, it was a recently built, terraced, neo-Georgian four-storied town house, backing on to open country. It was not quite like our old home in Hertfordshire but one could sit in the garden looking out over the fields and breathe air unsaturated by diesel fumes. The children all loved the house but schools were a different matter. John now faced a tedious one-and-a-half-hour's journey to school by tube. Fortunately his ability to concentrate, shutting out the external world, stood him in good stead and most of his homework was done on the train, but it was not an easy time for him. William detested his new school. He had become an accomplished 'thug', fighting for his place in the pecking order in a rough, tough Islington school and he found himself at odds with the gentler environment of Epping. Alison settled in quite well but as she approached transfer to secondary school, I found – like many of my constituents – the Essex County Education Authority obstinate, uncomprehending, bureacratic and paternalistic. Parental choice was not part of their culture. They knew best and that was that.

Our home in Islington had sold for £17,000 and we managed to make a small profit, even after the costs of improvements. The house in Epping cost only £11,750 so we had a small amount to tide us over the early months on my reduced salary.

In the meantime I had to buy a new car and, as a result, by the end of September I owed the bank almost £1000 and I remained in increasing debt to the bank through almost the whole of my life as a back bencher and a minister.

My relationship with BOAC was characteristically uncertain and difficult. My first thoughts were that I could continue flying – a New York trip once a month and something more during the long recess, being paid a nominal retainer to cover my pension contributions.

My flight manager was unable to decide what should be my fate and was unwilling to do anything but play for time. I too played it long and eventually was invited to lunch with the Managing Director, Keith Granville. By then events (plus Margaret) had convinced me that I could not stay on the flight deck. The chairman made me an offer to resolve the issue. BOAC would keep me in the pension fund, paying its contributions if I would pay mine, up to the next General Election and then I would have the choice of going back to the flight deck or retiring. Alternatively, if I wanted to make the break then they would pay me up to the end of October and put me on unpaid leave until 31 March 1971, and I could retire on my fortieth birthday with the choice of taking back my pension contributions, or drawing a small pension of £713 (index linked). Not an easy choice. The option of unpaid leave was by far the best, but I was desperately hard up and simply dared not commit myself to paying my pension contributions, however good a long-term prospect that was. Fortunately I rejected the option of taking back my contributions to the fund and compromised by taking what was in effect a generous offer of severance pay and an early pension.

The election of 18 June 1970 was seen as a triumph for Ted Heath. Against the odds he had led a campaign which brought down Harold Wilson, then at the peak of his abilities as one of the most adroit political tacticians of the post-war era. Looking back one can see that it was Ted Heath's campaign of 1970 and the Selsdon declaration which marked the Tory Party's first repudiation of the post-war Butskellite consensus. No one should doubt that at the time of the election in 1970 Ted Heath was committed to the end of that corporate consensus and to the new liberal economics. The Selsdon programme fitted well with his earlier battle to end retail price fixing, which was quite wrongly held by his critics to have cost the Conservative Party the 1964 election. Ted Heath's arguments at that time, and the 1970 manifesto with its commitments to the liberation of the economy from the web of Government controls, to denationalisation and its absolute pledge against state controls of prices and wages, were music to the ears of radical Conservatives like myself. I shared his belief that entry into a European market, governed by the strict provisions of the Treaty of Rome forbidding state subsidy of industry, would force our industry to look to itself, not to the state, for the solution to its problems. Although I had doubts over the excessively legalistic and complex proposals on trades union reform – I then favoured a simple change in the law to make contracts of employment legally enforceable – I admired the courage and judgement which had led to the commitment to tackle the abuse of trades union power which was the most damaging single poison in our economy.

At the time of the election I naively assumed that the conversion of both Ted Heath and the Party to the Selsdon programme was one of deeply rooted conviction. In doing so I overestimated Ted Heath's conviction and I underestimated the resistance to new thinking and change within the establishment of the Party. Even worse I was to find that although the Conservative Research Department under successive directors had introduced challenging responses to the accepted doctrine of the inevitability of creeping socialism, the establishment still ran scared of challenging the socialist consensus for fear of a defeat leading to a Conservative rout. They preferred as dignified and slow a retreat as they could muster, willing to concede defeat by instalments but never willing to risk sudden defeat in order to go for victory.

I could hardly wait to get to the House, attending at the first opportunity on 29 June to elect the Speaker, and on the following day to be sworn in as a Member of Parliament.

To reflect my claim that for me the road to Westminster ran through Harlow, I drove out of London to Harlow to be photographed boarding the train on my way to Parliament. Reading my Harlow local paper on the journey I enjoyed the sneering comments of its ill-natured political columnist who was clearly put out by Labour's defeat. I was, according to 'John Citizen's Diary', 'the short-notice little-impact Mr Tebbit.' It was the first, but not the last, time my critics would decry my campaign as second rate but have to admit that somehow I had won by a majority almost exactly as I had forecast and way beyond what they thought possible.

It was not long after my arrival that I realised how little I knew about Parliament. Looking around for help I turned to James Allason who, in no time at all, began to sort me out. As a result I acquired a desk – the first major achievement for any MP – which was conveniently situated in the cloisters at the foot of the stairs leading to the Members' Lobby. I had no idea how much post I would receive or how to handle it so I delayed looking for a House of Commons secretary and began to open my own post and employed a part-time secretary to work from my home in Epping. It was good training. Too many MPs see only the mail their secretaries think they should! I saw it all then – and still do so today. James Allason also advised me that if I wanted to make an impact in the House I should specialise in some way. Wisely I decided not to become just an aviation expert, nor to go for any of the other 'glamour' subjects of the day such as defence or foreign affairs. 'Go for something most people think is dull,' James advised me. 'Why not housing, like me?' As it happened, I was interested in housing, especially as like James I represented a new town, and took his advice. He then suggested I should become secretary of the Party's back-bench committee on housing. I gently protested that this might seem a little precocious as no one knew me and would hardly vote for an unknown new member. 'Leave that to me,' was James's response, 'I'll nominate you and speak to my friends.'

To my utter surprise, in a contested election I beat the former secretary, Robin Cooke, the Conservative Member for Bristol West. I had never met Robin until after the election when he took me aside and introduced himself. It was clear that he was upset at his defeat and I found myself lamely trying to apologise.

'No dear boy,' he said, 'you're more than welcome to the job – I only did it because someone has to and if you'd told me you wanted it I would never have let my name go forward, but it does make a bit of a fool of me to be beaten by someone nobody knows.' Why Robin, a notoriously prickly and difficult character, should have been so understanding I have never known, but over all the years until his sad and premature death in 1987 he was a good friend who extended to me all manner of kindness.

My electoral success rather puzzled me until James told me that I was invited to join a dining club of slightly right-of-centre Conservative Members. In those more discreet times such clubs were never identified in public, but now the names are common currency in the political gossip columns. The 92 Group which had welcomed me was one of the earlier, less hidebound and utterly snob-free groups, even though its membership included a large number of the knights from the shires. Designed for back benchers, those who achieved ministerial rank were then regarded as country members, not expected to attend too often, nor to throw their weight about. Whips were expected not to attend at all since it might lead to a conflict of loyalties between their Whips' duty to report all intelligence to the Whips' Office and the club duty to maintain absolute confidentiality about our discussions. During the elections of officers of the back-bench committees, including the 1922 Committee, those discussions led to agreement on a 'slate' of candidates whom members were expected to support – the explanation of my electoral success! I found the help and advice of members of the 92 invaluable. Not many of the members in those days were destined for ministerial rank – few indeed wanted or expected it. They were mostly very senior and whilst they were utterly loyal they knew how to apply pressure to ministers – an art I, too, learned – but above all they knew 'the form'. I now realise that the members of the 92 then had more in common with the pre-war style of MPs, many content to remain back benchers representing their constituencies as a form of public service rather than out of ideological conviction or ambition, than with the parliamentarians of the 1980s. We took it in turns to give dinner to the club, either at home or in a private room of a hotel or restaurant – money never changing hands between members. Although the 92 is happily still influential it has changed in many ways. We now have lady members – that was literally over the dead body of Ronnie Bell, the

Member for Beaconsfield, who blackballed the nomination of every woman put up for membership to the day he died. Today the 92 always dines in clubs or restaurants and we each pay our own way. Like the House as a whole, our members are more ideological and more ambitious and from a wider social background.

In Parliament I quickly realised that back benchers are noticed by the press and broadcasters only when they make fools of themselves or of other politicians, or when unexpectedly they display specialist knowledge in emotive areas. Sadly publicity about aviation is usually about a disaster so the crash of a Dan Air Comet approaching Barcelona Airport on 2 July captured the headlines. My own plea for better aids than the old-fashioned radio beacons on which the pilot had been relying, were carried by radio, television and the daily press. Despite my determination not to be a spokesman for BALPA, nor the airlines, nor even an aviation politician, every news editor would in future expect some comment from me on aviation stories.

At the same time my election as Secretary of the Housing Committee gave me a platform far removed from aviation – less likely to achieve headlines but more likely to make long-term political changes. Before the end of July I was speaking in my constituency of the need to 'press on a very receptive Minister [Peter Walker] ideas of radical reforms that may at long last begin to liberate housing from the prison of socialist dogma'.

The extension of home ownership, especially to council tenants, has probably had more effect than any other measure to change traditional voting patterns amongst C and D socio-economic groups – the traditional working-class trades unionist Labour voters. Neither Peter Walker nor Julian Amery (somewhat surprisingly cast in the role of Minister for Housing) were slow to move down the home-ownership road. The first step on 30 June was the issue of a local government circular from the Government urging the sale of council houses and, subject to certain restrictions, authorising discounts of up to twenty per cent. At that time it was left entirely to the local authorities to decide whether to sell, and, if so, whether to offer any discount. In Chingford the Waltham Forest Borough Council under Conservative control rapidly decided to go ahead, as did the Conservative-held Greater London Council which was also a large local landlord. In Harlow where home ownership was no more than ten per cent it was a different story. The left-wing Labour council had no intention of selling – quite the reverse; and the other major landlord, the Harlow Development Corporation was not covered by Peter Walker's first circular. Peter is no bad politician and before I could make an appointment to see him he caught up with me in the Division Lobby and encouraged me to put public pressure on him to allow discounted sales of new-town authority houses.

Together with James Allason I launched my campaign mainly through Parliamentary Questions to Peter and his Ministers who soon showed every sign of wishing to cave in. Fearful that Peter might be having difficulty in gaining the agreement of his colleagues we did all we could to help – even ensuring that both James and I questioned him whilst the Prime Minister was on the front bench awaiting his own Question Time. Our persistence was soon rewarded and the 'southern new-town swing' to Conservatives became a feature of every subsequent general election. Nor has the advantage been just party political, or just to a group of tenants given a good financial deal. The vast new-town estates which were built in the fifties and sixties and were often indistinguishable from the local authority estates of the same period, have generally been saved from becoming run-down ghettoes, financial and social disasters of the kind which have bred the misery and despair which is meat and drink to socialist managers looking for votes.

Some years earlier the Labour Party's strategists had correctly ident-ified the grammar schools as the most important escape route from the socio-economic prison in which able children of working-class parents are held. Then with the connivance of upper-class public school socialists within the Conservative Party, most notably Edward Boyle and Hum-phrey Berkeley, they had set about their destruction. The warders of that socialist prison were the trades union barons and it was to be over ten years before they received their come-uppance. In the meantime Peter Walker – himself a grammar schoolboy lacking university edu-cation – began the grammar schoolboys' revenge with the destruction of the prison wall of council housing, transforming it into the home-ownership road to independence. It is quite remarkable that so few people in 1970 saw the potential impact of his Circular 54/70 on house sales – perhaps because as in the grammar school controversy neither side was over anxious to plead guilty to political motivation.

Before the House rose on 24 July for the Summer recess I had found myself deep in controversial issues – arms for South Africa, support for independent radio, and the relationship between private enterprise British Caledonian airlines and the nationalised British Overseas Airways. Then, as in more recent times, I favoured private enterprise, arguing on BBC radio with trades union leader Clive Jenkins (also my constituent through his country home near Harlow) for a fairer deal for the independents. Even in 1970 the violence in Ulster was throwing a long shadow over Britain. The IRA sympathiser Miss Bernadette Devlin had been re-elected to Parliament; and a can of c.s. gas had been flung from the public gallery into the Chamber itself. In my end-of-term report to Conservatives in Epping I referred to these matters and the violent Cambridge riot in words that I would not alter today.

I wondered too how the Harlow Labour Party felt, having recently passed a resolution asking that the violent hooligans involved in the Cambridge riot should be let off more lightly. I still hope that it may sink in to those who, out of false sentiment, ignorance or stupidity, egg on, encourage, or sympathise with those who use violence against their political opponents, that they are treading a dangerous path. A path that can lead only to a breakdown of law and order followed by totalitarian rule.

One other very different shadow fell on the Government in late July with the sudden and tragic death of Iain Macleod. Perhaps because of my admiration for him – and I mean for the real man, not the image of him that has been posthumously created – I may overestimate the damage which his loss did to Ted Heath's Government. His successor as Chancellor, Tony Barber, a very good, decent and capable man, simply lacked the political weight of Macleod and he was unwilling to resist Ted Heath's reversal of the economic policies on which we had been elected. Sadly the reversal was to plunge the country into chaos and the Party into defeat within less than four years.

However, as Parliament broke up for the holidays I was busy selling our house in Islington – buying another in Epping, and looking forward to a family holiday in Gloucestershire.

In September the problem of hijacking, which until then had been a relatively localised problem between the United States and Cuba, exploded on to the world stage. In a series of co-ordinated actions, Palestinian hijackers seized three aircraft, forcing two to land at Dawson's Field in Jordan, the third in Cairo. The attempt to seize a fourth aircraft – an El Al Boeing over Britain – culminated in a shoot out. The Boeing landed at Heathrow with one hijacker dead and the other, Leila Khaled, taken prisoner and left in our custody. Later another aircraft, a BOAC Boeing with many children on board, was also seized.

As an ex-airline pilot I had no lack of platforms to express my views, nor any difficulty in coming to clear, even sharp, conclusions. The local press reports clearly drew on either a press release or my remarks on the BBC 'Today' programme when I debated the issue with Lord Soper.

If we give in to the terrorists we will have more skyjacking, and not merely from the Arabs... Whatever happens to these hostages – and I could easily have been one of them – if we give in even more people will be taken hostage and more lives will be laid at risk.

At the weekend I took part in Malcolm Muggeridge's TV series, 'The Question Why', discussing the same issue, and I was not unnaturally rather pleased with myself to read the *Daily Mail* TV critic, Olga Franklin, writing in her column on 14 September:

By this time things were really sizzling and I felt like cheering madly. This was due to a new man, new at least to me on television. Mr Norman Tebbit MP made the noblest speech of all. Mark my words, we're going to hear a lot more in future from Mr Tebbit.

My pleasure at such recognition was rather spoiled when a visitor from the local police brought home to me the potential dangers of standing up against terrorists. He was very reassuring but suggested that for a little while I should leave my car in the police pound rather than on the street at night and hoped we would not mind if he put an officer on duty outside our house for a few days. I expressed my thanks for his concern for my safety which gave him the entrée for the proposition that it was not just me but for my family, and asked that until the Dawson's Field affair was over we should keep our younger children at home and allow his men to take John to school. It was a preview of my life to come.

The Dawson's Field affair ended with a multilateral deal in which Khaled and other criminals were released in exchange for the hostages, and aircraft were destroyed – but so too was the power of the PLO in Jordan. There King Hussein took advantage of the opportunity to clear the Palestinians from Jordan and regain power over his own kingdom.

I was not so foolish as to ignore the fact that a resolute stand by Britain would have been undermined by deals done by other nations to save their own nationals. Nor indeed that had a refusal to release Khaled brought about a massacre of British hostages, public opinion would have condemned the Government. As a result I kept my doubts and criticisms to myself. Even then I realised that to be brave from the sidelines is easier than to make hair-trigger decisions with the weight of ultimate responsibility on one's shoulders.

Yet somehow I felt the Leila Khaled affair had cast a doubt over the

Government's determination not to compromise vital principles to avoid short-term problems.

Problems on the industrial relations front were particularly worrying. In July the Government had declared a state of emergency in the face of a dock strike and then appointed a court of inquiry leading to a foolishly expensive settlement. Talks between TUC leaders and ministers about wages became commonplace with too much talk of incomes policies. The so-called dirty-jobs dispute between refuse collectors and similar workers and local authorities worsened through the autumn and continued through the Party Conference in October.

At the Conservative Party conference in 1970 I found Ted Heath's speech reassuring. It had been clear and forthright, including passages that could easily be incorporated into any Thatcher Conference speech.

> We were returned to office to change the course and the history of this nation, nothing else. And it is now this new course which the Government is now shaping. Change will give us freedom and that freedom must give responsibility. The free society which we aim to create must also be a responsible society ... free from intervention, free from interference, but responsible. Free to make your own decisions, but responsible also for your mistakes. Free to lead a life of your own, but responsible to the community as a whole. This then is the task to which your Government is dedicated. This is the challenge and from it will come opportunity ... Opportunity to take our destiny, the destiny of this nation, once again in our own hands ...
>
> If we are to achieve this task we shall have to bring about a change so radical, a revolution so quiet, and yet so total, that it will go far beyond the programme for a Parliament to which we are committed and on which we have already embarked. We are laying the foundations but they are the foundations for a generation.

John Davies as Secretary of State for Trade and Industry echoed Ted Heath's tough line of disengagement from industrial intervention. Lame ducks it seemed would be helped only if they showed clear prospects of flying before long – or, as he put it, 'I will not bolster up or bail out companies where I can see no end to the process of propping them up.'

Tony Barber's October budget, cutting income tax and corporation tax, raising charges, reducing subsidies, replacing industrial grants with tax allowances, and axing the Industrial Reconstruction Corporation, seemed to emphasise the break with the old Butskellite consensus past. Even Nigel Lawson today might think it brave to do all that and cut free school milk, introduce admission charges to museums, increase prescription charges and school meal prices by sixty per cent, all in one budget. The abolition of the Prices and Incomes Board also seemed to confirm the direction of the Government's policy. But the storm clouds that were to surround the fall of Heath's government were already gathering on the horizon.

It was not long after the brave words at the Party Conference that, with uncollected refuse piling up and raw sewage going into the rivers and the government firmly standing back, the local authorities and NUPE agreed to appoint Sir Jack Scamp to head an inquiry into the dispute. That led to a swift and almost total sell out with an award on 5 November of 50 shillings (£2.50) which Scamp admitted was inflationary but excused on the grounds that so were lots of other settlements too.

Ted Heath was rightly highly critical of the Scamp settlement but spoke firmly against any legal pay restraints, saying that in a free society, 'people must face up to their own responsibilities'. Worse, however, was to come. Within a month the electricians began a work to rule which soon led to power cuts. There were shortages of candles, shops sold out of camping stoves, and the cuts twice left the House of Commons illuminated only by candlelight. Driving home through darkened streets, which only weeks before had been littered with rubbish, I wondered for how long this succession of strikes would continue. A Saturday Cabinet on 12 December decided to declare another state of emergency and appoint a court of inquiry under a High Court judge, Lord Wilberforce. That led to the end of the work to rule but like many of my colleagues I was becoming increasingly uneasy.

Not everything was going wrong by any means, but two proclamations of states of emergency in six months was worrying.

By the time Parliament had reassembled in late October I was better organised to pursue my new career. The children were reasonably settled, Margaret liked living in Epping and I was beginning to develop my own style as a constituency MP, although not even having made my maiden speech I had hardly begun to develop a Westminster style.

Inevitably my aviation experience kept me involved with aviation politics. The problems of airborne terrorism had been brought into stark relief by the Dawson's Field affair and, as a politician with technical knowledge and experience, I was bound to be caught up in the issues which it raised. Concorde was still a controversial project, none having been delivered to the airlines, and there were still those who doubted that it could be operated within normal civil requirements as well as those who opposed it on environmental, political or plain Luddite grounds. Aircraft noise was a far greater problem in the early Seventies than today. The early jet engines were far noisier than today's much more powerful high-bypass ratio types. That led to extravagant demands for restriction on hours of operation, the banning of jets from inland airfields near to centres of population and the construction of remote coastal airports.

The RB211 engine was destined to take the sting out of the environmental problem and designed to lift Rolls-Royce from a technically brilliant but commercially backward company into the world league. However, its technical problems threatened not only the survival of Rolls-Royce but that of the American Lockheed aircraft company whose Tristar passenger jet had been designed to us the RB211.

The high hopes for the RB211 faded and the ignominy of nationalising the company to save it from complete collapse fell to the Conservative government. I persuaded myself, as did many Conservatives, that Rolls was a special case. The defence and international considerations were paramount and the bail out was inevitable, even if unpalatable. The Rolls-Royce (Purchase) Bill was given an unopposed second reading but in the debate Enoch Powell's words of certainty expressed what were for me gnawing doubts: 'If there are profitable parts then the private sector would acquire them.' But not even he would vote against the rescue.

However, my first objective as the House reassembled was to get over the hurdle of my maiden speech. By tradition a maiden speech should not be controversial but I found it hard to find anything uncontroversial worth saying. To me it seemed that the only reason for that tradition was to balance the tradition that maiden speeches should not be interrupted – presumably to give the speaker an easy run at his first attempt, not least after the rough handling of the young Disraeli. Towards the middle of November I decided that when I made my maiden speech I would have to flout the convention but in the meantime I had already been trying hard to establish myself in the Chamber, doing what I like best, intervening on the spur of the moment as opportunities presented themselves.

I had taken such a chance on 27 October when the Chancellor, Tony Barber, presented his Autumn budget. It was skilfully presented, especially in the way that Tony casually announced, in response to persistent cries from Labour's Marcus Lipton, his cut of 6d – 2½ pence – in income tax. I sat amazed and amused at the histrionic denunciations of Tony's proposals from the Opposition. I had never before seen Roy Jenkins (Labour's Shadow Chancellor) in close-up on a big occasion, and marvelled at the welter of fake indignation that he sprayed out, his dewlaps wobbling in time to the vigorous tapping of his left foot. By the time Meyer Galpern (of whom in later years I became a fan) had all but forecast universal rickets as a result of charging for school milk, and Eric Heffer (whose charms I have been able to resist to this day) had forecast death for the industrial work force, indeed almost everything up to the death of the first born and a plague of frogs, I had had enough. Was there a way, I innocently enquired, by which those who had been protesting that the tax plans were vicious, class-ridden and savage could perhaps be excused their tax remissions?

From the row that caused I saw that I had discovered how to taunt and anger Labour Members. I was delighted. Within only a few weeks in the House I had stumbled upon the secret of using and playing them, a technique I was to employ over and over again. In the *Daily Telegraph* the next day Andrew Alexander (now City Editor of the *Daily Mail*) gleefully reported the incident in his parliamentary column which was in transition from traditional reporting towards the parliamentary sketch. He and Frank Johnson (now a leader writer on *The Times*) were to make the parliamentary sketch into a popular feature of their papers. In doing so they did more than anyone, except the Press Association reporter Chris Moncrieff, to make me into something of a national figure of the back benches.

Such incidents were fun but the maiden speech had to be made and eventually it came on 24 November on the Second Reading of the Civil Aviation Bill.

It was quite a short speech, dealing with the relationship and competition between the nationalised and private-sector airlines. I was critical of the unfairness by which the independents, having been virtually excluded from normal scheduled routes, and having developed the package holiday charter flight trade instead, were now to face cross-subsidised competition in that market from the state carriers. As I was to do in later years I suggested that route transfers from the big corporations to the independent airlines should not be made in the parts of the world where 'BOAC, Great Britain and good operating practice are virtually synonymous', but in 'other areas where the name of BOAC is not held in such high regard', suggesting that Eagle, then the leading independent, should be restored to the Bermuda route and those to the southern USA and Central America. Years later during the Ridley review I took much the same view but foolishly Adam Thompson of British Caledonian fought for and got British Airways' routes to West Africa and Saudi Arabia. That turned out to be a mistake for both Adam Thompson and the British interest.

Reading my speech again today I think Nick Ridley (then Parliamentary Under-Secretary of State for Trade and Industry) was more than generous in the traditional flattery of maiden speeches when he called it 'extraordinarily able and fluent'. However, it was over and done with – the barrier had been broken, I was really a Member of the House.

Returning after the Christmas break I concentrated on the subjects which I found most interesting and rather stayed out of the macro-economic policy debates and controversies, seeing them as areas in which I had neither specialised knowledge, experience, nor sufficient parliamentary seniority to make any impact. Significantly I said little about the Industrial Relations Bill. In fact I had serious doubts whether its formula would work. I remember expressing those one evening to Geoffrey Howe, then the Attorney General and the architect of the legislation. 'Are you absolutely sure we've got it right?' I asked. Geoffrey, characteristically, did not overstate his case with fake certainty. Had I known him better I would perhaps have read less into what he said but my unease was increased rather than diminished.

I felt that the Government did not seem to be in control of events – rather it responded to pressures put on it. To be sure, little had been conceded to the TUC over the proposed industrial relations legislation but in its attitude to the TUC the Government seemed to have conceded that the TUC was a representative body with which a Government backed by a sovereign Parliament should negotiate. To my mind the TUC was a sham. It was not representative even of the interest it claimed to represent and agreement with it was a waste of time since it could not deliver any agreement which employers or Governments with any guts and determination could not impose.

The first six or nine months of Ted Heath's Government had been difficult. What none of us knew was that it was going to get worse. Worse both because of outside events such as the oil crisis and because Ted Heath himself was to desert the Selsdon programme on which he had been elected and retreat into corporatism, and from there into a mish-mash of ill-considered centralist and socialist hand-to-mouth devices with no intellectual nor political cohesion, marked only by fits of obstinacy alternating with climb-down.

It was less than a year before I began to wonder whether Ted Heath ever had any real understanding of what lay under the Selsdon manifesto. He certainly understood the nuts and bolts of any issue with which he was concerned. Perhaps only Margaret Thatcher has shown a greater command of detail across such a wide range of issues but, for her, details are details, and they are built upon a general and usually consistent structure of belief and policy; for him details seemed always to obstruct commitment and obscure vision – except of course on Europe.

Ted Heath's path away from intervention involved the creation of the super-ministries, the Department of Trade and Industry (which, unlike its present-day namesake, included the responsibilities of both the Departments of Energy and Transport), and of the Environment. These were designed to increase, not to decrease, the power of ministers to intervene – and they did. Certainly the ill-fated Industrial Relations Act proved to be far more effective in dragging ministers into industrial disputes than dragging disputes out of Whitehall to their places of origin – which is usually the best place to look for their solution. So perhaps Selsdon Man was always a civil servant at heart even before his partnership with the head of the home civil service, Sir William Armstrong.

Events were to show that the Heath Government rarely persisted with any of its announced policies once the going got rough, except on Europe where Ted Heath's passionate belief carried him through every difficulty. I asked myself why. Could there be any other reason than the lack of either a long-term strategic view or of a bedrock of belief in a firm political philosophy? In our system – and a very good one it is – it is the politicians who should provide those beliefs and the civil service who provide the legislative and administrative counterparts. As Ted Heath's style of government gave singularly little opportunity to his colleagues to help him overcome his weaknesses (especially after the loss of Macleod) it may be that it was so unbalanced between politicians and civil servants as to be almost bound to end in tears.

However, at that time – before I had yet been in Parliament for a full year – I was unwilling to admit that my faith in the Prime Minister was faltering. I concentrated my efforts in areas where my loyalty was not strained.

Although Parliament had not then been cursed by the plague of departmental Select Committees, which these days provides a diversion from mainstream politics, their numbers had been growing. The Public Accounts Committee and Select Committee on Public Expenditure had been long established, doing an immense amount of useful work, but the number of Select Committees was beginning to increase to the extent that it was becoming difficult to find experienced Members of quality willing to serve actively on them.

As a result I was invited by the Whips to serve on the Select Committee on Science and Technology and I was sufficiently interested and flattered to accept, giving me another string of interest to add to my political bow. It soon began to occupy quite a lot of my time.

I played a considerable part in spiking an uncompleted report from the previous Parliament on population policy. To me, to talk of a population policy when political hysteria virtually prevented a rational discussion about family allowances (the predecessor of child benefit), was absurd. Nor was I of the view that the Government should have a population policy and in any case all previous forecasts had been wrong. The expert advice given to the Committee was no more than an extrapolation of trends which pointed to a UK population of 82 million by the year 2030. 'So what?' was my reaction, thinking it was all closer to theology than technology. (And more recent evidence has already shown this projection to be utterly wrong.) Mercifully the majority shared my view and the work was terminated and published incomplete. Studies by one sub-committee into the computer industry were continued – indeed they waffled on without significant conclusions for years, but I joined a sub-committee setting out on a new enquiry into policy on developments in space. Our conclusions were unremarkable and have been reached many times before and since. However, the gathering of information was fascinating, especially a trip by Sir Harry Legge-Bourke, Arthur Palmer, Ron Brown (brother of George Brown) and myself to Australia to see the Woomera rocket range installations in order to judge if any British assets there might be sensibly used in new programmes.

I learned as much about my colleagues as about the space industry. I found Arthur Palmer a good-natured ineffectual waffler, Ron Brown a limited but essentially decent man, immensely loyal to his brilliant but fatally flawed brother George. Harry Legge-Bourke was the very quintessence of a traditional knight from the shires. Tall, slim, moustachioed, with straight-as-a-ramrod military bearing, superficially something of a martinet, I found him uproariously funny, totally unstuffy, a wise and thoughtful friend, whereas I was a young and inexperienced colleague so widely different in style, background, education – indeed almost everything except political beliefs. Ron Brown had confided in me that he dreaded the thought of Harry as a wet blanket over the trip. Harry confided in me his fear that Brown would behave badly and let us down. Yet one of my abiding memories is of the pair of them demonstrating the steps of Zorba the Greek, arm-in-arm on the steps of the leading hotel in Canberra!

In fact we learned very little about the space programme that we could not have discovered in Westminster and I would never again agree to take part in a Select Committee trip outside Europe. Gradually I began to see the Committee, and later the proliferating new departmental committees, as overwhelmingly pretentious, expensive, time-wasting 'freebie' machines. They have disappointed the hopes of those like Norman St John Stevas who expected them somehow to invigorate Parliament and improve Government and those of the Whips and business managers who thought that boring or bolshie back benchers could be kept quietly and harmlessly occupied either upstairs in committee rooms or overseas and away from publicity. Even worse, they have become totally captured by single-issue pressure groups and are in my view amongst the most regrettable developments in politics. Indeed I was glad to use my appointment as Robin Chichester Clark's Parliamentary Private Secretary as an excuse to resign from the Committee in 1972. Although the Whips persuaded me to serve again later to try to keep the Committee on the rails (or else to keep me quietly occupied!), I was an uncomfortable and critical member of the Committee openly hostile to its globe-trotting ambitions and narrow vision.

Meanwhile in early 1971 I was still striking at targets of opportunity as they arose. My swipe at British European Airways for its sex discrimination policy on the recruitment of flight-deck crew brought me a sharp but private rebuke from Ronnie Bell, the noted anti-feminist Member for Beaconsfield, when I publicly upheld the case of his constituent, Miss Gray-Fisk. I had met Miss Gray-Fisk through friends we had in common. She was (and still is) a perfectly competent commercial pilot and, concealing her sex, had filled in the application forms for a job as a BEA pilot. All had gone well until she arrived for an interview when she was told in no uncertain manner that her application was deceitful and mischievous and that BEA did not employ women pilots. The case attracted a good deal of attention but the nationalised airlines maintained their sex bar to the very end and it is only since privatisation that British Airways has followed the example of the private sector in employing women pilots.

With Stansted airport only just ouside my constituency I had to tread warily on airports policy. I had flirted at one time with the Foulness or Maplin project but by March 1971 when the House debated the Roskill Report I had begun to hedge my bets. My hopes that aircraft technology might lead towards very short or vertical take-off and landing aircraft have been proved wrong, but my opposition to a huge new four-runway airport proposed by Roskill turned out to be soundly based. I still think it a pity that my suggestion of maximising the potential of Gatwick by the construction of a second runway was not taken up. Sadly by the time I was to have any chance to influence policy eight years later as a Minister, the Gatwick second-runway option had been deliberately destroyed by public undertakings and the construction of the M25 and various airport buildings, but at least I can draw some satisfaction from having rubbished the traffic forecasts and the anti-coastal airport lobby in its attempts to use seagulls in a scare campaign!

One of my early constituency cases was that of Pauline Jones, who abducted a baby belonging to another of my constituents from a pram outside a Harlow supermarket. There had been a spate of such abductions, some ending tragically. Happily the baby, Denise Weller, was found unharmed, and Miss Jones, pleading guilty to the abduction, was sentenced to three years' imprisonment. I was horrified. Miss Jones had been pregnant and had suffered a miscarriage shortly before the abduction and I guessed she had been suffering from a depression following the miscarriage. Three years as a punishment seemed outrageous. Nor, I thought, was it likely that when Miss Jones recovered from her depression (and prison did not strike me as the best place for that) she would commit another such crime so the public hardly needed to be protected from her. On appeal the sentence was cut to twenty-one months – still, I thought, far too harsh. The Home Secretary, Reggie Maudling, was unable to override the Appeal Court; Miss Jones was clearly guilty, there were no new factors of which the Court was unaware and quite rightly the Home Secretary would not, indeed could not, substitute his judgement for that of the Court. I had visited Miss Jones in Holloway Prison just before Christmas and described her cell as being more comfortable than the accommodation given to our soldiers in Ulster, but the atmosphere of the prison was grim, and I sought her transfer to an open prison where I felt her problems were more likely to be resolved than in the company of hardened criminals in a fortress prison.

Sadly a group of Labour MPs and Lord Soper, who had always appeared to me the epitome of sanctimonious ill-judgement, leapt upon the Pauline Jones bandwagon, turning a sad human case into a political weapon against the Home Secretary and the judiciary whilst she quietly served out her sentence, less remission.

On the national scene, things were getting worse as we went further into 1970. Despite the defeat of some minor strikes, I began to see a general picture of militancy paying, and of a Government unwilling to face up to strikes, passing the buck to 'wise men' whose conclusions turned out to be as foolish as only wise men can be.

By April 1971 the Employment Secretary, Robert Carr, was expressing concern at excessive wage settlements to both the TUC and CBI. There was growing interference in the pricing policies of nationalised industries and far too much talk between government, TUC and CBI about incomes and prices policies as our policy of disengagement began to crumble at the edges.

My hope that with the arrival of Ted Heath in Downing Street the TUC would be firmly put in its place faded when its general secretary seemed to be treated as though he was the ambassador of a powerful foreign state. In contrast the CBI was treated more like a disobedient colony – but increasingly it negotiated on behalf of the whole private sector and in July it undertook to limit price rises by members to five per cent.

In May with unemployment and prices continuing to rise and the Labour Party claiming that entry into the EEC would make matters worse, we suffered badly in the spring local elections. Defending seats won in 1968 when Labour had been at its nadir we did very badly indeed and, worse still, at the end of the month Labour won the Bromsgrove by-election – turning a Tory majority of 10,874 to 1,868 for Labour.

In June Upper Clyde Shipbuilders went into liquidation adding another twist to the spiral of industrial collapses and rising unemployment, amidst fears that unemployment might reach a million during the coming winter – a level thought to be beyond the ability of the political and social system to contain. It certainly seemed beyond the Cabinet's ability to navigate through these difficult waters on the course set out in the election manifesto, and one after another the Selsdon policies were being discarded.

I realised that things were looking difficult for the Government, and my doubts and worries grew. However, I hardly realised that the approach to the great U-turn had begun. But I began to feel that Ted Heath felt no unease – but rather relief – at shedding Conservative principles and returning to the policies of his predecessors. It was to be another decade before a Government would be really brave enough to avoid the interventionist policies and interventionist solutions of the post-war era.

Almost every back-bench MP wants to be noticed, either by the Whips and his Party leader, his constituents, the media or all three. By a combination of calculation, my natural style and views and a good deal of luck I seemed to be getting noticed often enough but never more remarkably than in early May 1971 during a debate on housing policy when I was deriding the Labour Party's double-talk.

Hon. Gentlemen opposite believe that when they impose a tax which raises the cost of living, and particularly the cost of housing for everyone, it can be called 'selective', whereas when we propose to get rid of it and hold back the increase in the cost of housing for everyone it is called 'divisive'. This is an extraordinary use of words, though 'divisive' has become the new parrot cry on the benches opposite.

I am willing to bet that on Judgement Day as the Lord divides those on the left from those on the right somebody at the back will be hard to shout, 'It is divisive' – and I know on which side he will be standing.

Some Labour MPs shouted, 'The Hon. Gentleman will not be there.' As I responded, 'Everyone turns up on Judgement Day,' a vivid flash of lightning illuminated the Chamber, followed almost at once by a colossal roll of thunder, recorded in Hansard as 'Interruption'. For a moment there was silence then a great chuckle from every corner of the House and, as I tried to regain the thread of my remarks, David Stoddart observed, 'I suggest that the Honourable Gentleman has upset somebody.'

Only after some moments of light-hearted points of order was I able to resume my speech which, or perhaps it was the 'interruption', was widely reported next day. I have wondered since how television would have reported it!

At this time, I was also vigorously supporting Peter Walker's policy of selling council houses. My view was not well known in my constituency – I had expressed my opinion as a candidate that councils should not be in housing at all except for special needs categories. As I have already said, the Labour Party's opposition to sales was inevitable. We were pulling down the walls which imprisoned tenants and forced them into voting Labour. It was, of course, bound to be a vote loser for Labour whichever way they played it. Never more so than when those who voted against the policy were caught out taking personal advantage of it.

At least one left-wing Labour Member was exposed as a hypocrite in that way. In my own Borough of Waltham Forest the incoming Labour council in May 1971 promptly stopped the sale of council houses, to the anger of many would-be purchasers, especially when it came to light that two councillors who voted for the sales ban had already bought their council houses during the Tory administration. I made much of that in Chingford where I was reported regularly in the local press, fighting not just for the political principle behind sales of council houses but for individual constituents whose applications had been in train when political control changed hands at the town hall and their hopes of home ownership were dashed.

It was a hard summer and before the break of 1971 I had taken part in two further debates in which I was able to speak with absolute conviction.

On 2 July I spoke on the Hijacking Bill which allowed Britain to ratify the Hague Convention of 1970. It was a short and unanimous debate. The earlier debate on the Upper Clyde Shipbuilders affair, however, when sharp differences of opinion were clearly expressed, was not. On this front at least the Government was standing its ground and John Davies made a clear and firm statement of policy that was in line with our election-time views. There could be no more bailing out of a business which had already failed. For Mr Benn the issue was equally clear. The businesses in which he had intervened (and was to intervene in future) were always about to break through into fantastic success. The workforce could do no wrong. The foolish bankers and Tory Ministers had no faith and wanted to destroy the splendid Upper Clyde Shipbuilders. It needed only a little more money and public ownership to turn this alleged lame duck into a swan. In fact it proved to be one of Ted Heath's albatrosses – but that was still months away – and I was then still confident in backing the Government's stand.

> This is a management that, in January, knowing that its guarantees were being withheld, said that all was well and that the future was bright, and then in June is struck by bankruptcy out of a clear blue sky at 48 hours' notice. When those deals were done UCS was given £20 million by the Right Hon. Gentleman [Mr. Benn]. He knew that they were financial boozers, and he turned them into financial alcoholics – as he did Rolls-Royce.
>
> What is more, now, when they say, 'Another little £5-million or £6-million drink will not do us any harm; we will give it up before long', he has the audacity to suggest that we should keep feeding them with the stuff. It is another of the Right Hon. Gentleman's white-hot technological marvels that has cooled down from the white heat into the red of the account books, and he knows it. His petulant, ill-natured, ill-considered call on the workers to commit the sort of industrial anarchy that he eggs them on in, ill becomes any man who has ambitions to sit on a front bench on either side of the House.

With speeches like that I was enjoying myself and, I believed, making some impact in the House. I realised that some of my colleagues thought

I was too brash and too aggressive, but equally many others including some of the old hands encouraged me to keep up my fire against the Labour benches. But it was an exhausting business especially in a torrid Summer session in which the Government looked less and less in control of events and we Tory MPs were all glad to get away.

All the family needed a holiday – even I owned up to that – and although not a sun-and-sand worshipper I had to admit that I was missing those relaxing days idling away the time until the next flight in some very agreeable spot. For once I had planned well ahead and discovered that it was cheaper to rent a house during August in Barbados than in Cornwall. The prospect was alluring, and as I had never until then taken advantage of my BOAC long-service entitlement to periodic free flights it was economically attractive too.

What bliss it was, at the end of my first full year in Parliament, to settle into the passenger seats of a 707 bound for the Caribbean leaving behind discounted house sales, Rolls-Royce, Upper Clyde and all the other problems, and heading for the sun and such nectar as Mount Gay Barbados rum at only shillings a bottle.

6

Ted Heath's Road to Disaster

The holiday in Barbados was a success and I returned to the fray distinctly less jaded and tired. Determined to avoid being typecast as an aviation-only specialist, I managed to be called to speak in the debate on housing policy at the Party Conference in Brighton. Well ahead of the 1980 'right to buy' legislation, I called for 'government action to ensure that councils did not gratuitiously nor arbitrarily prevent tenants from purchasing their houses'. That did me no harm at all in my constituency where, from Harlow to Chingford, house sales were a live issue.

In Parliament too I was soon rewarded for my interest in housing policy by election as Vice-Chairman of the back-bench Housing Committee. Perhaps less rewarding was to find myself on the Standing Committee on the Housing Finance Bill which had its second reading on 15 November and went into committee on the twenty-fifth. It was bitterly opposed by the Labour Party and in the fashion of the time it was not guillotined until 13 March 1972. By then we had broken most records for numbers of sittings and total hours of debate, with the Government Whips trying to break the determination of the Opposition with sittings in the mornings, afternoons and all night too. It was a most unsatisfactory way to do business and our morale depended very much on Spencer Le Marchant, the Government Whip on the Committee. Something of a *bon viveur*, Spencer arranged refreshments throughout the long night sessions, providing food and drink in a nearby committee room.

Julian Amery, who if he were a building would merit a preservation order as a representative of the political style of the 1930s, led for the Government. Julian's first love has always been foreign affairs but he has a strong social conscience and gave all his energies to his work as Minister for Housing. For all that, he could not change his style of the broad sweep of principle, the *tour d'horizon*, rather than the dry dust of detail. The latter was left to Paul Channon, able, industrious and likeable, who often had to calm the committee in the wake of Julian's impassioned and witty style. *Hansard* reports seldom do justice to such speechs but I still savour with delight memories of Julian in the small hours of the morning opposing Opposition motions to 'report progress' (that is to pack up and go home) with what became known as the St Crispin's Day Speech, and the monstrous effrontery of his claim (made with twinkling eyes) of an understanding of inner-city housing from his own experience. 'I was born and still live in a terraced house in inner London.' It was, of course, in Eaton Square. Never loath to gild the lily, as the laughter subsided Julian pointed to me, saying, 'And my Honourable Friend is a council tenant in an inner London estate.' That was a reference to a house we rented for a while in the City of London's Barbican development.

Perhaps the funniest session of the Committee came about as a result of Paul Channon's promotion in March to be Minister of State at the newly formed Northern Ireland Office. To celebrate his escape from the Committee Paul gave a party for the other Conservative members. For some reason the Labour Party wanted a longer dinner break too and so we had time for what was, in retrospect, too good a party. On the resumption of proceedings Julian was perhaps a little too lively, indulging in a few sedentary interruptions of Opposition speakers. They soon suspected they might be on to a good thing. We had no replacement for Paul so Julian would have to reply to the debate. Seeing the danger I passed to Winston Churchill (Julian's PPS) a note which said, 'Tell your Minister to shut up – Norman.' Winston grinned and passed it to Julian who replied to me with a derisive and rather unparliamentary gesture. That really put the fat in the fire and the Opposition members rapidly shut up to force Julian to make his speech in reply. Spencer seemed over relaxed, so I felt it my responsibility to protect Julian and, with a few others, kicked for touch with discursive if not illuminating speeches until it was time for the Committee to rise!

It is perhaps a mark of Julian's personality that we should all want to protect him. Indeed I have always valued his friendship, enjoying his company and his humour and knowledge. It was his habit to invite the officers of the back-bench Committee to lunch every month at his home in Eaton Square where we discussed the world (including housing policy at times) over marvellous food and good wines. Julian has outlasted his time – there are very few like him left today.

Despite the burden of the Housing Finance Bill I found time to take part in major debates such as the Airports Authority Bill in December 1971. Now that the old noisy jets have been banned and modern engines set new standards of low noise and absence of smoke it is becoming hard to remember how dirty and noisy the early jet liners were. I made no secret of my distaste for the Foulness (later renamed Maplin) project suggesting that it tackled the problem of aircraft noise in quite the wrong way.

> Our forefathers regarded the privy as a rather nasty, dirty, noisy and smelly thing and put it at the end of the garden, until some bright chap came along and invented the water closet which was installed indoors. We are taking the utterly negative approach of saying that we regard airports as nasty, dirty, noisy and smelly and should put them at the end of the garden when in fact they should be close to our cities.
>
> The contribution of this technically advanced country on the problem of aircraft noise will not be remembered in terms of adopting quiet engine techniques or of the fitting of engines with steep approach and landing paths. Our contribution will be seen as a long string of concrete stretching 50 miles from London to the East Coast, covered with vehicles, and another great slab of concrete stretching along the East Coast. This thought is utterly unacceptable. The sooner we turn away from the prospect of spending money on concrete and turn our thoughts to producing a decent, house-trained aeroplane which can be lived with and brought indoors, the better.

I also spoke about another problem which has since been resolved, the appalling restrictive practices and union Luddism in the baggage-handling and allied services at Heathrow. I had recently met Stanley Haggett, a British businessman who ran General Aviation Services Limited, a Canadian-based company which had set up at Heathrow and stirred up a hornet's nest by offering better, cheaper services to the airlines. In the fashion of the day, the Minister of Employment and Productivity had set up a committee of inquiry under Professor Robertson to deal with the rash of strikes which had been sparked off. Equally in the fashion of the day, although the inquiry came down clearly in favour of GAS having every right to be in business at Heathrow, not only the Government but the other employers were all for surrender to the unions in the interest of a quiet life. I liked Haggett, believed his firm was being treated disgracefully and worked for him for a while as an adviser. The last advice I gave him was probably the best, although I regretted having to give it. I told him that in the interests of the country I hoped he would stay and fight it out – but that in the interest of his company I advised him to cut his losses and get out. That is what he did and the sad policy of surrender to militancy continued its march towards the Winter of Discontent seven years later.

Whilst I seemed to be standing more firmly on my beliefs, the Heath Government seemed increasingly to be running away from the stormy political issues and straight on to the rocks on every issue except entry into the European Community. On that issue Ted Heath was indefatigable. Although our membership commitment had been only to negotiate for entry the three-line Whips cracked with no concessions to conscience. The European Communities Bill was made an issue of confidence, and the Prime Minister's resolve was there clear for everyone to see. In contrast, elsewhere resolution was in short supply, and the election commitment against statutory wage and price control was soon to be turned on its head amidst another fusillade of three-line Whips.

Early in January 1972 negotiations on the miners' pay claim (first submitted the previous July) finally collapsed in the face of a demand costing forty-seven per cent and an offer worth less than ten per cent. Coal stocks were high and the outcome of the dispute was soon seen to hinge on the success or failure of the secondary picketing of power stations to prevent the movement of coal. A coal strike was bad enough, but troubles seldom come singly and events took another turn for the worse in Ulster with bomb outrages, cross-border gun battles and the Bloody Sunday incident in Londonderry which led to Bernadette Devlin's physical assault on Reggie Maudling following his statement the next day. All this on top of the Labour Party's hysterical reaction to the entirely expected announcement that unemployment had exceeded one million reinforced the image of a government not in control of events. In contrast there was no lack of success on the European front with the signing of the Treaty of Accession and the brilliance of draftsmanship and political management which produced a European Communities Bill of twelve clauses rather than the hundreds which many of us had feared. Perhaps it was that contrast between the over-all sense of drift and the demonstration of drive and energy devoted to the European issue which began to drag me towards the conclusion that Ted Heath's administration was doomed.

The coal strike rapidly worsened in February, with more scenes of hysteria in the Commons following the death of a picket killed by a lorry whilst trying to prevent vehicles from entering a power station.

Labour MP Tom Swain's call for violence against the Government went unchecked by the Labour leadership, which soon gave total political support to the strike and the plainly illegal picketing. The turning point in the dispute was almost certainly on 10 February when the police gave in to massive violent picketing at the Saltley coke works. From then on the pickets were in charge and by mid-February, with huge stocks of coal still at the pitheads, power stations were fast closing down despite the declaration of a State of Emergency, and power cuts brought industry almost to a three-day working week. As usual when faced with a crisis, the Government passed the buck and appointed a judge, in this case Lord Wilberforce, to lead an inquiry and arrange the terms of surrender. Within little more than a week Lord Wilberforce had done his job, finding for the miners and proposing a settlement at almost triple the NCB offer, a capitulation hastily welcomed by the Government. Even so the final humiliation was to come when the NUM rejected the Wilberforce terms and were promptly invited to Downing Street in a re-run of the beer-and-sandwiches Wilsonian era so roundly condemned by Ted Heath before 1970. Having extracted a few millions more and trampled the Government's anti-inflationary policies into the ground, the miners returned to work triumphant at the end of February.

Inflation had been taking its toll on the value of the pay of Members of Parliament, too, and I was glad to find some outside interests to supplement my Member's salary which was considerably less than I would have been earning in BOAC.

Nor was it only my financial situation which was precarious. The Government had accepted in full the Boundary Commission Report which had led to Jim Callaghan's attempt at gerrymandering which had given me the lucky break at Epping, but now the ball seemed set to bounce the other way.

The Epping seat was to be broken up three ways. The Labour stronghold of Harlow, together with a few surrounding villages, forming a new seat, the heartland of Epping, Waltham Abbey and the other villages forming about one-third of a new Epping Forest constituency to which John Biggs-Davison's seat of Chigwell contributed the rest. The remaining quarter of the constituency, my stronghold of Chingford, was to be combined with the best of Michael McNair Wilson's highly marginal (528 majority) Walthamstow East.

Although Harlow turned Conservative in 1983 it was certainly not winnable at that time, nor ever under Ted Heath's leadership, so that was no place for me to go. It was unlikely that I could defeat John Biggs-Davison for the Epping Forest nomination, nor did I think it right as a junior MP to try to unseat such a senior and respected man. Gradually I realised it would have to be Chingford or somewhere quite new and although Central Office hinted broadly that I should seek the Braintree nomination I saw many disadvantages and risks in that. It looked as though I should try for the new Chingford seat, even though I would have to contest it against Michael McNair Wilson, a most decent and generous man, already a friend to my whole family.

A new Conservative Association had been formed but as usual with mergers there seemed little in common except for the name. Even worse from my point of view, Michael's constituency chairman, Ivor Swain, became chairman, and his agent, Bill Ottaway, agent to the new Association. The new Association had inherited no premises nor much money from Epping. From Walthamstow we had gained some very good people but neither money nor premises, and one third of Bill the Borough agent who covered three constituencies. I soon discovered that Bill, one of the nicest of men and formerly one of the best agents in the business, was fighting a losing battle against alcohol.

It was a difficult time, made more so when the Association, embarrassed at choosing between Michael McNair Wilson and me, opened the list to all comers. Michael and Fred Sylvester (a former Conservative Member who had won Walthamstow West at a by-election but lost it in 1970) being guaranteed no more than places in the last six. I was most unhappy about this and wrote a very sharp, perhaps intemperate letter to the Chairman, Ivor Swain, to say so. Fortunately Michael and I had agreed we would inform and consult each other about everything bearing on the selection process. It was just as well. I showed Michael the letter which he read carefully. After a pause he handed it back saying, 'Of course it's up to you, but I think it will damage your chances and I wouldn't send it if I were you. But if you do – I suggest you spell Ivor Swain's name correctly.' I tore up my letter and have never ceased to admire Michael's generosity.

In the end, the Selection Committee recommended Fred, Michael and me to a general meeting of members of the Association to make the final choice. I have lost the text of my speech made that night in early March 1972, but it reflected the turbulent times. The House of Commons had just given the European Communities Bill a second reading by a majority of only eight, the Government had surrendered to violence on the coal strike, and violence had spread from Belfast's bombings and Londonderry's Bloody Sunday to Aldershot where an IRA bomb had murdered five women, a gardener and a Roman Catholic priest. I warned that unless the violence was rooted out of Ulster it would inevitably spread more widely on the mainland and violent picketing such as that at the Saltley coke works would grow and spread to be a threat to democracy itself unless the law was upheld. It was a shamelessly emotional speech which carried the day and I won an absolute majority on the first ballot. Michael was among the first to congratulate me and although I had badly wanted to win there were few men I had less wanted to defeat. It was over a year before Michael, to my relief, secured his future being adopted for Newbury, a seat where he met his future wife and found great happiness.

During the late nights on the Housing Finance Bill I had realised that although our time in Epping had been a very happy period of our lives the move had been a mistake. I had no prospect of continuing to represent Epping and it would be no help to John Biggs-Davison in welding together the new Epping Forest constituency Association for me to continue living in the town. I was also finding the strain of travel too much for me. I had not secured a 'pair' to allow me to be absent from votes in the House – indeed as a very active back bencher I took a pride in voting in 444 of the 480 divisions during 1971. However, the long months of late-night and all-night sittings were taking their toll and I frequently arrived home just in time to give John a lift to the station on his way to school and I often found myself falling asleep on the last stretch home on the long straight unlit road through Epping Forest.

We agreed that a move to London would ease the travelling problems for John, resolve the problem of Alison's unsatisfactory schooling at Ongar, and William's distaste for his school too, and make life a good deal easier for us all.

Even in those days before the property booms we could not afford to buy a house in central London. However, driving into Westminster one day I diverted through the City looking for an easier route and, waiting at a red traffic light, I found myself looking at a huge notice board advertising houses and flats to rent in the Barbican – then still under construction. It seemed to be the answer. In April 1972 we sold our house in Epping and moved into a rented flat in the Barbican. My timing was almost a disaster. Property prices, fuelled by Ted Heath's policies, began to soar, the market becoming frenetic to the extent that at times estate agents in small towns had no property on their books to sell within normal price ranges.

We had to get back into the market and decided to concentrate our search on the northern boundary of Essex, since it was a convenient place from which to reach the Epping constituency, and not too far from Margaret's parents' home in Cambridgeshire. Perhaps, too, I had some sort of yen to settle near to my father's family roots, and at last we found an old timbered and thatched cottage in the village of Little Bardfield near Thaxted.

At first we all loved the house, its simple garden and the countryside, but Margaret's great enthusiasm for 'Gridiron' was to be destroyed by its association with the agonising months of 1974 when the illness which had followed William's birth struck her down twice again within the year. That, however, was still in the unknown future and for a while at least it seemed that although I had not managed our financial affairs very well – especially in retrospect when three or four years later I saw both our Epping and Islington houses selling for almost ten times the prices I had obtained – I had at least preserved my financial skin intact and found a long-term country retreat.

With a view to keeping my political skin intact, too, like many of my political friends and constituency supporters I was still suppressing my doubts and seeking out the issues on which I could readily support the Prime Minister rather than those where I questioned his judgement. I remember arguing with Tom Stuttaford, who had won the marginal seat of Norwich, that his rebellions against the Government would do more for the chances of his Labour opponent than for himself – as indeed proved the case. The Whips knew that I was a loyalist unlikely to do anything to help the Labour Party and not long after my adoption as prospective candidate for Chingford I was invited to become Parliamentary Private Secretary to Robin Chichester Clark, the Ulster Unionist Member for Londonderry, who was Minister for State for Employment. It was the second such invitation I had received: the first from John Peyton I had turned down as I thought it too early to accept the restrictions on freedom to speak on the Minister's departmental responsibilities. I thought that if I refused again it might look as though I had no interest in putting a foot on the first rung of the promotional ladder and although I had hardly ever before spoken to Robin, I agreed to work for him. The post of a PPS is a curious one. I defined it as being on the pay-roll vote but not on the pay-roll. It can amount to nothing more than arranging 'pairs' for the Minister or it can be a position of influence. A good PPS is the eyes, the ears and the informal spokesman of his Minister among back-bench colleagues, and in return he becomes a confidant and adviser, privileged in his dealings with the Department's civil servants. Robin treated me kindly and I hope I served him well in return. It was a dramatic time to be a PPS at the Department of Employment and to an Ulster Unionist MP. Robin was one of the most liberal of Unionists – absolutely committed to the union but entirely without taint of religious or tribal prejudice.

We enjoyed each other's company and Robin became a friend of my family, often exchanging schoolboy Irish jokes with my young children. From time to time I met and looked after his constituents on their visits to London whilst Robin was tied up in departmental work. I also moved my desk from the crowded cloisters shared with a dozen colleagues, where there was no privacy, to Robin's ministerial room in the House of Commons which was far more comfortable. It also contained a camp bed which Robin rarely used as he had an excellent pairing arrangement but which was very useful to me. I learned a lot about Northern Ireland and had the fortuitous advantage that out of deference to Robin I never spoke in debates on that issue. Just as well, as few English politicians have gained much for themselves or that unhappy province by doing so. My instincts were also leading me to doubt the Government's policy there, too, and I was unhappy indeed at its reaction to the report of the committee under Lord Parker (the Lord Chief Justice) on the interrogation methods used by the security forces. Lord Parker and John Boyd-Carpenter accepted that the methods could be justified but only where it was vitally necessary, whilst Lord Gardiner condemned them as illegal and unjustifiable. The Government promptly deserted the Lord Chief Justice and John Boyd-Carpenter and accepted the hostile minority report. It seemed to me a strange way to lead a country, a view reinforced by the abrupt imposition of direct rule following the impasse between Brian Faulkner and Ted Heath.

My doubts about the Government's judgement were compounded as the Prime Minister invited the TUC and CBI to Downing Street in a search for a new wages and prices policy to replace that which the NUM had destroyed. I simply hoped, without conviction, that whatever happened in those talks the tax-cutting Barber budget of 1972 would be successful. The decision to create and finance an Industrial Development Executive with a Minister for Industrial Development I saw as an incomprehensible reverse of the earlier abolition of the Labour Government's Industrial Development Corporation. U-turns and muddles seemed unending. On the industrial-relations front the container blacking dispute dragged through the National Industrial Relations Court. By June Sir John Donaldson, the Court's President, had been forced into a corner by the law which he had to administer, leaving him to choose between allowing three trades union officials to defy the law or to order their arrest. The dockers responded to the arrests with a widespread walkout set to develop into a national dock strike, when someone conjured up the Official Solicitor, who appeared (to the annoyance of the victims) to make application for the quashing of the Order. That was promptly granted by Lord Denning. This avoided a national dock strike, although the dispute dragged on as did the blackings. Midland Cold Storage, one of the businesses affected, took the dispute back into the NIRC but the dockers refused to recognise the court, again leaving Sir John no room for manoeuvre between a tough line against the individuals concerned or acceptance that the Industrial Relations Act could be defied with impunity. His Order for the imprisonment of five dockers for contempt of court gave them the martyrdom they needed to promote a national dock strike and several associated disputes, including newspaper strikes. Once again the Official Solicitor was 'magicked' into being, on the flimsy pretext that the publication of the Jones–Aldington report had created a new situation, and once again a brave effort to carry through the Government's own policy embodied in its own legislation was left in the lurch as Ministers clutched at an 'independent' report from a Government-appointed committee. In this case it was Lord Aldington, a former Tory Minister, by then Chairman of the Port of London Authority, and Jack Jones, the reactionary left-wing leader of the TGWU, who threw the Government a concrete lifebelt which was eagerly accepted. The dockers' victory was to prove pyrrhic. Its guarantee of jobs for life, regardless of whether there was work to be done (or indeed if available work was done or not), applied to all the significant ports of Britain in 1972. Today those ports carry many fewer seaborne cargoes than they might otherwise have done, with much of their former trade and considerable new business now going through ports like Felixstowe, so insignificant at the time that they escaped the 'benefits' of guaranteed jobs. Fresh from these fiascos the Industrial Relations Act displayed another fatal flaw when the Government imposed a cooling-off period to prevent a railway strike. The dispute was still unresolved as the cooling-off expired and, like actors in a Greek tragedy, Ministers asked the NIRC to grant an order imposing a ballot on the employer's offer. No one expected the offer to be accepted and instead there was a six-to-one majority for strike action. British Rail was then given permission for yet another climbdown to buy off the strike.

There seemed no end to the chain of Government defeats. The Pearce Commission which had been sent to Rhodesia to judge whether the independence terms negotiated with Rhodesian Premier, Ian Smith, were acceptable to black opinion, gave the provisional agreement the thumbs down and the Government's policy simply collapsed in failure. Ulster was going badly with only the success of the operation Motorman, to restore policing to the 'no go' areas, to set against a series of calamities, not least Willie Whitelaw's meeting with IRA men who had been given safe conduct for the occasion.

The May local elections were a disaster and by June a run on the pound forced up interest rates and the decision to float (or as it happened to sink) the pound. Not long after there came the sadness of Reggie Maudling's resignation as Home Secretary over the Poulson affair.

By the summer of 1972 I had little conviction that Ted Heath knew where the Government was going – except into the European Community – and I was far from alone in that. If faced with a choice between its friends and principles on the one hand and the expediency of placating its opponents on the other, the Government seemed always to dump its friends in an effort to buy its enemies. Even so I managed to avoid open criticisms of the Government – but as a PPS on the pay-roll vote voted with less and less conviction.

A combination of doubts and loyalty discouraged me from speaking in the House and I tended to confine myself to aviation issues such as the BOAC order for Concorde, the Trident disaster at Staines and airport security. In a debate in late July I maintained, as I have ever since, that whatever precautions are taken a really determined group will succeed in hijacking an aircraft and that the key was diplomatic pressure to bring hijackers swiftly to justice.

All in all I was thoroughly glad to get away for the summer recess. There was a lot of work to be done at our Essex cottage but before that we had arranged to rent a house on Hayling Island. I had never been there before but the house in a large garden, together with a sailing dinghy, canoe, outboard dinghy and a motor scooter, proved to be ideal for the children and we were blessed by fine weather. It was, however, during our holiday there that the Ugandan Asian issue came to the boil.

I had been able to contain my feelings at the succession of self-induced governmental disasters until events in Uganda proved too much for my constituents or me to suffer in silence.

It was that African outrage of Idi Amin's expulsion of the Ugandan Asians which inflamed still tender feelings in Britain over earlier unrestricted immigration. Of course it was hard on the Ugandan Asians, probably the most able and successful of all New Commonwealth immigrants, that they should have become the unwilling focus of yet another Heath Government U-turn. However, the British electorate had never approved of large-scale immigration, nor indeed had its consent ever been sought. At a time when the Government was extremely unpopular, its ready assumption that an outburst of black African racism was a problem to be solved at our expense was not widely shared amongst the electorate, least of all after the collapse of the Rhodesian agreement.

My Conservative Association Executive instructed the Chairman to write to the Prime Minister and to me in terms so strong that I advised them that neither the content nor the tone would be at all helpful – indeed they were unacceptable to me. After a number of telephone calls it was agreed that I should write instead to the Prime Minister and the Chief Whip telling them, 'My Association believes the Government is utterly and completely wrong.' I described the letters as 'rather brutal'. I knew that most of my electors felt that the original homelands of the refugees, India or Pakistan, should have taken a greater share of the responsibility for the Ugandan Asians and that the price of our acceptance of these hapless refugees should have been the return home of other Ugandan citizens in Britain.

I realised that in telling Ted Heath what the voters who put him in office felt, I had forfeited any prospect of preferment but I was already wondering not whether, but for how long, I could continue as a PPS if he continued to fly in the face of the policies on which we had both been elected.

Nor did the autumn of 1972 bring much political comfort, except in the problems of the TUC and the Labour Party. The TUC Conference was dominated by the expulsion of a handful of small unions, including BALPA, which had registered under the Industrial Relations Act; and the next month the Labour Party was split on both the usual left–right issues and on Europe. Our own Conference a week later was an equally unhappy affair with obvious discontent over policies on Ulster and economic affairs. It was, however, on the issue of Ugandan Asians that the discontent was most clearly seen when an amendment supported by Enoch Powell was defeated by 1721 to 736 votes in a secret ballot. Although the Prime Minister claimed it as a clear victory only just over half the representatives had supported the Government – a danger signal indeed at a Tory Conference.

Parties which have internal squabbles are heavily punished by the electors and it was the Liberals who benefited from the discomfiture of both Labour and Conservative parties with a spectacular gain from Labour at Rochdale in October and from us at Sutton and Cheam in December. Our only comfort was holding on at Uxbridge against Labour, Liberal, neo-fascist and anti-EEC candidates.

Feeling well out of sympathy with the Government I spoke less in the

House. I did, however, speak and cast my vote against televising the House of Commons, observing that I knew of nothing, with the exception of show jumping, which had not been trivialised or spoilt by having the cameras upon it.

It was another judgement that I have seen no cause to change.

As the Government pursued its tripartite talks with the TUC and CBI, I became increasingly depressed and uncertain whether success or failure would be worse. As I saw it, success would take us towards the politics of corporatism, not the liberal Conservatism in which I believed. But if the talks were to fail, what then? For weeks things dragged on with neither side wanting to take responsibility for a breakdown, but by 2 November an impasse was reached over the TUC's insistence on the repeal of both the Housing Finance Act and the Industrial Relations Act as well as control of all prices including food and rents. Four days later Ted Heath made his momentous statement to the House. There was to be a freeze on all pay, prices and dividends for ninety days with only fresh food and imported raw materials exempt. We had certainly now reached the great U-turn of the Heath Government.

Enoch Powell spoke the words that were in the minds of many of us. 'Has the Right Honourable Gentleman [Ted Heath] taken leave of his senses?'

I was close to despair. Parliament and the Party had avoided the humiliation of being required to rubber stamp a corporatist deal between TUC, CBI and Ministers, but we were faced with a crystal-clear breach of our 1970 election manifesto which had specifically rejected pay and price controls. I was sure that the policy would destroy the Government. Even worse, I feared it might wreck the party too for if we split it might well open the way to a decade or more of Socialism.

I found it hard to decide how to vote. To be part of a successful rebellion would lead to disaster within weeks. Ideally I wanted to be a failed rebel – but not quite a lone rebel. At least that way I would avoid voting against my convictions and undertakings without bringing down the Government. But what alternative policy would I put forward – except to say that we should never have got into such a mess? In the end I knuckled under and shamefacedly supported the Government which had a majority of thirty-five. I have often wished since it had been only thirty-three but loyalty, a deep dislike of voting with a party I utterly opposed, and a horror of precipitating years of Socialism dragged me into the Government lobby. I wondered next day if I ought to resign as a PPS then realised that at least that office gave me a plausible reason for not speaking on the pay and prices policy, so I soldiered on.

1972 ended as miserably as it had begun, with the Government now set firmly on a vast extension of its powers across the economy, taking the very powers which any Socialist or corporatist regime would want to control both businesses and private citizens.

After two and a half years my loyalty was tightly stretched and my support was given with a heavy heart. Quite rightly I feared that things would get even worse in 1973.

At least in private life, living in London was working out quite well. We liked the Barbican and began making friends there, finding it belied its unsociable reputation. It suited the children too. John was happy at the City of London Boys' School and did very well in his O levels in the autumn of 1973. Although Alison was less happy at the Girls' School William had cheerfully rejoined his old classmates in Islington. It was a chore taking him to school until we felt he could cope with a tube or bus journey on his own but worth it to see him happy. We all enjoyed our weekends at Little Bardfield even though we had little time for anything but work. Our financial affairs were still far from good, and my overdraft steadily increased throughout a year in which I had little luck in finding paying jobs compatible with being a Member of Parliament, although one bright spot was meeting a young publisher and aviation enthusiast, Brian Healey. I soon found he was a poor businessman and manager but writing for his aviation magazine made me an aviation journalist, with access to aviation shows and events. I regained my pilot's licence and began to receive invitations to fly all sorts of private and business aircraft in order to write articles and reviews about them. That was fun at a profit – a happy combination indeed. It was hard work but it also maintained my old flying contacts and created many new ones. Margaret, too, began to pick up her former career with part-time nursing at St Bartholomew's Hospital as well as learning to type to help me with my work. For a while I joined a small group interested in promoting an airfield for business use somewhere in the London area (a need for which the provision is still inadequate), but I found my prospective partners none too realistic, the venture became a liability and I cut my losses. More promising for a while was a scheme to market low-interest-rate, low-deposit mortgages in which the lender would share capital gains with the borrower. I had proposed this idea in a speech in the House of Commons and to my surprise was approached by a substantial Scottish-based insurance company who thought it an attractive concept. Sadly, in the face of legal problems and the financial shambles of 1974 the scheme was dropped, though in retrospect that proved a terrible mistake. Somehow, however, we managed, looking forward always to the eventual end of school fees and a successful enterprise of some kind.

I determined that whatever happened to the Government I had better get on with my political career and began 1973 more actively in Parliament. In February I spoke very critically on the Maplin Development Bill describing it as a 1930s' airport to be built in the 1990s. It would, I claimed, be the most expensive airport ever built and that the money would be better spent on quieter engines with tighter noise restrictions being imposed on aircraft. Again my loyalty to Ted Heath prevented me from voting against what I saw as a madcap scheme and I confined myself to abstentions. Hijacking remained a problem in the news, and so did I for expressing the views I still hold that the crime should be punishable by death and that regardless of cost no hijacker should ever be allowed to achieve his objective.

By this time I found myself more and more often amongst groups of friends in the House who were unable to see any happy outcome to the Government's policies. I belonged to several groups, one of MPs first elected in 1970, another of a dozen deliberately chosen to cover a wide spectrum of views within the Party, as well as the 92 Group. Without exception we doubted the wisdom of state control of prices and incomes but out of loyalty and an acceptance that the choice lay between supporting either the elected Government or a largely unrepresentative trades union leadership we rallied reluctantly to the Government flag.

In January the Prime Minister announced the second phase of his prices and income policy, taking unprecedented powers to control prices and incomes, including dividends and profits. It underlined his desertion of the free-market policies of the Selsdon manifesto but it was a mark of his mastery of the Party. Tony Barber, as Chancellor, delivered Ted Heath's economic policy to him, and Francis Pym as Chief Whip delivered the votes in Parliament. Like most of us they were loyal to a fault. Francis was one of the truly great Chief Whips, perhaps too good at his job for Ted Heath's own good. A few more rebellions from those of us who believed then in the policies which have since proved successful might have saved the Heath Government from at least some of its follies and the 1974 defeat, for although Francis always delivered the votes in the House of Commons the Party Whip has little effect amongst the electorate. In fact, in the end, we did little more than grumble and worry in private.

The national political situation began to seem more volatile. In a curious foretaste of the story of the Liberal SDP Alliance, Dick Taverne, who had resigned his seat, was re-elected as a Democratic Labour candidate, only of course to be swept away at the general election; but it was the Liberals who made most of the running in 1973, and they gave me some worry in Chingford where they had once been a powerful force. Unlike some of my colleagues who tried to hold them off by conceding political inches, only to find they had lost political miles, I never conceded anything to them.

In my book they were Enid Blyton Socialists, a dustbin for undecided votes, neither fish nor fowl, just pink herrings, an irrelevance in deciding the major issues of the day. As a result we generally held them in third place, even in the local elections that year which went very badly for the Government with Labour taking control of the Greater London Council and the Liberals storming home in Liverpool. The Government's by-election record was alarming; not only were we marginalised at Manchester Exchange, polling only 683 votes, but Harry Legge-Bourke's seat at the Isle of Ely fell to the comedian Clement Freud with the Liberals taking Ripon too, and in November Berwick-on-Tweed's 7400 Conservative majority was overturned by the then (and still) unknown Alan Beith.

Our own Government was still highly volatile too. One Socialist measure followed another, with even a thirty-per-cent levy on land having planning permission where development was not taking place as quickly as the Government wished. The Pay Board and the Prices Commission began to grind away suppressing market signals, misdirecting resources, playing God in the market place. At times there was an illusion of progress and by April Ted Heath claimed that the militants were losing support and that the acceptance of his policy had been 'a victory for common sense'. The truth was less palatable.

The Government was simply storing up trouble for the future, buying off unions with promises of future reviews which the unions read as commitments to more money. It would be unfair to Ted Heath to forget that the press, even *The Times* and the *Economist*, supported the incomes policy. With real living standards rising, the economy growing at a rate of at least five per cent, order books lengthening and unemployment falling, there seemed to be a good deal to crow about. However, the growing problem was inflation, and the conflict between rapid monetary growth inflating prices and legal controls trying to sit on wage and price rises was brewing up an explosive mixture.

We poor back benchers went away for the summer uneasy enough. Had we known more of what was going on in Government I think my unease would have become outright distress. As we now know Ted Heath had begun to by-pass his Ministers – a practice always fraught with danger – relying more and more upon Sir William Armstrong. Thus it was that only he was present at the Prime Minister's secret meeting in the garden of No. 10 on 16 July 1973, with the miners' leader Joe Gormley to stitch up a deal to settle the miners' claim within the limits of Phase 3 of the incomes policy. It was an act of supreme folly. Joe Gormley was in no position to deliver either the NUM or the TUC and I doubt whether his understanding of the conversation and Ted Heath's were the same. When Parliament returned we were asked to approve the regulations enforcing Phase 3, under which it was believed that the NCB's pay offer, amounting to about thirteen per cent could be made to work. Unaware of the Heath–Gormley conversation of July, the NUM Executive regarded the NCB package as an opening offer and it was duly rejected. With the Yom Kippur war raging and oil prices about to spiral the miners' leaders saw the chance to maintain their place at the top of the pay league, and if that smashed Ted Heath's pay policy and his Government then so much the better. Not only would that give much political satisfaction but, they must have reasonably thought, no one would ever again deny them what they demanded.

By mid November under the impact of the miners' overtime ban, Ted Heath declared the fifth state of emergency in his three and a half years as Prime Minister. By the end of the month, together with Maurice Macmillan and Tom Boardman (Employment and Industry Minister), the Prime Minister and the inevitable William Armstrong met the NUM executive at No. 10. I could never make out whether Ted Heath thought he might influence the NUM or if it was just window dressing, but in either case it was a failure.

From then on events moved inexorably as in the final act of a Greek tragedy. In a Cabinet shuffle on 3 December Willie Whitelaw replaced Maurice Macmillan as Secretary of State for Employment (potentially a shrewd move but it was too late and Willie was exhausted by Ireland). Ten days later amidst serious power cuts the three-day week was introduced, followed by Tony Barber's long-overdue cuts of over a billion pounds in public expenditure. There were crisis talks with the TUC and the Prime Minister chaired a meeting of NEDC in a welter of frenetic activity. It is an entirely misconceived notion that Prime Ministers should negotiate pay claims. It misled both Wilson and Heath; and five years later Jim Callaghan, too, was to discover that such notions are fatally destructive delusions.

By November I had given up the Government as a lost cause although right to the end I concealed my differences as best I could. In submitting my resignation as Robin Chichester Clark's PPS, I wrote: 'I have for some time felt increasingly restricted by the constraints imposed on my freedom to speak about industrial affairs and the related fields of incomes policy and employee participation.'

It was as gentle a way as I could find to break from a Minister I liked but a Government I found harder and harder to support. I was sad to leave Robin Chichester Clark. His life had disintegrated about him, his marriage, his province of Ulster, his constituency of Londonderry and his Ulster Association were all in tumult. I will never know whether I did Robin a good or bad service when one night, not long after my appointment, I had found him in despair over Ted Heath's Northern Ireland policy. Believing that he was on the verge of resignation, I saw the Chief Whip and asked him to talk to Robin before he went home that night as I believed the next day would be too late. Whether because of that or not Robin stayed in Government but sadly his liberal views were unwelcome in Londonderry and he told his local Association that he would not stand again for the constituency. I persuaded him to look for an English seat but his heart was never in it and his circumstances were hardly likely to win a selection contest. He was a loss to politics although happily he was succeeded by one of the best of the Ulster Unionists, William Ross, a very tough, brave and decent man.

1973 was not our happiest Christmas although, acting as usual as the focal point for the family celebrations, we managed to forget politics between the power cuts. However, the threat of a general election hung over us and I knew it was one for which my Association was ill prepared and in which I would have to defend a Government record of self-induced failures.

By late January all the creative accountancy within Phase 3 limits, and all the efforts of the TUC to persuade Ted Heath to allow the NUM to breach the limits on top of that, had failed. The NUM called for strike action to back up what until then had been only an overtime ban aided by effective secondary action. On 3 February the strike began.

The Government Whips had been sounding out opinion on a possible general election and I offered my opinion with no great enthusiasm. I assumed that it would be ignored by the Prime Minister who regarded the Whips' office channel of communication like all others as being one way only – for him to talk and us to listen. In any case, although I favoured an early election I had no great conviction that we would win and I had no idea what the Government would do to resolve the miners' problem if we did. The strongest argument seemed to me that the longer we waited the worse the defeat that awaited us. It became clear that the Party was split on the question, and the Cabinet and the Whips themselves. In consequence Ted Heath hesitated until 7 February when he announced the election date of 28 February. By then the window of opportunity for a successful campaign was fast closing.

Speaking to my own Conservative Association in January I had readied them for an early election.

> No one wants an election just for the fun of having one. The situation in Britain today is, however, close to the point where the people of the country must be asked to speak and speak clearly on the one great issue of the day.

The issue, I went on to explain, was 'Who Governs?'. On the merits of the Government's policy I must have sounded rather lame.

> I am, as you know, no enthusiast for statutory incomes policies, but at present Phase 3 is all that stands between Britain and runaway inflation.

The campaign was a miserable experience in every respect. My party workers worked for the Party and for me, but few had a good word for Ted Heath. On the doorsteps I found Tory supporters simply could not identify with the Prime Minister or a Tory Party which had deserted Conservative policies, led the country into a coal strike it could not win and called a general election without any idea of what to do if it won. It was clear that Ted Heath was an electoral liability.

I took a bold line in my election address.

> Most people know it [this election] is being fought because a tiny minority of communists and extreme leftists are trying to overthrow a legally elected Government and indeed Parliament itself by the use of the strike weapon.

I was perhaps rather tongue in cheek answering my own question, 'Can the election solve the strike?' saying,

> Yes. Agree or disagree with the result, the miners accept the verdict of their own national ballot. I believe they will accept the result of this national ballot too.

My election leaflets emphasised my local connections, support for capital punishment, tougher immigration rules and opposition to the Maplin airport scheme, and warned of 'the weakness of a Government without an overall majority depending for support on Paisleyites, Welsh and

Scottish Nationalists, Liberals and perhaps even National Front MPs.'

Fortunately neither my Labour nor Liberal opponents addressed the issues in the pamphlets which they issued. The Liberal campaign was based on no more than claims that their support was growing and, like the Labour challenger, their candidate avoided discussion of the miners' strike in his election address. The election was not only a political disaster. About a week into the campaign my agent, Bill Ottaway, succumbed to alcohol and disappeared until it was all over. My wife rose to the occasion superbly but towards the end of the campaign a terrible fear began to eat into me. Her enthusiasm and activity had become frenetic and a few days before polling day during the journey to dinner with friends I saw she was becoming agitated and fearful. During the meal she broke down, realising that the illness which she had suffered after William's birth was returning. The next day I called in our doctor and in a fit of clarity, before the clouds of depression and confusion overwhelmed her, she agreed to go into hospital again. Somehow I struggled through to polling day, getting the children off to school, cooking meals, canvassing and making political speeches between visits to hospital to see Margaret, once again changed by her illness into a stranger, alternately depressed, elated or simply confused beyond communication.

The events of the election, the damage done to Ted Heath's campaign by the leaking of statistical evidence from the Pay Board and the clumsy or prejudiced comments from Campbell Adamson of the CBI, and even Enoch Powell's advice to vote Labour, more or less passed me by. Throughout it all I stuck to my version of the election issues, campaigning on auto pilot with my mind on Margaret in hospital and the children at home, until I heard the declaration giving me a majority of just 5683 over my Labour opponent, with the Liberal another 2000 votes behind. From the count I went through the motions of the usual celebration party and then, bone weary, drove home to bed.

Next morning the radio and newspapers confirmed the defeat of the Government. Although the swing from us to Labour was minuscule, less than one per cent, the Liberal poll of twenty-four per cent was largely at our expense and we lost thirty-three seats. Labour with 301 was just four seats ahead of us, and the Liberals with fourteen had the power to put either Wilson or Ted into office. The old Ulster Unionists lost eleven seats, mainly to the new Unionists who refused the Conservative Whip. Had we retained their support Ted Heath would have still been the leader of the largest party, entitled to form a new administration and seek a vote of confidence, but his Ulster policy had robbed him of that option.

Like many others I thought we had been lucky not to have suffered a worse defeat. We could hardly have fought an election in worse circumstances and I had survived by a reasonable margin – certainly wide enough to ensure that Chingford would not be on the Labour or Liberal lists of a seat they might expect to win at a second general election which was sure to follow before long.

I was surprised that Ted Heath did not accept at once that he had lost the election, and as it became plain that he was seeking Liberal support for a coalition government my surprise turned to real anger. I was sure the Party was opposed to such a deal especially as it compromised our position on proportional representation. So far as I was concerned Ted Heath might enter a coalition, but I had not been elected to support one and was under no obligation to do so. I had no way of knowing that before long the private life of Jeremy Thorpe would be uncovered and the man who might have been Ted Heath's Home Secretary would face a charge of attempted murder. It was a lucky escape.

7

The Gang of Four

In some ways our defeat in February 1974 and going into opposition was a relief. I no longer had to defend policies which were indefensible and the way was open to take the Party back to Conservatism. The offer of coalition with the Liberals had been the last straw, and with Ted Heath now a political and electoral liability it was clear he would have to go once the inevitable second election was over.

At least our anxiety not to precipitate that election in what the country would see as a partisan or provocative way eased my domestic problems. A one-line whip, we joked, still meant turn up if you wish, but a three-line meant for God's sake stay away or we might defeat the Government! I endeavoured to keep up normal appearances, despite Margaret's illness. Once the children had gone to school I dashed out to do the shopping, usually in the street market in Whitecross Street just north of the Barbican, then back home to prepare an evening meal for the family. Even to this day the mention of my shepherd's pies and casseroles generates cries of 'No, not again!' from our children. Once the meal was prepared I dashed to the hospital and from there to Parliament, always trying to be in for Question Time and the meetings of the key party committees. Fortunately John and Alison were old enough to take on a good deal of responsibility and somehow we managed to keep the family together in good order.

This time Margaret's illness was not so severe. We understood it better and it was not many weeks before she was home again, fragile and insecure but gradually regaining her health and normal confidence.

In Opposition in Parliament I soon began to acquire the style which provided so much material for the political sketch writers – frustration for the Labour Party and a mixture of emotions among fellow Conservatives. Some thought my willingness to stand toe to toe against the more thuggish elements of the Labour Party and slug it out blow for blow rather vulgar. Others, especially in the country at large, seemed delighted at the idea of a Tory MP unwilling to be strangled into silence by his old school tie and quite prepared to take on all comers in robust terms.

There was more to the style than a lack of deference (which was uncharacteristic of traditional Tory MPs), and more behind it than my dislike of bullies, humbugs and Socialism. I had long believed that the Heath aberration of authoritarian centralist corporatism apart, most of the values, ethos and policies of Conservatism were strongly supported by working-class voters. Those voters – especially the socio-economic groups C1 and C2 – I saw as natural Conservatives who nevertheless saw themselves for tribal reasons as Labour voters. However much we tried to reach them by argument, we always failed because they were unable to identify themselves with the representatives of the Tory Party they saw. I was determined to be a Conservative who spoke their language, not just what is often described as my flat North-London accent – which was after all my mother tongue – but their practical realism, lack of humbug and strong attachment to many traditional standards and values. In my judgement they were ready to listen to blunt words – or even colourful words – but not to complex waffle. If we wanted to be heard in the pub or the street market our ideas had to be stripped down to their unambiguous essence and had to be delivered in a style which was familiar in those environments. It was a concept familiar enough today in any marketing strategy: use the potential customer's own words and present the product in *his* or *her* cultural packaging. It was revolutionary in the Conservative Party, where the formula had been to change the 'product' to what the voter was thought to want whilst retaining the packaging and style which had been putting him off.

In those early months of 1975 Harold Wilson handled the difficult business of minority government, in the midst of an economic crisis and under the looming shadow of another election, with great skill. His Cabinet balanced the left and right wings with great care although his appointment of Mr Foot as Secretary of State for Employment was something of a surprise. Mr Foot lost no time in settling the coal strike on the NUM's terms. The terms were close to those recommended by the Pay Board pay relativities report commissioned by Ted Heath which, in a bizarre twist of his own policy, he had announced in advance that he would accept. So the dispute was settled after Ted Heath's defeat on terms he had once refused to contemplate then subsequently pledged himself to accept.

Naturally the Labour Government built on Ted Heath's legislation to intensify price controls and consumer subsidies. Rents were frozen but Mr Healey in the first of his many budgets increased income tax, raised telephone and postal charges, rail fares, the price of coal, petrol and electricity, as well as increasing the tax on tobacco and alcohol.

All this was part of the background to Mr Wilson's promotion of the 'Social Contract'. The TUC were pressed to accept wage restraint in return for the Government's programme of price controls and subsidies but whilst the Government's obligations seemed to be a lengthy and specific shopping list those of the TUC were vague and without sanctions. The left wing was placated by the destruction of the Industrial Relations Act, a grotesque amnesty for illegal immigrants (rightly seen as a green light for further illegal immigration), the appointment of Mr Mortimer, a hard line pro-trades unionist, to head the industrial conciliation and arbitration service, and half promises of wealth taxes and gift taxes as well as more nationalisation through a National Enterprise Board.

Under Ted Heath's leadership the Opposition lacked credibility in criticising these proposals. All too many were all too close to the direction his Government had been taking since 1972. Whilst I hoped in 1974 that the second election would not come before some of the Labour Government's chickens came home to roost, I wanted to get it over so that we could start work on the reconstruction of the Conservative Party.

Parliament was in a pre-election hothouse mood right up to the summer break. There were excited scenes as the Industrial Relations Act continued to put Sir John Donaldson and the National Industrial Relations Court into impossible positions. The refusal of the AUEW to pay a fine resulted in a sequestration order. The Labour Government's equivalent to the Official Solicitor – a group of anonymous businessmen – paid the AUEW's fines to end the confrontation and only a few weeks later the court was abolished. Then, during the legislation on the Government's Trades Union and Labour Relations Act, which repealed Ted Heath's legislation, the Government was caught out improperly counting Harold Lever's vote when he was not in the House – a convenient error, or deliberate cheat, which precipitated an almighty row. A good many chances to defeat the Government were taken from time to time but never on issues serious enough to be regarded as matters of confidence.

The gathering economic clouds, the disputes in the NHS, where the nurses were bought off with a pay rise of fifty-eight per cent, and Mr Healey's second budget all pointed to an early election. His July budget cut VAT and subsidised both rates and food with a favourable impact on the RPI which eased the problem of 'threshold' pay increases overhanging from Ted Heath's pay policy. It was also the basis of Mr Healey's dishonest claim that inflation was down to 8.4 per cent. His arithmetic was achieved by quadrupling the three-month price rise which had been affected by the July measures and, alongside the claim of Prices Minister Shirley Williams that there were no price rises in the pipeline, it was widely used at the general election.

Having seen my wife through her illness and back home I was eager to get away to our cottage at Little Bardfield where we spent the summer. Margaret was very fragile and unsure of the security of her recovery, but despite that we enjoyed working on the house and playing with the children. William had begun to enthuse about cricket so I had some long bowling stints in the field adjoining our garden which was usually inhabited by horses and cattle – all adding to the hazards of the game.

My most successful commercial venture of the year came in October when I joined DEC – Digital Equipment Limited – the American multinational computer company, a very happy association which lasted until I became a Minister in 1979.

In the meantime I had to do all I could to hold on to my place in parliament. Although my majority of over 5000 seemed reasonably secure the opinion polls were putting Labour well ahead, the Liberals were riding high and the May by-election at Newham, although not representative, put us in fourth place behind the National Front. I spent a good deal of time encouraging my Party workers and being active in the constituency, fearing that as in February my agent might not be too much help when the time came.

By September everything was pointing to an October election. In August came Mr Healey's wealth tax and Mr Benn's nationalisation plans. Plans for Scottish and Welsh devolution followed in September, then more money for the building industry, plans for more environmental protection and effective municipalisation of building land. Finally Mrs Castle came in with big promises for pensioners, a sure pointer to the polls. In fact it was a blizzard of Government White Papers in a concentrated use of the Government machine for party electoral purposes of a kind not seen before or since.

The main Party manifestoes appeared before the official 'off' on 18 September for the election of 10 October but enthusiasm was hard to generate. Our supporters did not want a Labour Government but Ted Heath was even more unsaleable than in February. To make it worse poor Bill Ottaway went under once again, failing to turn up with my nomination papers and leaving me in the lurch on the town hall steps. Fortunately I had arranged my nomination with a few days in hand – a tip for any candidate – and we eventually tracked down Bill and the papers. Both Margaret and I were immensely fond of Bill – he had shown wonderful understanding of Margaret's illness and she in turn did her best to support him and get him back to work. Alas, it was too much for both of them. Bill went on another binge and Margaret suffered a relapse into her breakdown.

I was as sick at heart as I could be by polling day when once again I arrived at the town hall without her. The result was better than I had hoped – as was the result in the country. My vote had fallen some 900 to just over 19,000 and my majority of 4,645 was almost 1000 down, but the Liberal challenge had faded and my percentage of the poll had actually risen. Nationally the result was a bitter disappointment for Mr Wilson. We had lost twenty seats, Labour had gained eighteen to achieve a paper-thin over-all majority of only three.

Despite Margaret's illness, I felt a profound sense of relief as the election results came in. The Labour Government could hardly run full term and once we had jettisoned the Heath policies we could harry it to death. With any luck, I thought, it would be like the retreat from Moscow – a failed and dispirited army to be routed some day before October 1979 and I was confident that I would find a role in that action.

In fact the action had already begun. The Executive of the 1922 Committee (the Committee comprising all Tory MPs bar the Leader when in office, and all but Ministers and Whips when it is in Government) had agreed before the general election to meet shortly afterwards to be ready to respond to any situation which might arise. The meeting took place on 14 October at the home of the Chairman, Edward du Cann, and it decided unanimously what whilst an immediate election for the leadership of the Party was not necessary it could not be long delayed. Nigel Fisher's account of the leadership election (*The Tory Leaders: Their Struggle for Power*) is as good as any and I can add to it only from my personal experience. Until the leadership contest, like many colleagues, I hardly knew Margaret Thatcher. Indeed I think I had only ever exchanged a dozen words with her and had never thought of her as a potential leader of the Party. However, as Nigel Fisher records, the moment came when Ted Heath was forced into agreeing to a leadership election; and it looked as though there might be no credible candidate ready to challenge. Nigel Fisher favoured Edward du Cann, but I was concerned that the troubles of Keyser Ullmann, his merchant bank, might be visited on the party. Geoffrey Howe was a possibility, but I could not see in him the bite and sharp cutting edge needed to scythe down Harold Wilson. Willie, I felt, shared Geoffrey's shortcomings and in any case was unwilling to challenge Ted. Whilst Keith Joseph undoubtedly had the intellectual brilliance – and as I later discovered is one of the most honourable, decent, indeed lovable men in the world – I realised that not only did he lack that indefinable quality that makes a national political leader, but his very virtues were a disqualification!

We discussed the issue endlessly – indeed we had done so between the two elections almost wherever colleagues met and most particularly in our dining clubs and groups. My own feelings, and those of my friends in the 1970 intake of MPs, were very much those of the 92 Group – puzzled rather than split. The more left wing among them either favoured keeping Ted Heath or, if that was not possible, switching to Willie or even Peter Walker. The right wingers hesitated between Keith Joseph and Edward du Cann or Geoffrey Howe, but gradually Margaret Thatcher's name came more and more into play.

In the meantime all sorts of other names were being tossed around. Early in January Stephen Hastings asked me to call at his flat and told me that Julian Amery wanted to stand. We agreed that he stood no chance and would only be hurt if he did. I agreed that I would talk to Julian, and then to my astonishment Stephen told me that Christopher Soames was another possibility!

Nigel Fisher recounts how he chaired a group promoting Edward du Cann who was first very reluctant and then declared himself a non-starter. They turned to Keith Joseph, who also decided not to run. At that stage Airey Neave, a member of the group, proposed that it should transfer allegiance to Margaret Thatcher who, despite becoming a potential candidate, had no organisation beyond Bill Shelton and Fergus Montgomery, both of whom were friends of mine although neither had asked me to join them. Nigel Fisher felt he could not commit himself totally to Margaret Thatcher and on 15 January proposed that Airey Neave should take over the chairmanship to promote her candidature. About fifteen of the twenty-five members of the group followed Airey who, with Bill Shelton, then embarked on the campaign for Margaret Thatcher. A week later Ted Heath agreed that the election should be held on 4 February and the race was really on. By then I had told Julian that I was in Margaret's campaign team and advised him that he should not stand himself as he would be squeezed out in the Heath–Thatcher battle.

Under the rules for the election of Conservative leader the first ballot is decisive only if a contestant clears two hurdles, achieving both an over-all majority of those entitled to vote and fifteen per cent more of the votes of those entitled to vote than any other candidate. If a second ballot is required new nominations are needed, so new candidates can enter and a majority of those entitled to vote is decisive. If a third ballot is needed the top three candidates from the second ballot compete on a transferable preference system requiring a first and second preference choice from those voting.

It soon became clear that Margaret Thatcher was the only heavy-weight candidate willing to challenge Ted Heath on the first ballot, the rest of the Shadow Cabinet feeling inhibited from doing so.

Having come to know Airey Neave through our mutual membership of the Select Committee on Science and Technology I was pleased to join him and Bill Shelton at a Thatcher committee meeting on 20 January. I had already been canvassing views and was able to contribute my list agreeing to canvass a number of other colleagues. In order to avoid embarrassment for these colleagues and to elicit an entirely frank response I avoided asking direct questions or declaring my interest. Ted Heath's friends, however, too easily fell into the trap of putting junior colleagues into a position where answers were given to please rather than to inform.

Those of us close to the centre of Margaret's campaign never revealed how optimistic we were. We knew that a good many colleagues might want to get rid of Ted Heath but not necessarily to elect Margaret, and we needed their votes on the first ballot. A difficult balancing trick was required. We had to imply that her campaign was strong enough to win and strong enough to deny Ted Heath victory on the first ballot, but not to achieve either outright victory herself nor such domination as to prevent others, such as Willie, from coming forward on the second ballot. I recollect John Nott and myself persuading Michael Heseltine, who was a Whitelaw man, that unless he voted for Margaret on the first ballot there would be no second ballot and no opportunity for Willie to stand.

Our optimism, Airey's leadership and Margaret herself made us a happy campaign team – all the more so when Joan Hall, the former Member for Keighley, who had been defeated at the election, arrived to be Margaret's chauffeur, secretary, and all-purpose supporter. We worked to the very ballot itself. Erring on the side of pessimism I expected a vote of about 125 to 100 in Ted's favour and was happily surprised when Edward du Cann announced the figures. Margaret had polled 130 against Ted Heath's 119, Hugh Fraser's 16, and 11 abstentions. Our tactics had been successful. Whoever might come in on the second ballot would be fighting an uphill battle. It was quite a party at Airey's flat!

The second-round tactics were straightforward. The party wanted a change. Margaret would give it. The ballot gave her the decisive lead over Willie Whitelaw of 146 to 79.

At first I think she found it difficult to believe she had won so comprehensively. At a party that evening she radiated her delight, her excitement and her thanks to her friends – then suddenly she was whisked away to the television studios. It was all over. Knowing we had taken a huge gamble in staking the future of our Party on a woman leader we drifted away to dinner. I returned to the House where in the Central Lobby I found Denis Thatcher looking slightly lost waiting for Margaret, and persuaded him to join me for dinner.

For days the papers, few of which had seen Mrs Thatcher as such a clear winner, concentrated on assessing her and her appointments to the Shadow Cabinet and Central Office. Almost all of them reflected on the irony that it was the Conservative Party which had elected a woman as leader. She had never been thought of as a future Prime Minister and the political writers were not quick to refocus their thoughts. Wisely she tried to avoid offering too many policy hostages but unfortunately on a visit to Scotland on 26 February, which she took over from Ted Heath's diary, she committed the Party under her leadership to the devolution policy of the 1974 manifesto. Not being in her shadow team I could do nothing but watch in despair and hope that she would not continue to be misled by the 'Heathmen' who surrounded her. There was little point in changing the leader if we were to be stuck with the same policies! Ted Heath had been due to speak at the Conservative Trades Unionist Conference on 29 February and as I was President of their organisation Margaret, who was to speak in his place, asked me for my advice on what she should say. 'As little as possible until you have decided on your policy,' I advised her. 'No one expects a policy speech from you. I can talk about policy – all you need do is to say what a good lot they are, be nice about the Central Office people who are retiring and say that we have understood trade unions since Disraeli.' She thanked me and asked if I would write something for her as I knew the audience and she did not. It was my first shot at speech writing for her and it was so short, uncontroversial and so lacking in policy statements that I do not think it was reported anywhere. Just what was needed!

I could afford to be a great deal more pointed speaking in Parliament in my own name and I soon realised that asking hostile questions was a great deal easier than asking friendly or helpful ones. The latter had been particularly difficult during the Heath era as most of the questions I wanted to ask would have been highly unfriendly. I did not take long to improve my natural talent for getting under the skin of Labour Ministers.

A good deal of planning and thought is needed as Government departments come to the top of a roster to answer oral questions, and oral questions have to be tabled – that is put down – a fortnight ahead of the day for answer. In that time the Minister's civil servants provide briefing and draft answers. Then on the day the Minister reads the prepared reply and the contest of wits really begins as the questioner puts his supplementary question to which the Minister must give a reply, even if not an answer. It is an exercise in both careful preparation and quick thinking. There is time for relatively few questions to receive oral answers – especially if Ministers drag things out, or back benchers' supplementaries are long winded.

If I had a line of questioning I wanted to pursue I would often put down questions for written answer. Written answers usually come within days and if the questions were shrewdly devised they began to limit the scope for the Minister to avoid the point of the oral question I would then table. Enoch Powell once advised me, 'Never go into the Chamber of the House of Commons without a verbal grenade in your pocket.' I was usually armed to the teeth and invariably had a supplementary question in mind as I walked into Question Time. The secret of success is a mixture of preparation and opportunism and I was usually still completing my question in my mind as I stood up.

Quick wits are needed to follow up other Members' questions and often I found it best to junk my carefully thought-out supplementary and simply come back to a well-made point of a colleague. Few things put a Minister under more pressure, or give the impression he is failing to cope, than for several Members to hammer away on the same point. The style is simple but effective. 'That's all very well, but the Minister failed to answer my Hon. Friend's question. Is it that he doesn't know the answer or that he's ashamed to give it?'

Fortunately for Ministers, most MPs are too concerned with their often over-rehearsed supplementary question to hunt as a pack!

Once we were in Opposition I changed my regular seat from the middle back benches to that haunt of very senior ex-Ministers and the rough, tough parliamentary tricoteuse, the front bench below the gangway, linking up with Ian Gow, Peter Rees, George Gardiner and some of our more senior sharp-witted parliamentarians. Before long we were invited to join groups established by John Peyton and Jasper Moore with Whips' Office approval to co-ordinate parliamentary tactics to make life difficult for the Government.

There I found myself in one of my natural elements, preying on any weakness or division among Labour Members. Our success was noticed and in June Margaret Thatcher asked me to join her briefing meetings before Prime Minister's Questions. Success in those two fifteen-minute sessions each week is vital to a Prime Minister and even more so to a Leader of the Opposition. The ranks of MPs on either side are there to cheer on their champions. To be tripped or wrong-footed, to let down one's supporters in those battles of wits, can be the beginning of the end – especially for a new Opposition Leader lacking the trappings of office which lend authority to the Prime Minister. Experienced, wily, quick thinking, armed with an excellent memory, Harold Wilson was a difficult man to beat at the despatch box. Margaret, although intellectually severally classes ahead of him, lacked his wide experience and ability to turn a difficult question with a joke. Her strength was in the strength of her case, not in her parliamentary style, so the briefing sessions to select her line of questioning were vital to her.

Apart from members of her private office staff headed by Airey Neave and a researcher from Conservative Central Office, the team comprised three or four back benchers. Only rarely did she invite in a member of her Shadow Cabinet, as we were a tactical, not a policy group. I cannot claim to have invented, but I did develop, the tactic of using back benchers to prepare the ground for Margaret to come in with her questions to the Prime Minister. When the plan worked well and the right back benchers were called by the Speaker to put their questions, she was able to dispense with any preamble, making her question short and sharply directed to the point. Ideally it would place the Prime Minister on a Morton's fork – wrong either way – and forced therefore to avoid the question or rephrase it in his terms, giving her an opportunity to come back hitting at Wilson's weakest spot – his evasiveness and inability to give straight answers.

Working with Margaret we helped her hone down her questions to the shortest and sharpest formulation that could be devised and there could be few greater contrasts between her questioning of Wilson and Callaghan and Kinnock's questioning of her. Where she was disciplined

Kinnock is self-indulgent. Where she watched and listened to the inter-play of questions and might well have changed her line of attack using a second preference option, Kinnock blunders on in some pre-set plan even if has become totally inappropriate. Margaret Thatcher understood that it is the simple question which is most difficult to avoid, and her questions were precise and simple. perhaps 'Why?' is too short, but a Minister if asked six complex questions all at once will pick the ones he likes, ignore the others and get away with it. Kinnock's complex multi-faceted questions seldom reach their mark and his back-bench colleagues seldom prepare the ground or follow up for him; but Mar-garet's sharp questions and the support of her back benchers often put even the wily Wilson on the defensive.

Although in the battles at the despatch box Margaret Thatcher came out as over-all winner it was by no means all one way, and I recollect at one time quite late in the Parliament she had a bad run with some lack-lustre speeches and her confidence was in danger of being undermined. I felt she was often at her best when she left her text and spoke from the heart, especially since her speeches were being so re-written in the search for perfection that they became dull – indeed boring to her too. I was helping with the final briefing for one major debate which was not going at all well. I decided it was time for risks and gave her some entirely unconnected news about a Party matter which I knew would infuriate her. It certainly did. She was furious as she swept up her papers, stormed out of the office and into the Chamber. I turned round to the others. 'You know,' I said, 'I think she's at her best when she's angry – she's forgotten all her doubts and misgivings – well I hope so or I'll be in terrible trouble!' In the event I wasn't. The speech was a great success – she simply blazed power and authority and I breathed again.

It was not until July 1976 that I contributed again to a Thatcher speech. Prime Minister's Questions briefing was at 9.15 a.m. as Margaret was going to see M. Tindemans, the Belgian Prime Minister, and then on to the Free Enterprise Day lunch where she was due to make a speech. The draft she had was awful so I sat down in her office and wrote what became the second half of her speech. To my delight she used it and it was well reported.

I doubt if speech writing for anyone is all honey – certainly it was not so in my case. As in most things Margaret Thatcher is pretty much a perfectionist about speeches and a good many drafts finish in the waste bin before she is satisfied with a script. I soon learned that holding back my preferred phrases or paragraphs improved their chances of finding their way into the speech rather than the bin, but sometimes the writing sessions went on far too late for my liking.

I well remember once being approached by Margaret in the Division Lobby at 10 p.m.

'I've just got a draft for a speech – and it's awful – would you be able to look at it for me, Norman?' she asked.

'Of course, when is it for?'

'Oh good,' she replied, 'tomorrow lunchtime – do come round to the office.'

Somewhat taken aback I followed her to the office where fellow speech writers were assembling with pads and pens in hand. We were soon at work but it was hard going to hit the right note. Somewhere about three o'clock in the morning I was beginning to wilt and was caught in the midst of a great yawn.

'You're not very bright tonight, Norman,' she commented.

'It's not tonight,' I said, rather huffily, 'it's tomorrow bloody morning.'

Somehow that night, like many others, we got a decent draft for her and I have concluded that, like me, Margaret Thatcher works best under pressure – pressure which causes at least as much discomfort to one's aides as to oneself!

Our working relationship grew steadily over the years in Opposition. I never deluded myself that I was, or that she saw in me, a political intellectual in the class of Keith Joseph. I think she saw me as a tactician – perhaps a bit of a cowboy – rather than a general, although, having a good deal of specialist knowledge of aviation and trades union affairs, I could make a policy contribution from time to time.

Looking back after having served in the Cabinet and as party Chairman, I can see how irritating to senior members of the Shadow Cabinet these informal groups and speech-writing teams must have been at times because inevitably the material we produced for Margaret was coloured by our particular views which were no doubt held to have influenced policy.

I suppose in my case, if that had any element of truth it was in relation to trades union reform and devolution. I tried not to abuse what was a privileged position. However, I certainly took advantage of it, following a conversation over dinner in early July 1975 with Michael Mates, the newly elected Member for Petersfield. Michael had thrown in his lot with Willie Whitelaw in the leadership contest, acting as a sort of ADC during the campaign, and remained close to him. According to Michael, Willie felt hurt that although Margaret had named him as Deputy Leader she did not treat him any differently to other members of the Shadow

Cabinet. I offered no comment, nor did he expect any, but just thanked him, and when I reported the conversation to Margaret a day or so later it was received in the same manner. However, there is no doubt that she did subsequently take Willie far more into her confidence, and I am sure that by treating him as one apart she benefited greatly from his loyalty to her and his influence in the Party.

The activities of the briefing team inevitably became known to outsiders and we were comprehensively denounced by Miss Julia Langdon, a journalist writing in *Labour Weekly*. Picking up from the trial of Madame Mao in China she dubbed Margaret, Airey Neave, George Gardiner, the Member for Reigate, and me as the Gang of Four, the hard reactionary plotters of the Party. We were all highly amused and certainly George and I were immensely flattered. At first Airey enjoyed the joke immensely and exaggerating his naturally somewhat conspiratorial air greeted me as a fellow conspirator. 'Good morning, Three,' Airey would say as we met, receiving the reply, 'Good morning, Two', which led to some odd looks from passers-by!

However, the *Financial Times* ran the *Labour Weekly* story – without acknowledging its source – and highly coloured and exaggerated accounts of our alleged influence became an embarrassment to us all – not least to Margaret and Airey.

It was through the briefing groups that I met Michael Dobbs who joined us as research officer when his predecessor, Michael Jones, was promoted. Others, notably Nigel Lawson, joined the group whilst Geoffrey Pattie and Peter Rees were occasional members, too; but we, the original members of the Gang of Four, stayed together until Airey was murdered in 1979.

I never became a regular front-bench spokesman whilst we were in Opposition but was invited to be a sort of 'guest performer' at the despatch box from time to time. Usually this was for debates on aviation matters where I had twin advantages of professional knowledge and being Chairman of the Party's Aviation Committee. In that curious way in which Cecil Parkinson's career and mine have been interwoven, he opened on the Civil Aviation Bill in January 1978 for the Opposition and I wound up the debate. I remember us chuckling together on the front bench and Cecil saying 'We've come a long way from the soap box in Hemel Hempstead.' It was a remark we were to make more than once again.

Being in Opposition is in many ways a better life for back benchers than being in Government. Without the responsibillity for getting business through the House they can have an easier time, and the Whips encourage them to be more active too – in fact it is more fun. Of course it is depressing to see a Government pursuing the wrong policies (though even more so if it is one's own Government!) and in the end frustrating for those with expectation of office. But being in Opposition, especially if the Government lacks a working majority, is the time to learn how Parliament really works.

For a while, until it became boring, I revelled in my role as a leading member of the Opposition wrecking squad. We were the privateers of parliamentary warfare, licensed by our Whips' Office but told firmly not to expect support from our more respectable and senior colleagues. Whenever we created mayhem by ambushing the Government on votes or running procedural rings around them to hold up business our Whips complained that we were out of control – and sometimes we were.

I do not think Mr Speaker Selwyn Lloyd really approved of my style or tactics. I suspect he thought that only Labour MPs should be so brash and aggressive. I, in turn, found it frustrating sometimes to be the only Member standing up intent on following up a question only to be coolly ignored by the Speaker as he called the next question. I talked to Jasper Moore, the Member for Ludlow and one of the most delightful of the 'knights from the shires', about the problem and he advised me to go to see the Speaker. However, obstinate and a bit 'chippy' about it, I refused to ask for the treatment I thought mine by right; but things changed with the election of George Thomas to the Chair. He seemed inclined to call those with something to say and more than once when a Minister (even the Prime Minister) went too far in attempting a brush-off without an answer he called me again straight away for a second supplementary question, a rare event in Parliament!

Unlike many ambitious back benchers I never attached myself to the court of any senior figures in the Party – nor indeed when I became a senior figure ever had such a court myself. However, Michael Heseltine, then the Opposition spokesman on industry, asked me if I would act as his unofficial PPS – unofficial because such posts are officially recognised only within Government. It was a cheerful and not unproductive relationship for three years or so. I enjoyed Michael's company, as I still do today, whether I always agree with him or not, and I learned a good deal from him. Apart from the usual 'eyes and ears' role in the House I helped Michael in his attempt to initiate some dialogue with trades union leaders about industrial policy. The great majority simply refused to talk to him, saying that they had no interest in helping the Tory Party. However, a minority of the intelligent and moderate leaders, and at least one of the arrogant left, did accept invitations to dine at

Michael's home in Wilton Crescent, a street of lovely early-nineteenth-century houses just off Belgrave Square.

Without doubt it was the dinner for Clive Jenkins that lives in my memory. Nothing of substance was discussed at all, it was simply boastful posturing by Clive Jenkins and some witty counter attacks by Michael, both asserting the God-given right of Welshmen to dominate the conversation. Honours were still even as Clive left. He paused on the step.

'I must say Michael, it's a nice place you've got here.'

'Yes,' said Michael proudly. 'I did a good deal, picking it up on a short leasehold.'

'Oh did you,' responded Clive, dropping his voice as if speaking of an illegitimate birth amongst the congregation of a Welsh Baptist Chapel. Then, he added, brightening as he turned on his heel down the steps, 'I got mine freehold.'

I was also with Michael on the night of 27 May when the Opposition put down a motion to support the Speaker's ruling that the Shipbuilding and Aerospace Nationalisation Bill was, *prima facie*, a hybrid bill. If it had been carried, the Bill would have been subjected to a long and laborious procedure delaying it by up to a year but the vote was a tie, 303 votes to 303. The precedents curiously required the Speaker to use his casting vote to support the Government against himself. However, even then to escape the trap the Government still had to carry a motion to suspend the standing orders of procedures, and if that had been tied precedent would hàve required the Speaker to cast his vote against the motion. The Government cheated on this vote when one of the Whips broke his pair on the excuse that a Minister abroad had not been paired.

There was absolute uproar, with Labour Members having cheated their way to victory rejoicing by singing 'The Red Flag'. It was too much for Michael, and though I was seated just behind him I was unable to stop him from grabbing the Mace and swinging it around his head. It was a lesson for me, for that moment of reckless anger which got the better of him pushed us slightly off the moral high ground.

By this time, to my delight, I found I could keep dozens of Labour MPs up late at night to maintain the Government's majority over my troop of fellow parliamentary guerillas, merely by making sure that a few of us were seen sculling around the corridors looking mischievous. To my even greater delight, one evening when we were on a very relaxed whip and the Government had let most of its hard-pressed supporters go home, I arranged for a hundred or so back benchers to be gathered in several flats and houses in Westminster, waiting for the vote on the final stage of the Scottish Direct Labour Organisations Bill. To the horror of the Government Whips we all appeared as the division was called and their Bill, which had ground through all its stages, was lost.

My parliamentary style landed me in some unpleasant incidents and some laughable ones too. I was often the intended victim of the extreme-left ne'er-do-wells who occupied the front bench below the gangway on the opposite side and who were not above 'mishearing' what I had said and complaining loudly about it. Indeed on one occasion I am quite sure that Tom Swain, a tough old Derbyshire miner, believed I had said he was drunk. In fact I hadn't – though in the circumstances a fair case could have been made that a lesser man might have been – and he commenced a fairly vigorous exchange across the floor of the Chamber. Tom gained the impression I had offered to 'take him outside' – an unlikely idea as he had fists like hams but as hard as rocks and biceps to match. As we stood just beyond the bar of the House – technically outside the Chamber but still within its walls – he grasped me firmly by the lapels and suggested we got on with it! Happily he was persuaded by his friends to let go and I escaped with no damage, having given the parliamentary sketch writers a field day. Together with my wife I encountered Tom in the bar a few days later, and several drinks on, Tom was explaining to her the finer points of pruning grape vines. Parliament is a very odd place.

Such incidents did me no good with some of my colleagues but most of them recognised that I was an effective critic of the Labour Government. In those years I never imagined that I was commanding the intellectual high ground of politics, that position was for Margaret Thatcher and Keith Joseph. I was playing the role of a gadfly – or perhaps more correctly that of the picador tormenting the bull, setting it up ready for the toreador to deliver the fatal blow – and I cannot pretend that I did not enjoy myself at times.

Certainly I enjoyed myself at about 4 a.m. on 22 June 1977 during the passage of the Price Commission Bill. The *Hansard* report hardly captures the flavour of that night when the Opposition forced an all-night sitting which lost the next day's business too. Sally Oppenheim, as our main speaker, had moved that we should 'report progress', that is give up and go home leaving the Bill to be considered again in the following week. The deputy Speaker, Meyer Galpern, was reduced to near incoherence in some exchanges at about 4 a.m. when I advanced a complex argument about human circadian rhythms as a reason for ending the debate and going home. Some of the best of these exchanges went unreported as the packed House became so noisy that neither he nor I could be heard by the *Hansard* reporters or anyone else for that matter. Mischievously I observed quietly to my friends seated nearby that as no one could hear me I need not say anything but simply open and close my mouth silently. Eventually John Pardoe, the Liberal MP, was driven to protest that I must be breaking the rules of order not by what I said but by the fact of not saying anything and I yielded to Meyer Galpern's persuasion to allow the business to proceed. Such tactics, although apparently schoolboyish pranks, had a serious purpose.

The Government had lost its majority but was attempting to force through great amounts of highly partisan and controversial legislation. We were using the parliamentary system to restrain the Government from legislating with neither mandate nor majority, except that of the disreputable pact with the Liberals and periodic deals in which it bought the votes of other minority groups with promises of favours, such as devolution for Scotland.

If some of my colleagues were uncertain about my style there were few doubts amongst Ministers and Government supporters. I was quite amused to find that as a maverick back bencher with no formal standing I would lure senior Ministers into wasting their time and fire power on such an unimportant target. Mr Foot, supposedly a considerable politician, fell for the bait hook, line and sinker. Appointed by Jim Callaghan as Secretary of State for Employment, as a sop to the party's left wing, he presided over the worst industrial relations chaos the country had seen since 1926, the highest unemployment at that time since 1931, and the worst rift ever between the trades union movement and the Labour Party. I have no doubt that Mr Foot has always seen himself as a liberal but in his concessions of power to the trades union bosses he undermined parliamentary democracy and trod the same corporatist path as Ted Heath before him. Nowhere was Mr Foot's betrayal of his liberal past more clearly displayed than in the affair of the Ferrybridge Six.

The six men dismissed from their jobs as the result of the imposition of a closed shop were denied unemployment benefit on the grounds that they had brought about their own dismissal. In the words of Mr Foot, 'A person who declines to fall in with new conditions of employment which result from a collective agreement may well be considered to have brought about his own dismissal.'

As I saw it, such a dismissal, refusal of compensation and unemployment benefit amounted to 'pure undiluted fascism and left Mr Foot exposed as a bitter opponent of freedom and liberty'.

The next day, 2 December 1975, *The Times* first leader quoted my views and in a closely argued piece concluded that it was Mr Foot's policy to transfer rights and liberties from individuals to the corporate bodies concerned and to the State, ending,

> Mr Foot's doctrine is intolerable because it is a violation of the liberty of the ordinary man in his job. Mr Tebbit is therefore using fascism in a legitimate descriptive sense when he accuses Mr Foot of it ... The question is not therefore, 'Is Mr Foot a fascist?' but, 'Does Mr Foot know he is a fascist?'

Mr Foot was subsequently moved to describe me as a 'semi house-trained polecat'. I have always felt that the spilling over of his anger into such abuse was a sure sign that my attack had done more than wound his self esteem – it had penetrated his conscience.

I cannot recollect ever sharing a conversation with Michael Foot. He was always too securely wrapped in the armour of self-righteousness – the uniform of the arrogant middle-class intellectuals – for us to find any common ground.

No doubt in his own way, Jim Prior, who was Mr Foot's shadow, also had some hurt feelings about my views on union affairs and colourful style of expressing them. It is well enough known that I favoured a far tougher line and more radical reforms earlier in time than Jim. However, Jim's critics and even his friends forget the political atmosphere of the times. Successive Governments had been humbled by the threat or actual use of trades union power and the Heath Government's Industrial Relations Act, far from being an effective weapon against the abuse of union power, had been used by the unions to humiliate Mr Heath. On the doorsteps in the 1979 campaign Tory canvassers were asked, 'What if the trades union leaders won't talk to Mrs Thatcher if she was the Prime Minister?' The right answer to that question was and is 'So what – who cares?' But it was an answer which seemed credible only to a few radicals in 1975. By 1977 when the Grunwick strike crystallised many of the issues, our radical views began to seem less eccentric, but Jim was stuck firmly in the past. In 1975 a Conservative official spokesman would have been denounced in the press as a dangerous lunatic if he had taken my line but by 1977 public opinion was changing and the Grunwick dispute left Jim Prior dangerously behind the mood of the nation.

He was not alone. Grunwick was a dispute about union recognition. George Ward, the firm's proprietor, had no wish to recognise the trades union APEX to negotiate on behalf of his employees, and many of his employees had no wish to join a union. Unions, with Government

(*Above*) Earliest days.

(*Above right*) My brother Arthur (right), and myself aged five.

My father in 1919.

(*Above left and right*) Myself aged eighteen in 1949.

In the Royal Auxiliary Air
Force at North Weald.

With Joe Hoare at Summer Camp in Malta, 1953.

At St Paul's Bay, Malta.

Taken shortly after I was commissioned.

Our wedding, 29 September 1956.

Upwardly mobile with BOAC.

Inspecting Smith's Dock, Middlesbrough (1982).

A cartoon by TASS general secretary Ken Gill.

Campaigning during 1983.

The burdens of office. Secretary of State for Trade and Industry, October 1983.

'Finally, Norman, I'd like you to take a little test!'

On taking over from Cecil Parkinson at Trade and Industry.

(*Opposite above*) The family. Elizabeth, our first grandchild, on Margaret's lap. Behind us, from left to right: Ray, Alison, William, Penny, John, taken the Sunday before the Brighton bomb.

(*Opposite below*) 12 October 1984.

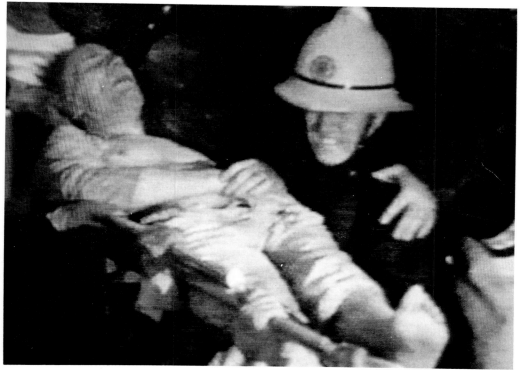

The Lord Mayor's Banquet, 1985. My Margaret's first public appearance after the Brighton bomb.

It was the TV lights rather than all the emotion that brought a tear to Margaret's eye.

At the Party Conference, 1985.

Garland

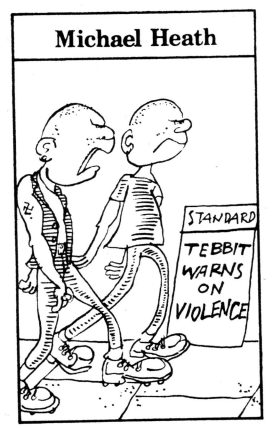

Michael Heath

" I WOULDN'T LIKE TO MEET HIM ON A DARK NIGHT"

JOHNSTON

The turning point at the
Bournemouth Party Conference,
1986.

With the Prime Minister at the
re-opened Grand Hotel in
Brighton, 29 August 1986.

The Party Chairman prepares for the 1987 election.

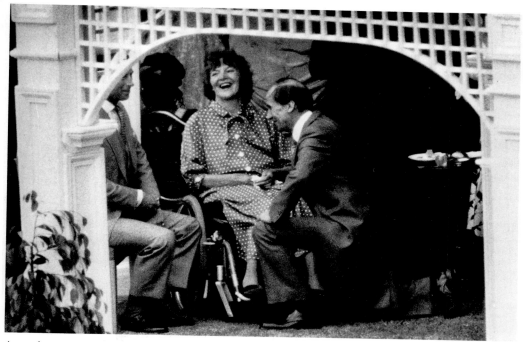

A sneak newspaper shot of us at the Buckingham Palace Garden Party, 1987.

At Central Office.

Proudly displaying my Companion of Honour outside Buckingham Palace in June 1987.

support and even a Ministerial presence on the picket line, tried to blockade the firm. The picketing subsequently became progressively heavier and then violent, and Post Office workers refused to deliver the mail. Although that was undoubtedly a criminal offence at the time, the Attorney General would not initiate any action and blocked others from doing so. The whole power of the union movement was used with Government backing in an attempt to crush a small, unimportant firm whilst the Government egged on its union friends and party paymasters. Despite the odds, Ward and his workers remained undefeated. The Government wheeled on ACAS to no effect and finally set up an inquiry into the affair under Lord Scarman.

It was the publication of the Scarman Report which outraged me and many others of liberal conscience. As we saw it, its main conclusion was that Mr Ward was wrong to stand by his rights under the law and that he should have bowed down to unlawful pressures. The dispute and the Scarman Report sparked off a speech from Keith Joseph which was seen by many as a clumsy intervention into Jim Prior's field of policy. The latter had spent two years courting the union leaders in the hope that he could persuade the electors that they would tolerate a Conservative Government and not bundle it out of office, as they had done in 1974, and resented any interference, as he saw it, with his job of building bridges between himself and the Party and those twentieth-century over-mighty barons.

A disagreement within the party had surfaced over Keith Joseph's views of the closed shop, and it was exacerbated by the Scarman Report on the Grunwick dispute and worsened by Jim Prior's comment that 'the unions had not behaved well'! In a speech in Chingford on 12 September I entered the controversy and, as a back bencher with no official position, I used some colourful language to ensure I would be reported.

I spoke of the threat to freedom posed by the Marxist powers abroad and continued,

Inside Britain there is a parallel threat from the Marxist collectivist totalitarians too.

Small in number, those anti-democratic forces have gained great power through the trades union movement.

Just to state that fact is to be accused of 'union-bashing' – often by people who know it to be true. Such people are to be found in the Conservative, Liberal and Labour Parties.

Their politics may be different but such people share the morality of Laval and Pétain ... they are willing not only to tolerate evil, but to excuse it ... and to profit by so doing.

The trades unions, like the press, the BBC, the CBI or the Army, are neither good nor bad in themselves.

They must be judged by their actions.

What would we say if the red-capped colonels of the Army used their military power for political ends? What if they insisted on conscription as part of their price for allowing a government to stay in office?

Would it be 'Army-bashing' to criticise that?

Yet today the cloth-capped colonels of the TUC use their industrial power for political ends. They insist on the conscription of the closed shop as part of their price for allowing a government to stay in office.

Is it 'union-bashing' to criticise that?

Both Jim Prior and Keith Joseph know that George Ward and Grunwick are not perfect, nor was Czechoslovakia perfect in 1938.

But if Ward and Grunwick are destroyed by the red fascists, then, as in 1938, we will have to ask, whose turn is it next?

Yes, it is like 1938.

We can all see the evil, but the doctrine of appeasement is still to be heard.

If an evil is so powerful that the faint hearts say it must be appeased, then that is all the more reason to deal with it before it becomes stronger still.

I was promptly accused of comparing Jim to Laval and it was clear that the row would surface at the Conservative Party Conference. I knew that to a considerable extent I could influence the mood of the debate on union affairs and somehow, without backing down from my radical line, I had to avoid open conflict and bitter personalised disputes.

What I needed was another colourful phrase. It was pretty late in coming. In fact it was still not quite formed until I was on the speakers' rostrum dealing with the difference between Jim Prior and me.

'I'm a hawk – but no kamikaze. And Jim's a dove – but he's not chicken.'

It went down well. It was not so much fudge as entertainment to divert the audience and give Jim Prior time to catch up with a changing mood. It was a chance he took, though never enthusiastically, and I think always believing I was going too far, too fast, too soon.

Although I found no point of personal contact with Michael Foot, I developed a wary relationship with Jim Callaghan. As Prime Minister, he was well aware of my role in Margaret Thatcher's team but was sufficiently astute, and I think broad minded, to look even to me when he thought it might pay him. On a good many occasions he indulged in good-humoured banter when we met in the corridors of the House but it came as a considerable surprise to me when one evening, as I was talking to Willie Whitelaw, he asked if he could have a word with me. He told me he had just set up a Cabinet committee to consider the options about the aerospace manufacturing industry and asked my views. I was taken aback, pleading that it was a complex matter. He suggested that we might talk again in a few days time and left me wondering how to react. We had several conversations reviewing the possibilities of collaboration with Airbus Industrie, McDonnell Douglas and Boeing, as well as the prospects for the BAe 146 project in which he was disarmingly and amazingly frank. I told no-one except Margaret Thatcher, and her advice was characteristic of her. 'Norman, if the Prime Minister asks you to talk to him of course you must.' Some time later a story of our meetings leaked. I refused to confirm or deny these reports whilst Jim Callaghan was an active politician, tactfully misleading journalists into believing them to be unfounded. However, ten years later, now that it can do Jim Callaghan no harm, it seems only fair to acknowledge the truth.

I cannot imagine Jim Callaghan heard much from me that his officials could not have told him but I gained a better understanding of the politician who concealed a complex tactical ability behind the bluff ordinary sensible Jim image.

My few conversations with Harold Wilson took place after his resignation as Prime Minister. On a couple of occasions I found myself standing up for him when I felt he did not receive the respect and courtesy due to both a former Prime Minister and a remarkable politician. Perhaps because of that, more than once he went out of his way to be kind to me.

I had always taken the view that the longer the Labour Government stayed in office the greater would be its defeat. The history of those years showed considerable swings in the Government's popularity and its ratings amongst political observers. There is little doubt that its overall record of economic management was appalling. Accepting that its economic inheritance from the Heath Government held in it the inevitability of high inflation, Mr Healey made things far worse. The collapse of the Social Contract, which neither side had ever really believed would be honoured, led inevitably to public disillusionment and the collapse of Mr Healey into the arms of the International

Monetary Fund bankers. For a time both he and Jim Callaghan took full advantage of the IMF monetarist medicine ramming it down the throat of a hostile Labour Party. The public expenditure White Paper in which a great deal of the agreement with the IMF was embodied, was debated on 17 March 1977, 'on the adjournment', a procedural device designed to avoid a vote on the White Paper itself, which was just as well as the Government was defeated by 293 votes to nil! Although the defeat was on a procedural motion, with the budget only a couple of weeks away, the Government's parliamentary position was desperate. A series of by-election defeats had eroded away the Government's majority and with a motion of no confidence down for debate on 23 March hanging over his head, Mr Callaghan hammered out the Lib–Lab pact to secure the votes of the thirteen Liberal MPs to avoid otherwise certain defeat. The standing of the Government was low and it would have stood a poor chance in an immediate general election. The Liberals too were at a low ebb, running fourth behind the National Front at the Walsall North and Stechford by-elections, and were in no mood for an election either. With the pact secured the Government won the vote of confidence by a majority of twenty-four. Had the Liberals voted with us the Government would have lost by two and a general election would have followed. I would never forgive Mr Steel for sustaining Labour at a moment when we could have won a sweeping victory.

The confidence vote cleared the way for a modestly reflationary budget which became more inflationary as the Government was defeated on some of its revenue proposals and chose neither to raise other taxes nor to cut expenditure. From there on the skids were firmly under the Government although the economic indicators were sufficiently encouraging for Mr Healey to tell the IMF we no longer needed to draw on our standby credit line, and promptly began a reduced tax and increased expenditure boom with his October 1977 budget. It was followed by another inflationary budget in spring 1978. From then on Mr Callaghan was trying to hold down wage inflation by incomes policy whilst at the same time inflating the economy, precisely the policy which trapped Mr Heath in 1974.

Although inflation and unemployment were unpopular the policies which lead to them were not, and in late May 1978 an NOP poll showed Labour five per cent in the lead and there were rumours of a snap election.

In the tactical group I had argued strongly that if he went in June Jim Callaghan might just have secured a majority. Certainly it would have been touch and go with little prospect of a Conservative working majority, and I believed a minority Thatcher government, inhibiting the appeal of her radicalism, would have been a disaster. My advice to her was based on many hours of Callaghan watching. As I saw it, Jim Callaghan was very bad at taking considered decisions. His capacity for making good quick instinctive decisions if he was given little time for consideration was not to be underestimated, but given time and an excuse he would always prevaricate. Having missed the favourable circumstances of 1977 our best tactic, I argued, was to keep facing him with distractions – to keep on the pressure by raising issues, to give him reasons for prevarication, and not to bring him down before the winter of 1978–9. By then I forecast the chickens would be coming home to roost and if we could strike then, we should have a handsome win. Within days of the NOP poll David Steel, under pressure from his activists, gave notice of the ending of the pact – effectively to expire after the summer recess, but our faint hearts were in a general state of jellied alarm.

Margaret, however, was characteristically determined at an early June briefing session, greeting me with, 'How are you – not depressed? Good. We'll beat the bastards yet.' She swore so rarely that I was taken aback but there was certainly an air of defeatism at that time. Over dinner in late June one of my 'wet' colleagues told me he would 'pack his stuff before the general election to avoid coming back to collect it'. In the event his majority went up from just over 120 to over 10,000 in 1979.

As June wore on, Jim Callaghan's luck seemed to turn again and he had some bad political days. The season for summer elections ebbed away and as Parliament rose on 3 August I felt it was six-to-four on an autumn election with a majority of twenty for us. The next day Jeremy Thorpe was charged with conspiracy to murder. With every prospect of a sordid trial it seemed to me the Liberals would hesitate to precipitate an election and we could continue our waiting game provided Jim Callaghan dithered. It was no wonder, some people thought, that Steel had not wanted a June election! If a charge of attempted murder against their former leader had broken during the campaign, it would have been bound to swing votes away from the Liberals. The affair must have influenced Jim Callaghan, too, since he desperately needed the Liberals to take votes from us if he was to have any chance of success.

Everything began to point to an autumn election. On the economic front earnings were still sprinting ahead of prices on the back of Healey's expansionist and inflationary budgets and mini budgets but there were clearly problems ahead. Stage IV of Labour's incomes policy – a five-per-cent norm – had little enough support in the CBI, let alone the TUC, and even less amongst employers and unions. The TUC could be relied upon to rally to the Government in October, but by the spring of 1979 the electors might be looking at a pay policy smashed by union avarice and stupidity. Although the formal end of the Lib–Lab pact was unlikely to lead to an immediate coalition between the Liberals, Nationalists and Conservatives to defeat the Government, the chances of an election forced to suit the Opposition's timing, not the Government's, would increase day by day once Parliament was back in October. It was no wonder that the Cabinet was absolutely amazed when Jim Callaghan told them on 7 September there would be no autumn election. The press were even more amazed with political journalists clearly feeling they had been led up the garden path by briefings from No. 10. Although I was preoccupied with personal affairs I remember my reaction. How right we had been in our psychological assessment of Jim Callaghan – and now we had got him. I did not think he had taken a decision against an autumn election but that he was simply unable to take the decision to call one. Joel Barnett tells us in his book *Inside the Treasury* that Jim Callaghan told the Cabinet that he did not mind them discussing the decision but it was made and he had told the Queen the previous night. I have often wondered whether he had made up his mind before his meeting with the Queen or if she had enquired whether he intended to call an October election, and rather than say, 'I cannot make up my mind and I will consult the Cabinet tomorrow,' he had taken the soft option and said, 'No'.

The Opposition years had not been easy in my private life. My Margaret had recovered only slowly from her illnesses of February and October 1974, and the summer of that year between her two illnesses had been a difficult time for her. We had spent a lot of time then at our cottage in Little Bardfield and I think it became unhappily associated with that time. Margaret's parents also died within weeks of each other in 1973 so we no longer needed a base on our way to Cambridgeshire and I no longer represented an Essex constituency either. The attraction and the *raison d'être* of 'Gridiron' had gone and we eventually decided to sell in order to buy another house near to our many old friends in Berkhamsted and Hemel Hempstead, which pleased my mother as she had been lonely living at nearby Tring since my father had died in 1975.

My finances had improved a little with my role as an adviser to Digital Equipment Limited and in the National Federation of Building Trades Employers (NFBTE) as assistant to the Director of Communications, Bill Bryant. The experience of work in the private sector was invaluable too. At DEC I participated in the company's decision to invest in its first UK factory and in the search for the optimum site. It was a brave decision in 1976 but it worked out well and that original factory employing 200 people at Ayr has been consistently profitable and trouble free, leading to far greater investments since. At the NFBTE I had the chance to see a really effective trade association at work and to learn a great deal about the building and construction industry.

At this time my wife had not been well again. On 5 September, after a reception I had sponsored at the House of Commons, Margaret and I joined friends for dinner. She was full of life until 3 a.m. and woke early the next morning unable to get back to sleep. It was an unhealthy 'high' and by the time Jim Callaghan cancelled the October election two days later I was seriously worried about her health. Fortunately we were now wise to the early symptoms and she agreed to see a Barts psychiatrist. He had no doubt that she should be admitted to hospital, but in a foretaste of the Winter of Discontent some NHS maintenance workers were in dispute and were refusing to allow the admission of new 'non-urgent' cases. It was their clinical judgement which over-rode that of my wife's doctors. Fortunately, not only did her doctors, to their great credit, find a private hospital that could accommodate my wife but one of them, furious and ashamed of her treatment, even drove us there and another continued to treat her even though she was not in his NHS hospital.

For the next few weeks I tried desperately to keep our family together and maintain an air of outward normality despite driving sometimes twice in a day to the hospital near Tunbridge Wells, wondering how we would ever repay the bank the money I had to borrow to buy the treatment wilfully refused by some cloth-capped corporal. This did wonders for my determination to break the power of union creatures of that kind.

The doctors of the private hospital in consultation with those of Barts made a new assessment of my wife and proposed a new medication using a simple inorganic chemical. Why in some cases it works with remarkable success and in others it is ineffective is still not clearly understood, but in Margaret's case it worked. Her recovery was remarkable, but by the time she was home and her confidence restored it was clear that the final collapse of the Callaghan Government and a general election could come at any time.

Everything was working out as I had foreseen four years earlier. Like the Russian generals of 1812 we had preserved our army intact, the winter was coming and Jim Callaghan had nowhere to go except to defeat.

The history of the last months of the Callaghan Government is well enough recorded. I can add little to it beyond an impression of my savage delight as not only the Government got its come-uppance from the unions, but the unions got theirs from Government, Opposition and public alike. The sheer spiteful nastiness of union leaders was displayed day by day, and displayed alongside it was the intellectual incoherence of the supporters of incomes policies. The statutory route to pay control had taken Ted Heath to defeat, now the social-contract route of deals with the unions was taking Jim Callaghan to his Waterloo.

At the same time the Government's devolution policy was falling apart as its inherent incoherence was ruthlessly exposed, most notably by the Labour MPs George Cunningham, Brian Walden and Tam Dalyell, giving me great satisfaction. On our side we were still somewhat divided on the issue but I had begun to appreciate Willie Whitelaw's genius for conducting difficult political manoeuvres under a smokescreen of apparent confusion. At the time he took on responsibility as our spokesman the Party had favoured devolution. By 1978 we opposed it but no one could quite remember how or when the U-turn had been made. It was the stuff of genius. We entered 1979 becoming more united, and at the same time the Labour Party fell apart.

The Government's pay policy, like Ted Heath's, was unenforceable and the devices used to try to make it stick made matters worse. The use of discretionary non-statutory powers to blacklist employers who had been forced to concede the demands of the Labour Party's union paymasters for pay rises of more than five per cent, was inherently corporatist, arbitrary and would have been repugnant even if it had been uniformly applied. In the event it was not. The TUC agreed a sixty-per-cent pay increase to be paid in three annual instalments of twenty per cent for its own employees without incurring any penalty whilst Fords were threatened with sanctions for conceding fifteen per cent. It was the subject for much of Prime Minister's Question Time on 7 November when the Conservative back benchers joined Margaret Thatcher in hammering away at the issue. A number of us helped to keep the issue live and running in Parliament. On 7 December Labour back benchers used time-wasting procedural tactics to avoid a debate on sanctions against firms breaking the Government's pay code. Under threat of withdrawal of all co-operation on the management of parliamentary business, the Government was forced to concede a full day's debate on 13 December. An Opposition amendment against 'the arbitrary use of economic sanctions' to enforce 'a rigid limit which Parliament has not approved' was carried by a majority of six, and the Government was then again defeated by 285 to 283 on the substantive motion. Jim Callaghan promptly announced he would put down a vote of confidence the next day. In that debate on 14 December he announced that the Government would no longer use discretionary powers against firms breaking his pay codes, and, although he won his confidence vote by 300 to 290, his pay policy was in shreds.

Before long the country was in the grip of the Winter of Discontent when the public sector unions, particularly those whose members worked in hospitals and local government, fought the Labour Government for huge pay rises. Strike followed strike, secondary picketing, even violent picketing was virtually unchecked. The Labour Party had sown the wind in supporting the strikes of 1973–4. Now it was reaping the whirlwind. The sheer viciousness and nastiness of unions such as NUPE in the hospital service was displayed day after day on every TV screen in the land as the sick, the old and little children were kicked around in a dirty fight between the Government and the trades union wings of the Labour Party. And to top it all, there was Jim Callaghan's famous remark, 'Crisis – what crisis?' which – while he may never have actually used those precise words, and certainly had not intended to refer to the hospital closures – was hung permanently round his neck because it fitted him so well.

During that winter of 1978–9 the Government's popularity slumped as its economic policies simply fell to pieces one after another. It was kept in office, above all, by the nationalist and Liberal parties, awaiting the outcome of the Welsh and Scottish referenda on devolution. By the time Parliament adjourned on 23 February for the final stages of those campaigns, Jim Callaghan had survived several more crucial votes by narrow majorities, but in the wake of the Government's defeat in the referenda pols in both Scotland and Wales his parliamentary position became precarious indeed.

Eventually it was the Scottish Nationalists who put down a motion of no confidence, promptly followed by our official Opposition motion, which took precedence and was debated on 28 March. Right to the end Jim Callaghan fought to survive with a special subsidy for state mining in Wales, which carried the support of the Welsh Nationalists, but the Scots were intent on the defeat of the Government.

Not for many years had the survival of a Government hinged on such a narrow vote as that night.

During the division I was talking to Margaret Thatcher. We knew that the arithmetic of the vote was finely balanced and tried not to be too optimistic. I waited at the exit from the Aye lobby – the motion was of no confidence – to hear the total of our vote.

It was 311. By our calculations, even without the support of the republican Irishman, Frank Maguire, or Gerry Fitt, but with the Government's supporters including the Welsh Nationalists and two Ulster Unionists, it should have numbered 312. 'We've lost by one,' the word ran through the House. Having waited to hear the count of votes I had no chance of a seat in the Chamber and was standing amongst a crowd of Members at the bar of the House when the tellers – two Members from each side who count the votes – appeared from behind the Speaker's Chair. To our amazement, our Whip, Spencer Le Marchant, was carrying the chit bearing the tally of votes cast – the privilege of the winning side - his face wreathed in smiles, a huge thumb raised towards Margaret Thatcher. The hubbub grew to a crescendo, then fell silent as Spencer read the figures. The Ayes 311 – the Noes 310. The noise was deafening. We had forgotten that two Labour tellers, like ours, did not vote so their maximum vote (without Maguire, who had attended in person to abstain, or Gerry Fitt) was not 312 but 310. The Clerk took the chit to the Speaker. The Ayes 311 – the Noes 310. So the Ayes had it. The House was in turmoil. Jim Callaghan did his best, defiantly declaring that he would 'take his case to the country'. It was not long before I found myself at the Whips' Office party, and by the time I left it was after midnight, and my birthday, which gave cause enough for celebration. In the succeeding days Parliament dragged on and overhung by the coming election took on an unreal air.

I played no major part in the election nationally, concentrating on Chingford and trying not to allow my wife to overstretch herself. We campaigned quietly and my pitch was simple. A weak Government which had clung to office by back-door deals with splinter parties had collapsed leaving a shocking mess. Prices, unemployment and debt had all more than doubled. There had been constant surrender to the union bosses. Socialism had not worked, it never had anywhere in the world. On trades unions, however, my election address deviated from the Party line.

We will protect people against the misuse of union power. Ordinary people damaged by unions should have a right of compensation. People denied work because of the closed shop should be able to sue the union for damages.

I would have liked to have gone further but felt that I should not rock the boat too hard. In fact it probably would not have mattered as I doubt if even the friendliest of journalists would have given much for my chances of becoming Secretary of State for Employment!

This time everything went right. My agent, although shared with other Conservative candidates for the Borough, was at least sober, and for the first time since 1970 my wife and I were together to hear my result declared. Both Labour and Liberal votes had fallen and the National Front and Ecology Party mustered less than 2,000 between them. My vote leapt more than 5000 to 24,640 and a majority of well over 12,000.

By the time my result was declared it was clear that Jim Callaghan had been defeated and that Britain had elected its first woman Prime Minister – one I had done something to help. As we returned home I was already anxious to know if I would find a place in the Government.

8

Into the Cabinet

I devoured every newspaper that Friday – and read somewhere that I was tipped as a likely Minister. By Saturday morning I had heard nothing, and we drove to Berkhamsted where over the weekend I wallpapered and decorated pretending that I did not expect to be offered a post. At last the telephone rang. The Prime Minister wished to speak to me. The familiar voice, bright and full of energy, came over the line.

'Norman, I would like you to work with John Nott at the Department of Trade. Would you be his Parliamentary Under-Secretary of State dealing with aviation and shipping?'

My resolution to say that I would say no to anything less than being a Minister of State crumbled!

'Of course, I would be very happy to do so,' I replied.

Before long I received a call from my Private Secretary, Jeanette Darrell. As I put down the phone I reflected how odd it seemed to be addressed as 'Minister' – but no doubt I would get used to it.

John Nott had been appointed Secretary of State for Trade with Cecil Parkinson as Minister for Trade, and Sally Oppenheim as Minister for Consumer Affairs. Sally was understandably disappointed not to be in the Cabinet but wisely Margaret Thatcher had decided to eliminate what had been a 'non department' of consumer affairs created for Shirley Williams. The Junior Ministers were myself and Reggie Eyre who was to look after the companies side of the Department. I took over direct responsibility for civil aviation, shipping and, oddly enough, the film industry, helping Cecil out on trade matters when needed. As we met at the Department for the first time I am sure we both wore rather silly grins – our careers, we agreed, seemed destined to run closely parallel, with even our first taste of office coming on the same day in the same Department.

I found John Nott to be a mercurial character with strong upbeat moods when he would tackle any issue with enormous energy, insights of lateral thinking, great style and determination. At other times, in his downswings, he was difficult to work with, listless, refusing to take decisions, a prey to defeatism claiming that, anyway, no decision would improve matters. Fortunately the upbeat John was dominant and he understood his own moods very well. He ended one meeting at which his indecision was proving a trial to all of us saying, 'I know what you're all thinking – you think that I'm kicking up my heels because I can't tackle the fence – but don't worry I've never refused one yet and I'll jump it when we get there.' He was, of course, quite right – he always cleared the fence on the day.

The week after the election found John in splendidly upbeat style, gathering us all around the table in his office (to become mine only four years later) telling us that now was the time to take the critical and radical decisions. If we delayed, he said, we will be enmeshed in all the detailed arguments against doing anything, so let's get on. In no time at all we concluded that all controls over prices should go. This left the Price Commission without a role but we agreed that the question of its abolition would have to be further considered by the Cabinet. Although John faced some opposition from the old guard who still hankered for incomes policy, I think none of us had any doubt about the outcome – and it soon went.

John's appetite for radicalism suited me very well. There was a need for a Civil Aviation Bill in 1980 and I suggested we should use it to give authority to denationalise British Airways as soon as circumstances allowed. John took up the idea with great enthusiasm, although in the end he could obtain agreement only to the sale of a minority shareholding. His statement to the Commons on 20 July brought some predictable reactions of pleasure and fury from Opposition sides. We both enjoyed it hugely – we were the first Ministers to nail our colours to the privatisation mast, just beating Keith Joseph's statement on British Aerospace. Sadly the troubles of British Airways and the legal actions by Laker delayed the flotation until February 1987 but the process was under way.

Full of cheerful radicalism I firmly put my foot in it by asking why I had been given responsibility for policy on the film industry. 'Why do we need a films policy? Let's get out of films as fast as possible.' Leo Pliatzky, our extraordinary Permanent Secretary, simmered, and with a restraint quite unnatural to him, suggested that he should come and talk about it to me later. Leo was a film buff – an enthusiasm he shared with Harold Wilson – and it was not until after Leo's retirement that, as Secretary of State for Trade and Industry, I won that battle!

I certainly came out second best in my first contest with Jeanette Darrell. Ministers' private secretaries, particularly principal private secretaries, are civil servants of high quality marked out for promotion and it is the principal private secretary who is responsible for running the Minister's private office. A great deal depends on how well that office works as it is the interface between a Minister and his Department. A good private secretary (and over eight years in government mine varied from good to superlative) is the Minister's eyes, ears and voice within his Department. Jeanette was very good indeed and as a Junior Minister I was lucky to have acquired her. She was tall, slim, smart in a sort of jolly-hockey-sticks blue-stocking way, possessed of good judgement and a rather unfemininely wicked sense of humour. She was also highly efficient and protective, organising everything I asked for (and some things I didn't) with perfect efficiency, even discovering from my wife my likes and dislikes in food and drink.

Naturally many of my friends asked me in those early days what it was like to be a Minister. One thing, I told them, is that although when I was a child I never had a nanny nor a governess, I now knew what I had missed, saying I had acquired a governess called Jeanette.

One day unknown to me one of my friends telephoned whilst I was out of the office and spoke to Jeanette. When I arrived back she followed me in to my office and stood rather menacingly beside my desk.

'Yes?' I asked.

'What's all this governess business, Minister?' she demanded.

I flannelled.

'One of your friends,' she told me, 'on being told you were not in, said, "Oh is that Mr Tebbit's governess?"'

I flannelled rather harder, receiving only a 'Hmph' in acknowledgement before the matter was dropped – or so I thought.

It was a couple of weeks later that I attended an excruciatingly long-winded meeting of the Merchant Navy and Airline Officers Association's Executive Committee to discuss safety at sea and in the air. As it dragged on I caught Jeanette's eye, giving her a 'get me out of here' look. She responded with a smile, got up, walked around the table, bent over my shoulder and in an awful stage whisper, said, 'Time for walkies, Minister.'

We never mentioned the matter again!

I soon became immersed in my own responsibilities. There were opportunities and problems in plenty: some in areas familiar to me, others like marine policy, the coastguards, and ships' pilotage, entirely new. I had no doubt that my portfolio was the best of any parliamentary under-secretary in Whitehall. It was a fascinating mix of policy work – on airports for example; and real operational control – as in dealing with shipping incidents, particularly the oil-tanker accidents which were making spectacular headlines at that time.

Needless to say, I took a particular interest in the affairs of British Airways and airline policy, happily carrying forward the work to prepare BA for privatisation. The question of competition between the then State carriers and the private sector was as live then as that of competition between the privatised British Airways and the smaller airlines today. In those days the Labour Party was devoted to securing a monopoly for BOAC and BEA and bitterly opposed to allowing the small carrier a living at all. Curiously, nine years later, it has become bitterly opposed to the privatised British Airways and full of support for the smaller carriers it tried to put out of business ten years ago!

In opposition I had had the good sense to steer a measured course on these issues. The Laker Skytrain case was perhaps one of the most important. Laker had won its case with Lord Denning finding that the Labour Government had misused its powers under the legislation. The implications flowing from his judgement were widespread and in my first weeks in office I read the Denning judgement with great care. Having thought about it for a while I asked the Deputy Secretary responsible for aviation policy and the Department's lawyers to see me.

'I've been reading Denning's Laker judgement,' I said. 'He was wrong, wasn't he? Peter Shore [Labour's Trade Minister] was within his powers wasn't he?'

'You're quite right,' they both said. 'But we hadn't expected you would come to that conclusion.'

'Well,' I asked, 'why didn't Peter Shore appeal?'

It was not, of course, a question my officials could answer in that form. The reasoning of Labour Ministers was not a matter they could discuss with me, but it was not difficult to guess that Peter Shore had made a sensible political decision not to fly in the face of public opinion, although I believed he would have had a good chance of winning if the case had gone right through to the House of Lords.

It was to be several years before Laker's luck, much of it well deserved, deserted him. His contribution to breaking up the great flag carriers' cartel and bringing airline travel into the mass market should never be underestimated, but even by 1979 I could see evidence of the two shortcomings which were finally to bring him down. First, Freddie Laker tried to manage what had become a big business without a proper management structure and, second, his splendid self-confidence grew to the point where I believe it led him into *folies de grandeur* and the eventual collapse of his overstretched business.

Most of my time at the Department was taken up with civil aviation issues. One immediate problem facing us was the succession to Sir Frank McFadzean as Chairman of British Airways. I was anxious to avoid a quick decision which might become a long-term problem and persuaded John Nott that in the Chief Executive, Ross Stainton, we had available a 'safe pair of hands', who was due to retire within a year or so. That gave us time to search for a long-term chairman to take BA into the private sector. There were candidates enough, but none seemed quite right. Eventually the name of John King was put forward and John Nott invited me to join him when they met. The idea had been that as usual we would compare notes afterwards and consult our officials, none of whom were at the meeting. Any meeting with John King is an experience and at that time I had neither met him nor knew anything about him other than his c.v. The impact was extraordinary. He is a man full of controlled, sometimes concealed brute power with a razor-sharp brain often masked by his apparently naive or simple questions. To my surprise, and I think John Nott's too, our conversation, far from being a gentle probing exercise to establish if John King was a possible candidate, ended with King agreeing to accept the job. John Nott and I looked at each other, slightly shell-shocked, as King left. 'I hope I've done right,' said John in a somewhat unsure way. I think my reply echoed his half question. It is curious how uncertain one can be at the time about what turns out to be the best of decisions.

Whilst the Civil Aviation Bill took up a good deal of my time – although I managed to talk it through, including the privatisation proposal, without a guillotine or an all-night sitting – I was also well occupied on the European scene. In the Council of Ministers I achieved agreement on the progressive banning of the noisy jet airliners, and in Eurocontrol (the international air traffic control organisation) began the process of getting to grips with that organisation's inability to control costs and its excessive pan-European zeal. I enjoyed the challenge of negotiation and dealing inherent in the Community system and first became aware of the extent to which Ministers and officials were benefiting from the cross fertilisation of ideas and experience. Sometimes, however, the misunderstandings bordered on the hilarious.

At one Eurocontrol meeting with the French Minister in the chair, the Irish Minister, Padraig O'Flyn – a staunch republican – was being particularly difficult, perhaps because it was his first meeting in Brussels. It was clear that the impasse could not be broken in formal session round the table and the French Minister sent his senior official to me with a remarkable message.

'My Minister is going to adjourn the meeting for half an hour and he says as you understand the Irish would you talk some sense into him.'

I thought for a minute and said, 'Okay – I'll try.' As the meeting adjourned I buttonholed O'Flyn. 'Mr O'Flyn,' I said, 'Our French colleague says that as we English understand you Irish, would I talk some sense into you.' It was a high risk tactic – but the problem was solved and O'Flyn and I still exchange Christmas cards!

Negotiating became a near full-time task, first to renew the air service agreement with Malaysia and then I had to negotiate with the Chinese the opening of services from London to Beijing. It involved delicate handling of the Hong Kong issue and the rights of the airline Cathay Pacific. However, when all was settled I received my reward – a trip to China on the inaugural flight in November 1980.

A good deal of negotiating was also needed to arrive at an agreed airports policy, as John Nott and I did not at first see quite eye to eye! I saw the problem as one of a growing potential shortage of both runway capacity and passenger-handling capacity (passenger terminals and surface transport facilities) in the South East and a lack of sufficient demand elsewhere to provide comprehensive services to overseas destinations. My thinking had led me to prefer putting London's fourth runway at its second airport, Gatwick. Unfortunately the undertakings given in the time of our predecessors ruled out that option so the fourth runway had to be at Stansted, the third London airport. I struggled, not without success, to prevent similar undertakings being given on Stansted, to avoid the nightmare of seeking yet another site in the late nineties merely because Heathrow needed a fifth runway. Similar common sense dictated that a fifth terminal at London should be ruled out, at least until it was established that its runways could cope with the traffic to utilise it, that the surface access links could cope with the traffic generated and that a new site could be found for the Perry Oaks sewage works – the only possible fifth terminal site.

Airports policy, like many other problems thought to be very difficult in the sixties and seventies, yielded quite quickly to common sense. Had the late 'Rab' Butler not misused his Cabinet post and influence to block the development of Stansted (which was on his constituency doorstep), we need not yet have developed Gatwick as a major airport nor wasted time and money on the public enquiries and the ludicrous Maplin project. Sadly it was too late to deal sensibly with Scotland's needs, so now there are three airports where just one would have been better and cheaper. Fortunately, we were in time to prevent a similar wasteful failure to provide the best possible services to the North of England. By rejecting the parochial pleas of other cities and concentrating international services on Manchester, not only is that airport now viable but it serves far more destinations than would have been possible from a scatter of lesser airports.

Fortunately throughout the difficult process of persuasion of colleagues in Government and the House of Commons I had the help of Norman Payne, Chairman of British Airports Authority. I could not have wished for a better man. Not only was Norman Payne an excellent manager (as he has proved himself to be in the private sector) but I could always rely upon his total loyalty. Norman always argued his case with clarity and force, but if I had to refuse him what he asked (including immediate privatisation) he would come back within days with no trace of resentment, full of enthusiasm for whatever I had asked of him.

I was similarly well served by my civil servants. On the aviation side I could rely on my own experience and knowledge but I knew little about shipping, and training came on the job. In fact the worst of the great oil-tanker disasters were already behind us but there was well-justified public concern over safety standards and the serious pollution risks.

Aviation had been virtually born into an internationally regulated environment but shipping, with a history vastly longer than modern internationalism, was, and is, far less regulated. IMCO – the International Marine Consultative Organisation, is, like its aviation counterpart ICAO, a United Nations body, but it has far fewer teeth. Fortunately its long-time Secretary General, Mr Chandrika Prasad Srivastava, an assiduous and skilled Indian civil servant, is a considerable diplomat and I found myself working closely with him in the design and implementation of the safety standards which have greatly improved the safety of the huge bulk carriers which came into service in the sixties and seventies.

Nor were my responsibilities solely legislative. I had considerable executive powers and responsibilities to deal with marine disasters or emergencies in, or near to, British waters. In these matters I was advised by a retired naval officer, Admiral Stacey. An admiral of any calibre packs a good deal of punch and one so competent, tough and clear-thinking as Stacey was a handy man to have around in international negotiations, public meetings at home or when I had to deal with operational problems. He always kept me well informed of potential disasters, and usually it was a Sunday morning telephone call which brought me the bad news, prefaced by the words, 'I don't want to alarm you, Minister, but I thought you should know . . .' Typically the potential problem would be a supertanker with disabled steering or broken-down engines drifting none too far off the west coast in a westerly gale. Fortunately I only had two really difficult operational decisions to make in my time in office.

One concerned a small German tanker, *Tarpenbeck*, which had capsized following a collision in fog and was drifting towards the south coast. Without formally invoking my powers to take control I steered the salvage operation nonetheless. It became a political hot potato when I authorised the salvors to tow her into Sandown Bay on the Isle of Wight – first to empty her of oil, then right her before she was towed away. It was right in the summer holiday season and not surprisingly the Island's hoteliers and the Member of Parliament expressed some doubts about my decisions. Fortunately all went well, only a gallon or so of oil was spilled and I was forgiven!

A Channel collision involving a supertanker just within the French zone posed an even more difficult question. The bow section had sunk but the stern half, laden with crude oil, was drifting in heavy seas, threatening to break up. With a north-westerly gale blowing, my French opposite number telephoned to ask my agreement to the hulk being towed into Torbay in Devon, the best and nearest place for shelter. The thought of defending my decision if it all went wrong with thousands of tons of crude oil coming ashore in Devon was intimidating but I decided I had to agree to this best option to avoid a massive potential disaster – even though if things went wrong I would have transferred the disaster from France to Britain. Happily within an hour of giving my agreement the wind swung round to the south west, making Cherbourg the best place to take the potential disaster!

Sadly, I had several times to report from the despatch box the loss of fishing vessels, all too often with the loss of all those on board. Fishing, deep-sea or coastal, is a desperately dangerous business and a mixture of the men's pride in their ability to cope with any weather, commercial pressures and, I have to say, alcohol abuse at times, in what is always a dangerous and unpredictable environment, costs many lives each year. In my search for ways to minimise such loss of life I spent a couple of days at sea off the West Coast of Scotland in a modern purse-seiner trawler fishing for mackerel. It was one of my more memorable min-isterial experiences! Fortunately my ability to use Loran, a radio navi-gation aid common at that time to ships and aircraft, established me as a human being, not just a Minister, in the eyes of the crew and I learned more about fishing in forty-eight hours than in the previous forty-eight weeks.

Such experiences and my travels around the coasts dealing at first hand with the problems posed by supertankers in Sullom Voe in Shetland, meeting lifeboat men, coastguards and all manner of mariners, made my first job in Government one of the best I ever had. It had its less happy side, too, for the decision to take away the 'tickets' of ships' officers guilty of professional negligence or misconduct, or those of ordinary seamen for disciplinary offences, fell to me. Happily even that was balanced by the privilege of making far, far more awards for gallantry in saving life at sea.

Looking back, I think I was lucky to be given the one job in Govern-ment where as the most junior of Ministers I had the chance to take decisions and manage difficult issues. I was also lucky that some of those decisions came early in my career and were ones which I was particularly well qualified to take.

Just such a one was over the grounding of the Douglas DC10 airliner after the Chicago disaster. In America McDonnell Douglas, the manu-facturers, were in all sorts of trouble amidst wild allegations of bribery to gain contracts, bad management of design and manufacture, improper pressure of the airworthiness authorities and a great many other mostly unsubstantiated wrongdoings. The US authorities yielded to an intense campaign and for several weeks refused to allow the aircraft to fly.

It was a time for some calm judgement. The easy option would have been to arm-twist safety authorities (I had no powers as such) to change their recommendation. It would have been wrong to do so and I found myself facing some near-hysterical questioning in the House of Commons with none too many colleagues willing to support me. I was proved right. The aircraft was not inherently unsafe and the DC10 has since proved itself with an excellent safety record.

As 1980 drew to a close the regular press talk of Government shuffles increased and when Margaret Thatcher and I were talking on our own or with her close friends such as Keith Joseph, she had made it plain that she wanted to begin the reconstruction of the Government to bring forward more of those who believed in the policies on which we had been elected rather than those who still hankered after those on which Ted Heath had been defeated. And Thatcherism in those days was fully accepted by very few of the political and economic journalists, indeed most of them were waiting for the U-turn back to traditional consensus politics.

The shuffle came on 5 January. In the Cabinet Francis Pym was moved gently sideways, losing his department and taking over from Norman St John Stevas as Leader of the House. John Nott moved from Trade to replace Francis at Defence. John Biffen replaced John Nott at Trade, making way for Leon Brittan as Chief Secretary to the Treasury. It was not just a matter of 'drying out' the Cabinet. Margaret Thatcher was very sad to lose Norman St John Stevas (who may have been a 'wet' but fought a valiant battle with almost no support but mine to abolish the Inner London Education Authority in 1979). It was felt that Francis Pym had not coped well with managing a large department and John Biffen, regarded as a 'dry', had not taken a sharp enough axe to public expenditure. On this occasion I was asked to see the Prime Minister who told me what she had in mind and asked if I would go to be Keith Joseph's Minister of State at the Department of Industry. My brief was clear. Keith, for whom the Prime Minister has always had both high regard and great affection, had been taking a lot of flak. I was not only to take some of that to ease the political pressure on him, but to return some fire on his behalf too.

I could not have been happier. I greatly admired Keith Joseph and had felt that he had been pretty badly treated by the Opposition and the media, mainly because he was pressing on with the new Conservative policies, well ahead of most Ministers. His reduction of ineffective regional industrial support spending and his controversial appointment of Ian MacGregor as chairman of British Steel were brave and right but not many of our colleagues were over-willing to stick out their necks to support him. Although I was only to work for Keith for eight months they were amongst the happiest of my ministerial life. Few men have been so cruelly misrepresented. The portrayal of Keith as an insensitive axeman, or the mad monk, was unfair and totally remote from reality. I found in Keith not only one of the major intellects of the Thatcher Government but one of the kindest, most highly principled, thoughtful and decent men in politics – or anywhere else. His very goodness rendered him vulnerable to misrepresentation. Keith, for all his Jewish upbringing, was less likely to act on the Old Testament doctrine of an eye for an eye and a tooth for a tooth and more likely to follow the New Testament injunction to turn the other cheek than most Christians I have met. His intellectual integrity – which sometimes threatened his common sense – needed a touch of political street-wisdom, and it was my job to supply it.

Keith made it plain to our officials and to the chairmen of nationalised industries for which he was responsible that I had his complete confidence – something which was of immense help to me. Men like Ian MacGregor of British Steel, Michael Edwardes of British Leyland and Austin Pearce of British Aerospace were rightly used to dealing with the Secretary of State, but by making it plain that I spoke in his name he made it easy for me to take a good deal of work from his overloaded shoulders.

Ken Baker, Keith's other Minister of State, and I had quite separate areas of responsibility. He looked after the modern high technology industries – with the exception of British Aerospace and Rolls-Royce; and I took on the 'smoke stack' industries – steel, motors, engineering, textiles and the like. Traditional business it may have been, but there was plenty going on in my sphere.

In the motor industry BL, still in long-term difficulties, despite the achievements of Michael Edwardes, was negotiating the collaborative deal with Honda, whilst unknown to either party the Government was negotiating a deal with Nissan to establish a manufacturing operation in Britain. The first major denationalisation – that of British Aerospace – was only a few weeks away; the steel industry was, in the words of the European Commission, 'in a state of manifest crisis'; so, too, in anyone's words was our shipbuilding industry; and the national Enterprise Board was also in a state of turbulence.

Fortunately, the Department's officials, like those at Trade, were of excellent quality, and my private office worked well. I quickly found myself on excellent terms with Keith's principal private secretary, Ian Ellison. Like me, Ian was devoted to Keith and fought internal departmental battles on his behalf with a formidable mixture of zeal and aggression. Shorn of diplomatic official niceties he firmly told me that my job was to do the same in the political battles, both in public and within the Government, and I assured him that was how I saw it too. Between us I think we covered the field of battle pretty well! Sadly for the civil service, Ian is but one of the many extremely able officials who have left for greener and more exciting pastures in the private sector.

It was typical of Keith that he allowed me to take over much of the final negotiations with Nissan and to make the House of Commons statement on the agreement just over three weeks after I had joined his Department. The deal was not in the bag until only a few days before the statement on 30 January and both its conception and completion owe much to Mr Botnar, an East-European immigrant who had created and owned the Nissan–Datsun British distributorship. There were very awkward points concerning the measurement of the 'Britishness' of the cars produced as the operation moved from assembly to manufacture. I think it only fair to say there were doubts on both sides about how the agreements would work out but Nissan has more than fulfilled my hopes that it would become a major industrial asset in a region of Britain which desperately needed investment and jobs. The case for an effective Official Secrets Act, covering commercial as well as defence and security matters, could not be better illustrated by the need of total confidentiality in such negotiations. However tight the circle of those involved is kept, the need to secure final agreement with Ministers in other Departments inevitably requires wide circulation of information in the final stages when a leak could seriously damage the prospect of completing the deal in question, or indeed others. Fortunately, news of the Nissan deal only began to leak after it was concluded.

I approached the Commons statement with some concern. Not everyone on there Government benches would like the idea of inviting a Japanese car manufacturer into Britain whilst our own industry was in such disarray, so BL's friends might be hostile. The purists would criticise the amount of financial aid involved, the xenophobes would oppose anything Japanese and the cynics would say the agreements on British content would not stick. I assumed the Labour front bench would be hostile, particularly as the deal had been done by Keith and me. It all looked tricky. I saw no point in being apologetic or even accommodating to the critics.

To my amazement instead of being congratulated for crushing Labour's Stan Orme, our Chief Whip, Michael Jopling, told me that he had received the strongest representations from his opposite number that my behaviour had been quite unwarranted and that I should publicly apologise. 'What the Hell for?' was my reaction. As I realised I was being asked by our Chief Whip to accept the Labour Party view I became very angry. I explained very firmly what I had been asked to do as Keith's number two and if that had changed then it would be best to find someone different to do it – but apologise I would not. 'No wonder we get a bad press – no wonder we lose – we're bloody well apologising for winning,' I exploded, and marched off in a considerable huff, bumping into Ian Gow, the Prime Minister's PPS, who received the full force of my indignation in colourful language. I later received a note from him. It said simply '*Reculer pour mieux sauter*.' It was advice I detested but I agreed I would mollify Stan Orme with a word when we next met in the corridors and some emollient phrase at a suitable time in the House, but I was left wondering if the Tory Party yet had the will to win.

The British Leyland problems were so large and so political that Keith personally steered the policy. The business has brought every Minister associated with it into conflict with Margaret Thatcher – whose instincts about it have been undoubtedly right – but who like the rest of us, when faced with the human, financial, industrial, economic and political costs of the scale of surgery required, played the issue long. Always she hoped that a Minister would find a short cut at little political or financial expense that would get the Government out of the BL morass – instead of a route to get further in, in the hope of getting out on the far side. Just as many of those Ministers have from time to time vented their frustration on hapless chairmen or officials, so they have suffered from Prime Ministerial frustration too. Keith rightly saw that there was little point in taking BL's corporate plan to 'E' – the Economic Committee of the Cabinet – without gaining Margaret Thatcher's consent to it first. Discussions between our officials and those from No. 10 had cleared some issues but it was obviously going to be a difficult meeting. As we left the office on our way to Downing Street one of our officials asked, 'Is there anything more you need?'

With a weary smile, Keith said, 'No, thank you – well, yes, ambulances for two at 3 o'clock.'

We survived and so has BL! Indeed I survived a hostile debate on BL in which an Opposition spokesman accused me of 'stabbing BL in the back,' a charge I deflected with the remark, 'If I did – it was with a cheque book.'

At that time, although John Egan had taken charge of Jaguar the survival of the business was in doubt simply because customers would not buy the product which had acquired an appalling reputation. Quite how I managed to convince myself first and the Treasury next to agree that the first large expenditure on the XJ40 – which became the new XJ6 – should be authorised, I do not know. It must have been mainly on a basis of faith – faith which happily proved well founded.

During that first month in the Department I had been dashing from the Nissan meetings to BL meetings and on to the British Aerospace flotation meetings – Keith had also given me much of the detailed work which remained to be done.

Writing the prospectus was not easy. In particular we had to ensure that proposals within the Ministry of Defence which would affect the view of potential investors were properly dealt with, in the knowledge that a misleading or incomplete statement would not be just a political embarrassment or hostage to fortune but a criminal offence. Nor was pricing the shares easy. Whilst our merchant bank, Kleinwort Benson, and stockbrokers, Hoare Govett, had handled many flotations, this one was not only very large, it was controversial, the first of its kind and no one could be sure how the public and the markets would react. in the end the issue at £1.50 a share was $3\frac{1}{2}$ times over-subscribed and the shares began trading at £1.72 to ignorant and hysterical wailing by Labour spokesmen that we had underpriced by twenty-two pence and cost the taxpayer some twenty million pounds. In fact the number of people prepared to pay £1.72, though unknown, must have been very small against the number we needed to take up the 100 million shares on offer, and an issue at £1.72 would have been the flop the Labour Party wanted. Perhaps in retrospect we could have got an extra few pence a share – but the risk was high and above all we needed a successful, not failed, flotation to pave the way for an enthusiastic response and good prices for future offerings.

After the years in which denationalisation had been condemned not only as immoral or foolish but accepted even amongst most Conservatives as impracticable, it was immensely satisfying to have achieved the first stage of our economic revolution – the sale of BAe – successfully. Even such Thatcherite economic policies as medium-term financial strategy were still only intents at that time rather than achievements. In many ways it was the BAe flotation which first proved that the socialist ratchet could be reversed.

Clearing up the mess left by that lame-duck farm, the National Enterprise Board, was a tedious and messy business. The old corporatist and interventionist board had resigned in 1979 and the new Chairman, Sir Leslie Knight, sadly had to stand down for personal reasons. Fortunately Sir Freddie Wood of Croda International Limited took over shortly after my arrival in the Department and with Keith we began to extricate the taxpayer from some pretty awful commitments. There were some good businesses in the portfolio but all too many were eternally cash hungry, 'losses-today but hopefully profits-tomorrow' firms. The losses always arrived but in general the profits never did and in many cases we were contractually locked into money-losing deals with other businesses. There were several with names like Nexos, Araxos Inmos, which, when I took the usual bad news to him one day, prompted Keith's agonised cry, 'Oh no – not those damned Greeks demanding gifts again.'

However unwelcome, the NEB's calls for cash hardly compared with those of British Steel. The steel strike of 1980 had been a disaster for the

Corporation and its workers. Both the recession and technical change were hitting the market for steel and British Steel was an over-manned, inefficient, high-cost, poor-quality producer in a market where the customer was king. Somewhere inside BSC there was a viable business with good managers, technologists, production and sales workers. Whether they could be extricated from the shambles that was BSC at the beginning of 1981 was still an open question.

We were not alone in our problems. The European Commission and the Council of Ministers had declared a state of manifest crisis in steel production. The task was to restore an orderly market in a Community in which most countries blatantly poured operating subsidies into their loss-making, nationalised steel industries and others covertly subsidised their private-sector producers, all in breach of the Treaty. Keith had no taste for the wheeler-dealer negotiating world of the Council of Ministers and I was given a very free hand to negotiate in the Council. It was a difficult hand to play as our objective was to stop the competitive subsidisation, and force a cutback to bring capacity into line with demand. Awkwardly, however, only the Italians were subsidising more heavily than ourselves and if operating subsidies were prohibited too quickly our industry would face collapse. Our aim was to achieve a compulsory scheme of price fixing to prevent the dumping of steel at below reasonable-cost prices, of output quotas and plant closures, to bring supply and demand into balance and to impose a time limit by which national subsidies would be ended in order to allow price and output controls to be ended and the free market restored.

The German industry, in the private sector, was the best, most profitable and least subsidised (covertly through coal and freight rate subsidies) in Europe, and the German Economics Minister, Count Otto Lambsdorff, came to see me to set out his views and discover mine before the first Steel Council I attended. For political reasons the Germans advocated a voluntary agreement between the steel producers, although with no real conviction it could be reached or would work. At our meeting Lambsdorff and I were seated facing each other across the table, both flanked by our advisers. In his excellent English Lambsdorff set out the case for a voluntary agreement. As he concluded, I asked, 'Minister, I have spoken to your steel producers and I do not believe they will volunteer. If I am right, what will you do then?'

Lambsdorff's face remained almost straight, but with a ghost of a smile and a clear twinkle in the eye he emphasised his almost imperceptible accent. 'Then we shall have to find ways to make them volunteer,' he replied.

I knew at that moment that Otto and I would become friends!

The negotiations at numerous Council meetings in Brussels were long and difficult. Stevie Davignon as the Commissioner responsible for industrial affairs and Franz Andriessen responsible for competition policy, made a nicely balanced pair. Stevie, always dealing, fixing, persuading, compromising, and Franz always principled and correct. The Ministers were a mixed bag, many represented unstable coalition Governments and had imprecise industrial policy briefs, but the great divide was between the Italians, who wanted to pour public money into new and bigger loss-making steelworks, and the commercially minded Germans. We, as I explained to Stevie Davignon, had behaved like Italians but we wanted to behave like Germans.

The most crucial meeting came soon after my appointment. It soon became very clear that either the Italians or the Germans would walk out of the meeting whatever proposals were tabled. Wisely the president adjourned the Council for an early lunch with Ministers, two translators and the two Commissioners. It was over lunch that the serious negotiations began and six hours later we emerged with a text partly in French partly in English, forming the basis of what became the agreement that has restored profitability to Europe's steel producers. Our advisers were almost distraught – what had their Ministers done without them? Mine were soon reassured – the agreement was within our negotiating mandate. We could return to London in good order. I reported the next day to Keith Joseph who asked how the meeting had gone. I could not resist pulling his leg.

'A triumph, Keith', I said. 'I have helped create Europe's biggest cartel designed to force up the price of a commodity already in surplus against the interest of the consumer.' Keith put his head in his hands, and I added, 'Don't worry, Keith – it will all come right in the end.'

I also concluded the first denationalisation in the steel industry with the first 'Phoenix' steel company, Allied Steel and Wire. In Allied we merged the rod and wire businesses of private-sector GKN and BSC with a rationalisation and reconstruction plan. In doing so I achieved a reputation as a hard negotiator. I felt that the deal being proposed was too generous to GKN, and I tightened the terms quite considerably. Happily, the structure, financing and management have all turned out well and Allied recently achieved a full quotation on the stock market.

Looking back on my time with Keith Joseph at the Department of Industry, it is clear that once again I had been lucky. One after another, major decisions came up to be made and difficult negotiations presented themselves to be resolved. My first two years in ministerial office had been a testing time but not only for me. By the summer of 1981 the Government seemed perpetually on trial. The Brixton riots in April were followed by others in London in June, then in July the Toxteth riots, followed by those in Manchester, Brixton, Southall, Reading, Hull and Preston. It is far from well known that before the Toxteth riots it had been decided that a single Minister should be appointed to co-ordinate and improve Government programmes to assist Liverpool but no decision had been made on who, or from which Department – Industry or Environment – he should come. After Toxteth it was a clearly a Cabinet-level initiative and Michael Heseltine saved me from any risk of becoming Minister for Liverpool!

Although inflation was firmly under control (without an incomes policy or price controls), unemployment was rising in the great industrial shake out. In fact we had been at the trough of the recession with recovery imminent when in March 364 economists declared our policies could never succeed. By October, when fourteen of the most eminent of them called for reflation and an incomes policy, Thatcherism was just beginning to be seen to be working. Their longing for the old ways of compromise was echoed by those who wanted to give in to the threat of jailed IRA criminals to starve themselves to death in a hunger strike. Few people believed the Government would stand firm in the face of even one death, but it did and after nine more it was the will of the IRA not Margaret Thatcher's which broke. Gradually it was becoming clear that she was a Prime Minister unlike any since Churchill. Nonetheless, the 'wets', the weaker willed, the craven-hearted and the embittered failures amongst the Conservative Party still hoped she would go away and let them go back to their old ways. Indeed when David Owen and Bill Rodgers led the split from Labour to form the SDP there were many who forecast that a dozen or more Conservative MPS would join the new party. In the event only Mr Brocklebank-Fowler (who lost his seat to a Conservative two years later) defected.

In the face of the rising tide of unemployment, Geoffrey Howe's brave anti-inflationary budget of 1981 caused a good deal of dissent within the Cabinet with several Ministers openly trying to duck their collective responsibility. By September Margaret Thatcher had decided that after six years as Leader of the Party she should have a Cabinet with a majority of her own supporters. There had been plenty of speculation about a shuffle and I had been worried when I heard that my name was being touted as Lord Thorneycroft's successor as Chairman of the Party. That was not what I wanted. I could not accept an unpaid job and I liked ministerial life too much to want to change. I took a chance and went to see Margaret, telling her that the man for the job was Cecil Parkinson. Urbane, good looking, a competent, if not a great speaker, a former constituency chairman, a reliable organiser, who could afford a couple of unpaid years, he was, I suggested, just the right man. However, whoever she appointed, I said it would be essential to give him a place in the Cabinet.

As usual I was at home on Sunday afternoon in Berkhamsted when the Cabinet Secretary, Robert Armstrong telephoned to say the Prime Minister wanted to see me the following morning. I was due to leave that evening for the west country ready for an early engagement on Monday morning.

'It's very inconvenient,' I told Robert. 'Is it really that important?'

'I think it would be very much in your best interest to cancel your engagement and see the PM,' he replied.

Next morning at No. 10 Margaret told me that she wanted me to take over from Jim Prior at Employment – to increase the pace of trades union reform and argue our case on unemployment. Jim, she told me, she hoped would go to Northern Ireland, and to my delight Cecil Parkinson was to become Chairman of the Party with a Cabinet seat as Chancellor of the Duchy of Lancaster.

I left No. 10 in a slight daze but, I suspect, wearing a silly grin. Ossie (Miss Osborne), my faithful driver, looked quizzically at me. I had inherited her from John Nott when he went to Defence where Ministers have military drivers, so she had lost 'her' Rover as Ministers of State rated only an Austin Princess. 'Am I going to have a Rover?' she asked as we drove away. Looking in the mirror to see my grin was still there she drew her own conclusion.

The Cabinet shuffle was rightly seen as a turning point in Margaret Thatcher's premiership. She needed to strengthen the Cabinet with colleagues who believed that the policy of the Government was right and that it could be carried through. With the departure of Ian Gilmour, Christopher Soames and Mark Carlisle and the arrival of Cecil Parkinson and myself the balance in the Cabinet was decisively changed. The change from Jim Prior to myself was widely seen as significant. To some it was a calculated insult to the unemployed, to others a welcome challenge at last to the abuses of trades union power and the closed shop in particular.

I started my new job with a number of advantages. Not least, most of my opponents still thought of me as no more than a thick-headed, sharp-tongued brawler. Even better, they deluded themselves not only about public opinion but the opinion of trades unionists themselves. Even Terry Duffy, that sincere and generally sensible leader of the

AUEW, was quoted in *The Times* as saying, 'Tebbit has not got the barometer of opinion; he is out of touch with the movement.' Like the military establishment in 1914 and 1940, the cloth-capped colonels of 1983 were readying themselves to fight the last war. Totally blinkered to the changing realities of public opinion or the new tactics I intended to employ, they were expecting another 1972-style confrontation. It was to be some weeks before Moss Evans of the TGWU was to wonder aloud, 'if Mr Tebbit was the cleverest and nastiest Secretary of State or the most stupid and dangerous holder of that high office.'

It seemed to me that the first place to establish a clear understanding of my intentions was in the Department of Employment. In comparison with Industry, Employment was a small central Department, having only two Deputy Secretaries (the rank immediately below the Permanent Secretary), but enormously larger in total numbers, mostly in the benefit offices and hived off into the Manpower Services Commission's Jobcentres and training operations.

My Permanent Secretary was Denis Barnes, a thoroughly decent, traditional civil servant. I soon realised that he was anxious to retire, only staying to help smooth the succession of Permanent Secretaries across Whitehall. He was slightly 'demob happy' and, although a valuable source of sound advice, too conservative (with a small 'c') for my taste. I teased him early on by asking him if he thought that his Department was any longer necessary. Surely, I suggested, its functions might better be split between the DHSS social security wing and the Department of Industry. He refused to rise to the bait, pointing out that with three million unemployed whatever the merits of my argument the abolition of the Department might be misunderstood!

I had rather more fun at my first meeting of my key eight or ten officials. I told them that I wanted no misunderstandings. I was totally determined on my programme of union reform. I would not be thwarted. To their growing consternation I went on,

> If necessary I will surround every prison in this country with police – and if needs be the army. I am willing to seal them off with barbed-wire barricades. Under no circumstances will I allow any trades union activist – however hard he tries – to get himself *into* prison under my legislation.

From there on, the ice was broken and once again I found I had the benefit of officials of the highest integrity and ability. Once I had laid down policy they were tireless in finding ways to deliver what I wanted. Taking their lead from my teasing, my officials also allowed fuller rein to their sense of humour, to the extent that I eventually had to warn against overdoing the circulation of spoof memoranda since some were so good as to be almost believable.

We also became the subject of some Whitehall gossip over the Chelsea Flower Show gnomes dispute! I received a wonderfully funny letter from the owner of a garden gnome factory who had been refused a stand to exhibit his gnomes at the show. He was, he said, going to put gnome pickets outside the show but wanted guidance on the laws relating to picketing. 'Not for us,' I observed, flippantly. 'Pass it to the Gnome Office.' Never lacking in zeal my officials went further, inventing ever-more fantastic gnome jokes asking the help of their colleagues in the Department of Elf and Social Security.

I believe that in a curious way my arrival at the Department, once the initial culture shock was over, improved morale amongst the senior staff. They all liked and respected Jim Prior but were conscious that he lacked the Prime Minister's support and was unlikely to win Cabinet battles. Like all organisations, Departments like to be on the winning side and they saw in me a winner in the Whitehall civil wars. The discovery that I was not a humourless and rigid fanatic also helped, and before long, morale and self-confidence returned to a Department which had been very unsure of itself.

I soon realised that I had three interlinking major problems facing me. Unemployment was just on three million and still set on a rising trend; training in industry was old fashioned and insufficient; and the power of trades union leaders was excessive and widely abused. I had little doubt that the union problem had a good deal to do with the first two.

I was also presented with a decision which was to have unexpectedly far-reaching repercussions. As the officials put it to me, there was the matter of the reappointment of Sir Richard O'Brien as Chairman of the Manpower Services Commission. I pointed out that I had not yet considered the matter and asked who were the other candidates, only to be told that my predecessors had not considered any and that they had expected the reappointment of Sir Richard. 'Well,' I said, 'I have not yet decided so let me see the papers and draw up your short list of possible candidates. In the meantime I will see Sir Richard.'

Richard O'Brien was a man of the Wilson–Heath corporatist era. He had come into public life in 1966 as an Industrial Adviser in the first Wilson Government's ill-conceived Department of Economic Affairs. He had been appointed to the MSC when it was accepted that a candidate for his office had to be vetted and approved by the TUC, and not actively opposed by the CBI. Decent and nice man that he was, he was not my man, nor a man for the times, and I thought it fortunate that his term of office was about to expire. My officials soon produced a list of worthy men whom they thought sufficiently insipid to be acceptable to both CBI and TUC but I decided to seek my own man.

I had been impressed by Keith Joseph's special adviser at the Industry Department. Keith, though sorry to lose him, recommended him to me and I secured the Prime Minister's agreement to the appointment of David Young. When I consulted Len Murray, the General Secretary of the TUC, his advice was, as always, crisp, amusing and delivered in total confidence. It did not lead me to believe I would be popular in trades union circles, nor did it cause me to draw back for fear of the consequences. Oddly enough it was a *Times* leader which criticised me for abandoning the consensus approach in what they saw as the field of industrial training. Consensus on trades union terms had got us nowhere in that field or any other, but the writer also failed to envisage how David Young and I were to steer the MSC on to a rather different course. Indeed, had I had my way, the direction would have changed more sharply, and sooner than has since been accomplished.

My main preoccupation was to frame and secure Cabinet agreement to the White Paper which would set out the shape of my 1982 Employment Act. I have no doubt that Act was my greatest achievement in Government and I believe it has been one of the principal pillars on which the Thatcher economic reforms have been built. I had inherited Jim Prior's consultation document (the 1981 Green Paper) on the next step in trade union reform and my position on the closed shop had been strengthened by the findings of the Strasbourg Court in the case of certain former British Rail employees dismissed for failing to join the 'appropriate' union. However, I was determined not to enact unenforceable legislation – the memory of the collapse of the 1972 Industrial Relations Act was very much in my mind.

I had a clear game plan for my programme of reform before I made the first move but it existed only in my mind and I had no intention of exposing more than one move at a time. I was determined first to form public opinion and then to be always just a little behind rather than ahead of it as I legislated.

Too few reformers had faced the fact that the power of trade unions is based on the privilege of immunity from liability in tort. Broadly that means unions have licence to commit unlawful acts without those who suffer loss as a result being able to sue for damages or seek an injunction requiring the mischief to be ended. From 1906 until my 1982 Act that immunity was almost total, and unions which could not be held responsible in law for their actions were behaving with greater and greater irresponsibility. The closed shop – a form of conscription – gave the unions the power to put people out of work with no possibility of redress if they refused to obey orders. This gave the leadership of unions enormous power which they used as they pleased. Whilst they had no personal immunity from the law, as the 1972 Act had shown, it was useless to bring legal actions against them as individuals. The situation was absurd – the rich and powerful unions were beyond the reach of the law which could only touch individuals who were in general not worth suing.

Jim Prior's Green Paper on the next steps in union reform had been published just before I arrived at the Department and it gave me a good basis for my White Paper which I published in late November. I decided it should have three main thrusts – on the closed shop, the tightening of the definition of a 'trades dispute' and the restriction of the unions' immunity from legal actions for damages for unlawful acts.

The first closed shop measures were quite straightforward. I rejected the pressures to 'ban' the closed shop – it simply would not have worked – but I did set out to undermine it. I proposed that compensation for those dismissed as the result of a closed shop should be sharply increased, that the workers concerned could in effect seek compensation from not just their former employer but the union concerned, too, and that unless there had been a recent ballot approving the closed shop any dismissal on grounds of a union non-membership would be construed as unfair. I also decided to make void and unenforceable contracts which specified union-only labour and to remove immunity from those organising industrial action in support of the closed shop.

My solution to the second and third problems was also simple. I decided to bring the immunities of unions into line with those of individuals organising or taking part in industrial action. That would make the unions themselves 'liable in tort' (that is, open to damages) if they committed unlawful acts except in 'pursuit or furtherance' of a 'trades dispute', and for both unlawful secondary picketing and actions to enforce union membership. However, the definition of a 'trades dispute' which was contained in what was known as the 'golden formula' in the 1974 Act was far too wide. Under it there could be a 'trades dispute' in a firm in which no employee had any grievance against his employer! That definition had to be tightened, and to achieve immunity disputes would have to be not just 'connected with' but 'wholly or mainly concerned with . . .' industrial relations issues. Thus neither what people called 'political' strikes nor strikes about matters outside Great Britain would any longer have immunity.

By a quirk of the law it had been established in the courts that, even if a strike was virtually over, employers could not dismiss those who refused to return to work without also dismissing all those who had returned to work – an absurdity which I also decided to end.

Together with some other minor provisions it made a much tougher package than I think Jim had in mind. It was carefully designed and did not of itself compel the unions to do anything – so there could be no mass refusal to comply with what came to be known as 'Tebbit's Law'. Nor did it create a complex new legal structure – it simply tilted the balance of power away from the unions by chipping away the privileges and legal immunities which gave them their ability to ride roughshod over the legitimate rights of the general public.

Regretfully I decided that it would have been a bridge too far to remove immunity from strikes called without a ballot. That provision, which was to have a crucial effect in ending the coal strike in 1985, had to await the 1984 legislation. Had it been in force earlier the strike might well have been far shorter and less vicious.

There was not time to clear my proposed reform package with the Cabinet before the Party Conference at Blackpool, so I had quite a difficult speech to make. Unemployment was about three million and rising and the faint-hearts were hoping and calling for a U-turn. There being nothing new that I could say I had to concentrate on style as much as on content.

My approach to industrial relations law reform was a mixture of menace and reasonability.

> We are not union bashers, I have never bashed a union in my life, but in the Winter of Discontent how many of the old, the sick, unemployed, disabled were bashed by the unions? . . . My conclusion is that there is need of further steps and it is time another step was taken. With that in mind I have prepared proposals for legislation in the next session of Parliament which I will shortly be putting to my colleagues.

I rightly claimed that nothing in the package would have impaired my work as a trade unionist in BALPA, and promised I would use the power of the law to protect the weak against the strong and to provide redress for those unjustly harmed by the action of others.

I had already agreed with Cecil Parkinson a campaign to defuse the issue of unemployment by initiating a debate on its causes and asking in my speech who was to blame.

Was unemployment a surprise, an act of God, an Act of Parliament, or an inevitable retribution for the follies of governments, workers, unions, managers, financiers and employers?

Not many, I declared, could make a plea of not guilty.

A Conference speech is made in reply to a debate and quite naturally I added to my speech to take up points raised by speakers from the floor. One speech by a Young Conservative, Ian Picton, angered the Conference by implying that rioting was a natural reaction to unemployment and I could not let it go by. I reminded him that Britain had experienced worse unemployment amongst my father's generation in the 1930s when I was growing up, but that generation did not riot. 'My father,' I observed in a graphic phrase that it seems will never die, 'got on his bike and looked for work.'

The speech was well received. I had passed my first test by giving the Conference hope and holding the line against the trimmers, and I headed back to London well satisfied.

My proposals had to be cleared by 'E' – the economic committee of the Cabinet – before going to the Cabinet itself and I rightly expected some difficult arguments. A number of my colleagues had become besotted with three media hobby horses – political strikes, procedural agreements and the so-called lay-off provisions. I soon convinced them that political strikes could not be defined in law and there was no need to try as I had skinned that cat in a better way. It was more difficult to persuade them that industrial procedural agreements could not be made legally enforceable and that to try would risk making the law an ass. 'Lay off', the concept of a legal right for employers to send workers home without pay whenever their firm was affected by an industrial dispute, was a popular idea which I bitterly opposed. Employers had always had the right to lay off hourly-paid workers but in the newspaper and engineering industries in particular many had negotiated that right away in deals with their staff. I thought it totally wrong – indeed improper – for employers even to ask me to give them back by law what they had freely sold in negotiation. I won my argument in Cabinet but sustained some unpleasant attacks in part of the Conservative press as a result. Indeed at the end of a long leader advocating 'lay-offs', *The Times* concluded, 'Mr Tebbit should therefore proceed boldly. The roars before his entrance have made Mr Prior look like a mouse but that is more honest than a cowardly lion.'

Some of the tabloids were rather nastier but in time the newspaper proprietors would learn that the lion had enough courage to face union leaders and employers alike, however powerful they might be.

The really difficult issue, however, was the reversal of the provision in the 1906 Act which had given unions total protection from being sued for damages. In the end I think it was only the Prime Minister's open support for me that carried the day. Had she not given it I would have lost, and I believe Mr Scargill, not Margaret Thatcher, would have won the coal strike.

With my Cabinet battle won I could complete my White Paper on industrial law reform but I also had on my plate the awkward problems of training in industry. The old statutory industrial training boards with representation from unions and management were a hangover from Britain's corporatist period. Few of them had been effective, most were wasteful, but each and every one was a sacred cow to the brahmins of the TUC. My announcement that sixteen of the twenty-three would be scrapped was received by the unions as an act of heresy and desecration, giving them an opportunity to rehearse their attacks for the real battle. I also set in train steps to abolish the Wages Councils. They had little impact – some had hilarious titles, like the 'Wage Council in Ostrich and Fancy Feather and Artificial Flower Trade' – and, over all, I believed they contributed to unemployment by raising wages above market levels.

On 23 November I published the White Paper and made my statement to a well-attended House. According to Paul Routledge, the left-wing but very straight labour correspondent of *The Times*, I 'took even some of the Government's opponents by surprise', by the extent of my proposals. The reactions were predictable. Mr Len Murray claimed I was deliberately going out of my way to pick a fight and Eric Varley, the Labour front-bench spokesman, gave a pledge that the next Labour Government would wipe out my legislation as they had done with the 1972 Act. Despite some regrets about the lack of 'lay-off' provisions, I enjoyed a good day in the House of Commons and a generally good press.

It soon became apparent that the TUC campaign against the White Paper and later the Bill itself was to be based on a mixture of misrepresentation and misjudgement. They misrepresented not only my intentions but my legislation; they misjudged the mood of their own members and, disastrously for their own purposes, they even believed their own quite false propaganda. Mr Moss Evans of the TGWU constantly proclaimed that he would be willing to go to prison by defying my law. If only he had cleared his mind of preconceptions and read the Bill he would have realised I had no intention of letting him, or anyone else, go to prison. Mr Bill Keys of the print union SOGAT wrote that he did not believe the opinion polls showing I had the support of trade unionists, and in a newspaper article claimed that the main proposals in my package were 'dynamite' which, if used, would 'blow a company's industrial relations sky high'. In fact it was the militants who were to be blown sky high, as Mr Keys' SOGAT was to find out in its ill-judged dispute with the Murdoch press at Wapping.

I was enjoying myself hugely. In Parliament, at public or private meetings, in press briefings or on television and radio, I was winning the arguments with ease, because I had designed my legislation, arguing through virtually every clause with my officials and I knew it from end to end. My opponents, however, were too prejudiced to try to understand my proposals and made themselves very easy meat.

It was much the same when I introduced my December package of employment and training measures and published my White Paper on industrial training. The main feature of the statement was the announcement of what was to become YTS, the Youth Training Scheme, building from the rather inadequate YOP (Youth Opportunities Programme to a full year's training open to all sixteen-year-old school leavers by the autumn of 1983. The statement went well although I was strongly attacked for suggesting that the supplementary benefit of unemployed youngsters refusing to undertake training should be cut. In fact I wanted to go further but failed to persuade my colleagues that supplementary benefit should be entirely abolished for those who could join a scheme and earn money but simply refused to work.

Next day I savoured Frank Johnson's parliamentary sketch column: 'Mr Tebbit is now the complete master of his craft. Yesterday he moved though 45 minutes of hostile questions without encountering the slightest difficulty from his enemies – many of whom are on the Labour benches.' Frank Johnson's perceptive innuendo was well judged. I had had to work very hard with my own back benchers to sell them the YTS concept and even more to gain at least neutrality on the issue of pay and supplementary benefit, a task in which Iain Mills, my PPS, was of enormous assistance.

I believe the creation of YTS was a major achievement, not just in the sense that it was none too easy to extract £1 billion from the Treasury, but more importantly in that it began to restore the concept of preparing young school leavers for the world of work. Eventually YTS became a two-year scheme, but in late 1983 the first priority was to find enough employers willing to offer training of the required standard and enough education institutions to provide off-the-job training. For all my frequent criticisms of both CBI and TUC, on this occasion they each delivered what I asked.

I had been working extremely hard and I greatly enjoyed the Christmas break which we spent quietly at home with our family. The end of the holiday came all too quickly and in January 1982 I introduced my Bill into the House of Commons. It held one surprise. I had added a provision to pay compensation to closed shop victims whose circumstances were like those of the four former BR employees who had won their case at Strasbourg; they were believed to number about three or four thousand.

The reactions to the Bill were predictable. Arthur Scargill advocated defiance of the law, Len Murray called for constitutional resistance and Eric Hammond told the special TUC conference called to discuss my Bill that, 'there was little feeling among the membership for confrontation'. It was neither the first time nor the last that Eric Hammond showed himself to be much closer to his members than any other trade union leader.

Progress in Parliament on my Bill was slow, but I was not worried. I knew that Eric Varley, Labour front-bench spokesman, was under attack from many of his colleagues for his moderate views and that he would have to put up at least a pretence of a tough fight, although neither he nor I could see any sense in all-night sittings of the Committee on the Bill since they would achieve nothing. However, the least he could decently do in evidence of his struggle would be to force me to guillotine the Bill and impose a strict timetable to end the discussion. When, after 100 hours of debate, we were still on clause 2 of 14 clauses I obliged Eric by bringing in a guillotine, amidst a great ritual of protests. Once the ritual was over the Bill sped easily through the Commons hilariously splitting the Liberal–SDP Alliance three ways (to the annoyance of Liberal Cyril Smith who had generously supported me in the Committee) – between those voting for it, those voting against it and those unable to decide what to do.

It was not only in the House of Commons that resistance to my legislation was ineffectual. Despite a TUC levy of ten pence per union member, raising over a million pounds to 'Kill the Bill', as Eric Hammond had rightly predicted, there was little grass-roots support. The protest rallies and marches, featuring many of the same 'Trots', Militants, Communists, Socialist Workers Party members and the like were well reported in the media. The huge banners proclaiming 'Kill the Tebbit Bill' were a matter of hilarity for my younger son William's friends (he is known as Bill) and made me the second best-known Conservative politician after the Prime Minister herself.

The rows over my appointment of David Young to head the MSC had soon died down. A very persuasive talker, David soon brought the trade unionist representatives on the Commission round to the view that he was really apolitical, and that his aim was greatly to increase public expenditure on the unemployed.

This all fitted into the plans Cecil Parkinson and I had developed to neutralise the political damage of unemployment. These were not confined to educating the media and the electorate to see the real causes of unemployment – the world recession and the uncompetitiveness of British industry which had been brought about by earlier Socialist policies and the activities of trade unions in wrecking businesses through excessive pay claims, constant strikes and a refusal to modernise working practices. We also realised we had to show a proper concern particularly for the young unemployed who had never had a job and the adult long-term unemployed. The YTS coped with the first group, and David and I with the Chancellor, Geoffrey Howe, developed the Community Programme to deal with the second. I did not get all my own way in either scheme since I had failed to secure the withdrawal of supplementary benefit from those sixteen-year-olds who preferred idleness to useful training, and I had to agree to paying 'the rate for the job' to those on the Community Programme rather than a premium of £15 a week over the cash benefit they would have received whilst unemployed. As a result Community Programme was able to benefit fewer people than I had hoped and too many youngsters continued to be given money for nothing. However, six or seven years later my successor, Norman Fowler, is achieving what in 1982 I could not.

Like most people, I was also well aware that although the great mass of the unemployed desperately wanted to get back to work, the official total listed in the statistics included a number who should not be there. Those people fell into a number of categories. Some were retired – usually from well-paid jobs on good pensions but not yet sixty-five – some were married women, who had not previously been in the labour market, were ready to work if the right job turned up but not prepared to take anything else. Others had found a job but had not taken their names off the list of job-seekers at the job centres. It was possible to identify and enumerate all those, but although it was common knowledge that there was a large number of people drawing benefit and working, or drawing benefit with no intention of taking a job at all, there was no way of knowing how many. Indeed at the time no politician dared speak of them for fear of the abuse he would receive.

This latter group had grown hugely through a penny-wise and pound foolish application of a well-researched and sensible Rayner efficiency audit of the payment of unemployment benefit. The study had recommended that the weekly or fortnightly 'signing-on' to collect benefit should be abandoned. It was bad enough to be unemployed in areas where job seekers outnumbered vacant jobs by a hundred to one, but to be required to attend regularly and solemnly to attest to the fact was a needless burden which also imposed an unnecessary cost on the civil service machine. The recommendation to end signing-on and send Giro cheques by post to claimants instead, was accepted but the recommendation simultaneously to increase the number of officers preventing fraud was not. As a result fraudulent claiming grew to a serious abuse. (First David Young and then Norman Fowler, as my successors, bravely and cleverly tackled the problem of 'claiming whilst working', uncovering such widespread abuse that I think it is now quite reasonable to doubt if unemployment ever reached three million at all.)

I decided to end the requirement for unemployed people to register at the job centres and base the unemployment statistics on a count of those drawing benefit – a more precise figure. This eliminated the early retired, a number of married women and some 100,000 employed people, but included for the first time the severely disabled job seekers. Because, however, it reduced the official total of unemployment my move was much attacked by Labour politicians and trade union leaders.

I was in a reforming mood and before the summer, after a long struggle to convince my Cabinet colleagues, and still having failed to convince some employers, I announced my intention to rescind the 1946 Fair Wages Resolution. Originally conceived as a measure to prevent government contracts from being won on the basis of 'sweated labour', it had become a mechanism for upholding the concept of the 'going rate' of pay increases, an important help to unions to leapfrog wage claims and a barrier to the employment of unskilled workers. Like the Wages Councils it was a cause of unemployment and had to go and I doubt if even many of those who abused me in 1982 would now reintroduce the Fair Wage Rules or extend the Wages Councils.

David Young and I worked well together although I had to be firm over his more ambitious and expensive plans vastly to increase the size of the MSC. However, together with Keith Joseph, Secretary of State for Education, we devised an inexpensive scheme, the Technical and Vocational Educational Initiative, to restore the provision of technical education for fourteen- to eighteen-year-olds. Sadly my idea that this should include a few entirely new schools in inner cities funded through the MSC was eroded away until the TVEI became simply part of the curriculum in some comprehensive schools. It was a great opportunity sadly missed but now being taken up by City Technology Colleges.

However, I took the view that as I was securing all my major objectives and at least progressing in the right direction on all those where I could not get entirely my own way I had little cause for complaint. The Parkinson–Tebbit tactics seemed to be holding the line on the political consequences of unemployment. The polls showed that the Government was not seen by the voters as the villain of the piece however hard the Opposition tried to make it seem so. In Parliament I had no difficulty in dealing with the Government's critics, either on the other side of the House or my own. The Labour spokesman, Eric Varley, was so sensible and reasonable that he must have found it difficult to believe much of what he was compelled to say to please his left wing and the union bosses and he seldom seemed to have his heart in his arguments. By the autumn of 1982 we had weathered a vicious NHS strike, not least due to the calm, resourceful and much underestimated team of Norman Fowler and Tony Newton at the DHSS, and the long-running British Rail dispute too.

In great contrast to the Heath era inflation had been falling sharply and industrial relations improving without either incomes policies or cosy *tête-à-tête* meetings with union leaders. Indeed I scarcely saw them at all except at meetings of 'Neddy', the NEDC or National Economic Development Council. Somehow this old corporatist tripartite forum escaped the axe, much to my personal irritation as I detested wasting a morning in an agony of boredom when I had better things to do. From the trade union side I enjoyed the rare but pithy contributions from Frank Chapple, admired the decency of Terry Duffy and the dry self-deprecating wit of Len Murray, but everyone (except perhaps the sec-retariat) knew that Ministers, union leaders and employers would all rather have been somewhere else, doing something else. It was hardly the stuff of productive discussions.

The pattern of the eighties was being set – strikes in the private sector diminishing rapidly, those in the public sector dragging on at great expense and inconvenience, ending in considerable personal loss on the part of the strikers. Time and time again we simply stood firm and won – gradually the lessons were being learned.

The most spectacular example of the capacity of the Government to stand firm was not, however, in my field but on the world stage with the invasion and liberation of the Falkland Islands. There had been some concern at the provocative tactics of Argentina, most particularly the illegal landing on South Georgia of a party of scrap merchants, but more worryingly at the end of March there were reports of Argentine warships in the area. The Foreign Office assumption was that this was no more than sabre rattling for home consumption or to reinforce a negotiating position, but it was decided that *HMS Endurance* should remain in the area rather than return home. She was of no military significance, unarmoured and scarcely armed, but was a symbol representing the Royal Navy. Despite these alarms, even as late as 1 April 1982, when the United Nations Security Council met at Britain's request and issued a call for restraint and avoidance of force, no one in London foresaw the Argentine invasion next day. At first it was hard to believe but after some three hours of resistance the handful of Royal Marines in Port Stanley were instructed to surrender to avoid needless loss of life.

The Cabinet met next morning, Saturday 3 April. Never in my wildest imagination had I expected, when I joined the Cabinet six months earlier, to be faced with the decision before us that day. We reviewed the events leading up to the invasion and the options available. The military advice was clear. An invasion at such a distance, against a numerically superior garrison with air cover from nearby land bases, would be not only hazardous in the extreme but unprecedented. There would be a risk of heavy casualties, even failure. Taking into account the superiority of our men, however, the odds became distinctly better, though we could have no guarantee against failure. After some general discussion the Prime Minister put the decision to the Cabinet. Should a task force, prepared to take back the Falklands by force, be despatched to the South Atlantic? We had no illusions about what we were being asked. If diplomatic pressure failed to dislodge the Argentine invaders, were we prepared to risk the military option? There could be no question of despatching the fleet and then recalling it with Argentina still in occupation of the Islands.

Cabinet is not a place for votes although if a decision is finely balanced the Cabinet Secretary keeps a tally of views for the Prime Minister's summing up, but that morning the Prime Minister asked each colleague directly, 'Should the fleet be despatched – Yes or No?'

That afternoon when the Commons met, the Prime Minister was able to announce that whilst we had called for an emergency meeting of the UN Security Council the Cabinet had also authorised the assembly of a naval task force.

Sadly, the Foreign Secretary, Peter Carrington, resigned, feeling that responsibility for the failure of his Department properly to assess and warn of the Argentine intentions fell upon him. Humphrey Atkins, the

Government's foreign affairs spokesman, and Richard Luce, a Junior Minister, followed suit in what I felt was a needless sacrifice, and of course John Nott, as Defence Secretary, eventually went, too, after the successful conclusion of the war. Francis Pym succeeded Peter Carrington and in true Foreign Office style pursued every avenue which might lead to an accommodation with Argentina, ending each journey in a cul-de-sac blocked by the complete intransigence and incompetence of the military dictator Galtieri and his junta.

The full story of the Falkands War cannot be told for many years to come. There are no British skeletons in cupboards but it would be against our national interest to expose how, sometimes with the help of friends and despite the efforts of our potential enemies, some things were achieved. It is sufficient to say that the wild conspiratorial theories of the more spiteful or unbalanced critics are total rubbish – the product of fevered imaginations. The invasion itself was not launched to scupper a peace initiative – there had been weeks of those and all had foundered on Argentinian obduracy. It was launched because the fleet could not be left heaving around in heavy Atlantic seas at serious risk from Argentinian submarines or, before she was rightly sunk, the cruiser *Belgrano* and her attendant destroyers.

The story of the campaign has been well told and I can add little to it. My experience was confined to the Cabinet room where I shared the burden of responsibility, the anxieties, the grief of war and the eventual joy of the peace and liberation. I made only one unique contribution. The Prime Minister formed a Falklands inner group of herself, the Foreign and Defence Secretaries and her deputy Willie Whitelaw, but it was at my suggestion that she included Cecil Parkinson. As Chancellor of the Duchy of Lancaster, Cecil was in effect a non-departmental Minister who could bring a detached view to bear and effectively represent all the rest of the Cabinet. It was a significant move making him a national figure and giving him far greater personal authority almost overnight.

The Argentine garrison surrendered on 14 June, and the $2\frac{1}{2}$ month war was over, at a cost of 255 British lives, many terrible injuries and a huge but unknown toll on the Argentine side. In Argentina the Falklands adventure was to bring about the downfall of the military dictatorship and there was a political fall-out in Britain too.

Support for the Government had begun to recover before the Falklands affair, partly as the novelty and media infatuation with the Alliance went slightly off the boil, but the Government's handling of the crisis brought about a surge of popularity in the polls. Between

December and June the Prime Minister's popularity rating doubled, and the so-called 'Falklands Factor' had entered the political vocabulary. There is no doubt that it was real but some commentators quite wrongly associated it with national chauvinism. In my view the affair reminded voters that amongst the most important qualities of a Prime Minister are clear judgement, determination, incisiveness, courage, patriotism, leadership and an ability to keep one's head whilst many others are losing theirs. The harsh light of the Falklands crisis, illuminating the character of the Prime Minister, displayed those qualities in abundance – and in falling on Mr Foot, the leader of the Opposition, it cruelly illuminated his complete unsuitability for her office.

Amongst the casualties of the Falklands War was the relationship between the Government and the BBC. Whilst the BBC correspondents with our forces in the South Atlantic upheld the highest standards of courage and journalism of their wartime predecessors, the unctuous 'impartiality' of the BBC's editorialising was a source of grief and anger. Few of us directly concerned will ever forgive the phrase, 'the British authorities, if they are to be believed, say . . .' or the regular references to British and Argentinian forces rather than 'our forces' and 'enemy forces'. The elaborate even-handedness jarred cruelly with those whose lives were at risk, those of us who took ultimate responsibility for committing our forces, knowing the human costs of what we had to do, and with the general public. Nor did the excuse that the Overseas Service broadcasts would lose credibility with their foreign listeners unless the BBC remained 'impartial', hold water because it confused truth with impartiality and balance. It was not impartiality that impelled Germans to risk punishment by tuning in to the BBC during the Second World War. For me the British Broadcasting Corporation might have better called itself the Stateless Persons Broadcasting Corporation for it certainly did not reflect the mood of the British people who finance it. The wounds inflicted by the BBC have still not healed – indeed the recent decisions to broadcast one play hostile to the campaign and to black another presenting a favourable view ensured that the wound would fester.

With the Falklands War over, except for the ghoulish search of some Labour politicians and journalists for a way to find within a great victory some incident to discredit the Prime Minister, political life resumed as normal.

9

On to the Second Term

By the close of 1982 we had begun to focus on the coming general election. There was no doubt that industrial relations would be the issue to counter-balance concern over unemployment and I was already planning my campaign.

In December I allowed some speculation that if the unions publicly accepted the permanence of my reforms after a second Thatcher election victory relations with the Government could easily be restored and that if I was seen as an obstruction I could easily be moved. Then in January 1983 I increased the pressure again with the publication of my Green Paper on union democracy, on which I had been working since July.

As a consultation paper it canvassed solutions to the three problems it addressed: the lack of democratic elections within many unions, the frequent lack of pre-strike ballots and the system of press-ganging union members into Labour Party membership without their consent.

It had not been easy to write and I had to fight off a number of 'improvements' suggested by well-intentioned colleagues and lobbyists. Some still hankered after the lay-off clauses, others wanted a legal requirement for pre-strike ballots.

I was determined that my second Act like my first should be foolproof, vandal-proof and lawyer-proof and that required that the law should be simple. I favoured simple requirements that voting members of the national governing bodies of unions should be directly elected by the members in fair ballots; that strikes called without the approval in a ballot of the workers concerned should not enjoy immunity; and that union members should not be required to contribute money to the Labour Party without their consent. In the end I had my way on the more important issues but I had to back down on the political levy.

Indeed that was to be kicked into touch until after the election as it was made plain through the party whips' offices that any attempt to introduce a requirement for union members to give their personal consent to payment of the political levy would be met with really implacable opposition. That would include the deliberate disruption of parliamentary proceedings and the threat that any future Labour government would totally cut off financial support from industry to the Conservative Party. In the end we legislated to require unions to ballot their members to authorise political funds, but gave individual trade unionists no better protection. And, even worse, no attempt was made to engender a fair debate before ballots were taken. In my view almost without exception the ballots which have approved union political funds were conducted so unfairly that if challenged they would have been overturned by the courts. However no trade unionists could afford such a challenge without substantial financial support as the case would inevitably have been fought up to the House of Lords. I believe that this issue was shirked partly at least because it might have led to the cutting off of corporate funding to both major parties and to further pressure for state funding. I never accepted that logic, and in retrospect it seems to me that the preservation of trade union funding, and therefore of trade union domination of the Labour Party, may well be a key factor in the inability of that party to come to terms with reality and offer a credible alternative to Conservative government.

Quite rightly Paul Routledge, labour editor of *The Times*, saw what he called my 'astute and persuasive' Green Paper as part of a struggle for trade unionists' votes in the forthcoming general election, a popular issue which could be kept on the boil right up to and through the campaign. At the same time a vicious strike in the water industry involving a highly suspect ballot which almost certainly breached the union's own rules raised great public concern over strikes in the essential services. That caused me a great deal of difficulty within government as I came under heavy pressure to do something to stop such strikes. None of the suggested remedies, which even included the foolish ideas of making strikes in essential services a criminal offence, or wildly expensive and unenforceable no-strike agreements, would have been effective. I argued strenuously that the measures already enacted together with those I had proposed would be the best – but inevitably imperfect – deterrent. In the end I had to canvass and hint at some way of enforcing procedural agreements (which had been blatantly broken in the water strike) but I did so with neither conviction nor enthusiasm and the idea was never taken up. The strike was very badly handled by the employers, a weak, divided and barely competent group of negotiators; and the intervention of ACAS (the Advisory Conciliation and Arbitration Service) I found generally unhelpful. Indeed its chairman, Pat Lowry, and I were badly at odds over his part in the affair. Pat, a man of considerable ability and integrity, was still thinking in the 1970s' terms of splitting the difference and compromising half-way between unreasonable demands and perfectly reasonable offers, having not adjusted to the idea that unions which overplayed their hands should be forced to face up to the consequences. To be fair to him, nor had the employers adjusted and he had no easy task; but I found myself profoundly wishing he would leave things to run their course rather than perpetually trying to secure a face-saving formula in a dispute where both sides deserved to lose face.

Much of my time in the first half of 1983 was spent on planning for the forthcoming election, attending the first major discussion on tactics at Chequers on 5 January. Tim Bell and Michael Dobbs represented Saatchis, Gordon Reece and Ian Gow (Margaret's PPS) were there together with a team from Central Office and Ronnie Miller, the playwright. Apart from Cecil Parkinson, I was the only Minister present and I realised that I was to have a major role in the campaign. As the talk turned to who I wanted as my Junior Minister after the shuffle, I also realised that the talk of a move to Defence in the mini shuffle caused by John Nott's resignation (which I would have liked) had come to nothing.

I did not worry too much about that but having done so much at Employment I hoped for a new challenge after the general election. At about that time, I was irritated by a trivial incident which caused me a great deal of trouble. In answering a question about unemployment at an industrial relations conference I observed that despite the three million unemployed I had been unable to find someone to paint the gates of my home in Berkhamsted. For days we were pestered with reporters and photographers around the house, then Socialist vandals daubing the gates with red paint, and demonstrations outside. My wife was very upset and we spent some unhappy weekends in our London flat, to avoid the demonstrations.

Meanwhile, I pressed on with more reforms. I wanted to repeal the Truck Acts – obsolete laws which gave workers the right to be paid in cash rather than by goods or credit notes for goods which had been interpreted to include cheques or bankers' drafts. Naturally the unions opposed such a sensible idea. More to the point the Chancellor, Geoffrey Howe, was not too keen but I persuaded him to agree to another Green

Paper on a new Protection of Wages Bill to achieve the same end after the general election.

That election began to loom over everything we did and I had become convinced that subject to the May local election results Margaret should call an election in June. October looked to be a difficult month and to leave it over until the following spring risked leaving ourselves at the mercy of any unforeseen events with no time to recover before the deadline of June 1984. All Margaret's instincts were against such an early election. In her own words, 'It would be out of character,' so I knew that before long Cecil and I would have to put all the options fairly and squarely to her. The subject soon came up after a Sunday lunch at Chequers. As the other guests were leaving Margaret indicated that Cecil and I should stay on and once we were alone she returned to the question of election timing, expressing her concern at the build-up of expectations for a June election. Cecil as Chairman of the Party wisely held back his view whilst I pointed out the hazards of October. Inflation would be edging up from its mid-summer low and unemployment would have begun its seasonal climb. Uncertainty surrounded trade figures, currency and interest rate levels so far ahead and I had no taste for a long summer election campaign. Margaret thought about it, still concerned that it would be out of character to go so early but agreed she would not rule it out until after seeing the May election results.

I was now working extremely hard – days of meetings in Cabinet committees alternating with regional tours on departmental and party business, with the awful red boxes piled two or three high waiting for me each night. The water strike was dragging on as I became more impatient with the employers, ACAS, Pat Lowry, my officials and my colleagues, none of whom seemed to me to have the will to get out and win. At least I found some comfort from Frank Chapple who came to dinner with his wife one evening to our flat and told me more about the causes of the dispute and the roles of the union leaders involved than anyone else before or since. Such insights were all too rare, only men like Frank Chapple were willing to discuss such things at all – let alone so bluntly.

Perhaps we were all feeling the stress but I began to realise that I was uncharacteristically touchy and found myself in a pretty fearsome row one day with Arthur Cockfield (the Secretary of State for Trade) who wanted us to renege on our agreement to finance British Leyland's corporate plan as sterling's depreciation was favourable to the company. It irritated me that someone who knew little enough about BL and absolutely nothing about winning elections should put up such a stupid idea. If it had leaked it would have cost at least a dozen seats. I backed Patrick Jenkin (Secretary for Industry) more strongly than he backed himself in stopping further discussion of Arthur's madcap scheme and remained in a bit of a huff for the rest of the morning. My visits to the Council of Ministers in Brussels came almost as relief from pressures at home and by the end of the month my spirits had recovered to the state when I could laugh at the discovery of terminal rust in my car and accept with equanimity my Margaret's wish to sell our home in Berkhamsted and buy what would be our retirement home, preferably in the West Country.

By the spring things seemed to be going our way. The opinion surveys showed that my Green Paper on union reform was bang on target with the electorate; Scargill was decisively defeated in the miners' strike ballot; the Budget was well received and the polls looked good. In his Budget Geoffrey Howe announced increased spending to help the unemployed and the expansion of the Enterprise Allowance Scheme from a few small pilot exercises to help about 25,000 unemployed people to set up in self-employment whilst continuing to draw £40 a week in benefit for up to twelve months. It was another scheme, invented by David Young and me and our officials, which from its small beginnings has become a major job creator.

The Darlington by-election result on 24 March was encouraging enough to intensify the election speculation and after a long discussion Cecil Parkinson and I agreed that there were only four sensible choices of election dates in 1983: June 9 and 23, September 29 and November 10. I plumped for 9 June, and in a cheerful mood, despite the interminable water strike and a dispute in the docks, headed off to clear my desk before flying to Portugal to join my wife for the Easter holiday, before things became really busy.

I returned ten days later to go to the key meeting on the election manifesto. To avoid publicity we met in the Chancellor's house in Downing Street on a Saturday. David Howell, Nigel Lawson, Keith Joseph, Cecil Parkinson and the three authors of the first draft – special advisers Adam Ridley and Peter Cropper and Ferdie Mount, the journalist and policy unit chief at No. 10 – had all agreed to arrive by different routes – through St. James's Park, by Downing Street, and through the Cabinet Office and No. 10 – to avoid notice by any watching press men. Geoffrey Howe proved an excellent chairman, his splendid sense of mischievous irreverent humour, which is seldom seen in public, cheering us on until by ten o'clock that night the job was all but done.

By Thursday 14 April when Geoffrey reported to the Cabinet on our work, election fever was running high and although election timing was not formally discussed it was clear that June had become the favourite choice. In the following week the best inflation figures for fifteen years did nothing to arrest the June bandwagon and in a further meeting with Margaret Thatcher I pressed the case for 9 June, despite her commitment to attend the Williamsburg Conference in the United States during what would be the campaign period.

Somehow, despite the pressures, I seemed to be on top of my work, even making time for a first house-hunting trip to the West Country. We were also delighted to hear that our daughter Alison, who had married in 1981, was pregnant with our first grandchild and we were speculating on the probable engagement of our elder son John to his very attractive girlfriend Penny.

There was, however, to be little enough time for our family for the next few months. The local elections of 7 May would almost certainly determine the election timing but because of the substantial boundary changes which affected more than half of the parliamentary constituencies it would be a complex task to interpret them correctly. However, Cecil had prepared an excellent team for the task and by Sunday 8 May the rather mixed local election results of the 7th had been translated into a forecast of Parliamentary seats likely to be gained and lost.

A meeting had been arranged at Chequers on Sunday morning to hear Cecil's review of the results and to consider the election timing.

The weather was foul that weekend and my Margaret and I were at Berkhamsted quietly relaxing on Saturday afternoon when Ian Gow rang. Ian wanted Cecil Parkinson and me to see the Prime Minister before the others arrived. He felt that she was hardening her views on timing and to avoid a difficult meeting in a larger gathering wanted us to set out the case for 9 June in private. I am not sure that Margaret Thatcher felt it was a terribly good idea but it was agreed that we would arrive at 11.30 a.m. on Sunday.

It was another awful wet day and as I approached the drive of Chequers I could see a mob of reporters and photographers waiting. My elderly little Citroen did not look like a ministerial car and, pulling my hat well down and switching off the windscreen wipers, I kept going at high speed until the last possible moment, then slammed on the brakes and was in the drive before being recognised. Cecil and Ian Gow were already with Margaret and we began a difficult discussion. She was adamant that she could not let down President Reagan and must go to the Williamsburg Conference of Western leaders from 28 to 30

May, which ruled out 9 June. In what was to be a rehearsal of the discussion in the larger group, Cecil and I advised that speculation was such that she would have to let her intentions be known the following day or it would be thought we could not make up our minds and the financial markets would soon be in great disarray. So whether she named the 9th or the 23rd the campaign would begin, making it either a four-week or a six-week campaign. By then the others were arriving and we broke off the discussion without reaching a conclusion.

We resumed with a presentation by Cecil on the polls and the local election results. By then we were all present: Willie Whitelaw, John Biffen (Leader of the House), Michael Jopling (Chief Whip), Cecil Parkinson (Chairman of the Party), myself, Ian Gow (Margaret's PPS), Tony Shrimsley (Central Office Press Officer) and David Wolfson from No. 10.

Cecil's analysis was based on some superb concentrated work by the Central Office psephologist Keith Britto. In two days the voting figures had been analysed ward by ward, compared with 1979, and constructed to forecast the results on the new constituency boundaries. The evidence showed that the Alliance was fading, the Liberals remaining the stronger partner, with Labour closing the gap. If Healey had been the leader or if he were to replace Foot before a 1984 election it would be touch and go. Cecil concluded, saying that on the most rigorous pessimistic assessment we should gain a majority of twenty-two in a June election.

We broke off for lunch and when Margaret asked our views we were unanimous for 9 June. To balance the discussion I suggested we assumed it would be the 23rd and looked at how we would handle that decision. The problem soon became clear. There was no way to avoid a statement by Friday at the latest. Margaret was rigorous in the extreme, pushing and pushing us to substantiate our advice. After all, we were only advisers, the decision would be hers and hers alone and we all knew it was a decision crucial not only to Britain but the whole Western Alliance. She had to be sure. Suddenly, still without giving her own view, she said we could not go for the 9th because we were not ready. Her speeches were not written – they never would be until the last moment, I thought. She could not let Reagan down – she could go by Concorde and be away only twenty-four hours. The manifesto was not ready – so at 3.30 a.m. we sat down to improve and revise it. By 5.30 it was almost done and I excused myself, escaping unrecognised once again, still not knowing what the decision would be.

Cecil told me afterwards that when everyone else had gone she told him she agreed it would be the 9th. She had certainly tested our arguments and our commitment and we were all on the line.

On Monday morning No. 10 phoned my office calling a Cabinet at 11.15. The Prime Minister told us that after consulting colleagues she had decided there should be a June election – on the 9th. 'Does anyone want to turn that decision over?' No one did. A short campaign is better than a long one for a government. We agreed to meet the next day to clear all outstanding business and the Prime Minister left to see the Queen.

Before the start of Tuesday's Cabinet we had a small meeting to agree the manifesto line on strikes in essential services and the political levy. With a great deal of help from Geoffrey Howe and Willie I convinced everyone that the criminal law would be useless against strikes in essential services, as would the imposition of no-strike agreements, and anyway we could not define an essential service in legal terms. I was unenthusiastic about making immunity conditional on observance of procedural agreements but agreed to say we would consult on the idea. The levy discussion was easier, everyone quickly agreeing my formula that we should invite the TUC to achieve a free and effective choice of whether or not to pay political levies and undertake to legislate if they failed to do so.

The Cabinet endorsed these proposals and we also agreed to add the abolition of the Greater London Council to the manifesto.

It was a productive morning and to my delight I was due to answer questions in the House at 2.30 p.m. where we had a marvellous time completely dominating the Opposition.

By the middle of the week, although Parliament was still sitting to clear up the legislative programme and to enact an interim Finance Bill following the budget, the election campaign was on. On Thursday I was in Scotland, on Friday in Wales, with lightning visits to my constituency in Chingford to ensure that my own campaign was ready. Apart from speeches by the Prime Minister, the main burden of the national campaign was to be carried by Cecil, Geoffrey Howe (as Chancellor) and me. It was hectic going and I saw Cecil regularly at Central Office to co-ordinate our efforts. Quite early in the campaign we fell to discussing what post I would like in the new Government. 'I don't mind,' I told him. 'Don't take the Home Office,' he advised. 'No one has gone on from there, it is the real bed of nails.' There had been a lot of speculation that I might go there but I told him I was unenthusiastic, saying, 'I prefer an economic department, Trade or Industry would be best.'

The days whirled past, with little time even for sleep and I almost missed the briefing for the Central Office press conference on Monday

23 May. After it was over I stayed on for a chat with Cecil Parkinson, partly to apologise for being late, but I had noticed he looked worried. I asked if anything was wrong and he told me he had 'a personal problem.' I invited him to share it, as perhaps I could help, and he told me that his secretary, Sara Keays, with whom he had had an affair, had told him she was pregnant. I told him to say nothing to anyone and do nothing except to play for time and we would talk about it again shortly.

In the meantime the election was going very well. A huge Labour split on defence was emerging with Foot and Callaghan clearly at odds. I was quite enjoying myself, my Margaret was taking the strain very well indeed and I was enjoying the great advantage of having the help of Michael Dobbs who was both my special adviser and a key member of the Saatchi campaign team. I was not able to spend as much time as I would have liked in Chingford and I began to think that my ambition of a 15,000 majority might not be achieved. To complicate matters I had to attend a Council of Ministers in Luxembourg a week before polling day to settle a directive on the control of the use of asbestos. It was a relief from electioneering – almost a holiday, especially as it was on 'wobbly Thursday' when much of the press, bored with our success, started pushing stories of a surge in support for the Alliance. So in 1983 I missed the trauma of the Prime Minister's worries. Despite these worries, it was so clear that we were winning handsomely that Cecil felt able to cancel a huge weekend press advertisement campaign.

By eve of poll everything pointed to a great victory, but I simply felt exhausted. I had another long talk with Cecil who knew he would be consulted about the new Cabinet and wanted to know what I hoped to do. I told him I did not mind but I did not want another two years at Employment.

We also talked about the problem of Miss Keays. I told him that he should not think of resignation and that I would stand by him whatever happened, but he was clearly worried, and torn between loyalty to his wife and his sense of responsibility to Miss Keays' child.

At last it was polling day and by the time my result was declared it was clear that we had won the election. In Chingford the Labour vote had collapsed, the Liberals had taken second place and my majority was increased by just thirty-one votes, a disappointing result. From the count I drove to the BBC to take part in their election night coverage. The atmosphere in the studio was terrible – almost everyone on the staff seemed to be in mourning with no attempt to conceal their regret that their side had lost – which added to my enjoyment of the night.

The day after the 1983 election, Friday, passed in a haze of exhaustion but by Saturday we had recovered enough to get away to Berkhamsted for the weekend, picking up our son William from the friend's house where he had wisely stayed during the election, which had coincided with his A levels at school. During the afternoon the Prime Minister telephoned to say that Cecil was going to the new combined Department of Trade and Industry and she hoped I would stay on at Employment. I could not conceal my disappointment, but that was that. Later in the day Cecil rang telling me that he had taken my advice and told the Prime Minister about Miss Keays. Subsequently, there was a good deal of press speculation that the Keays affair had tipped the balance against Cecil going to the Foreign Office and led him to the DTI, which otherwise might have fallen to me. I told him I was pretty fed up but I would not complain as I had always said I would do any job which Margaret asked.

At least on Sunday it was gardening weather and I was interrupted only by a call to consult me on my new team of Junior Ministers. I managed to keep the excellent Peter Morrison and secure his promotion, and gained John Gummer and Alan Clark as my two new juniors. At least that was satisfactory, and my spirits began to recover. By Monday life was back to normal, with a very cheerful lunch at No. 10. I decided that there was a lot to be done in the Department and I could enjoy getting on with it.

Generally the political scene looked good. Inflation had fallen to 3.7 per cent (although it was expected to go back to 5 per cent or 6 per cent in a winter peak), the Labour Party was tearing itself to shreds and my Margaret and I had spent a happy weekend with friends in the country.

The next day I had a useful talk with Len Murray, telling him how I intended to proceed on my proposed legislation and offering to consult the TUC about the political levy. I took his advice not to do so before the conference season and allowed the conversation to run more widely. He asked what I would want of the unions and I told him their prime role should be to help improve the performance of the firms which provided their members with jobs, and a more general role in supporting better training and vocational education. Len Murray suggested we might talk about where more jobs might arise; but I was cautious – that could easily slide into asking Government to become involved in job creation. However it was a positive step in line with my call for unions to accept the new Thatcherite *status quo*.

Life settled down to the usual ministerial round of meetings. Those on the special employment measures, the Technical and Vocational Education Initiative and YTS went well, and we also agreed on the sort of papers we would need for our discussions on the employment outlook in September. Others, notably those on public expenditure where Nigel Lawson as the new Chancellor took a tough line on public expenditure, and those on the pay of Members of Parliament, were less easy.

I was busily preparing my statement of 12 July on the next steps in industrial relations law reform: the requirement for fair elections by secret ballot to the governing bodies of unions, pre-strike ballots as a condition of immunity for any strikes, consultation on the need for adequate procedure agreements in essential services, periodic ballots on political funds and consultations on the operation of the 'contracting out' system. In the absence of Eric Varley, Giles Radice acted as Labour's front-bench spokesman and managed to miss or muddle every important point.

The statement had a very good press, except in the *Morning Star*, the *Mirror* and, to my irritation, the *Daily Express* where I was described as 'timid tiptoe Tebbit'. Quite by chance I was due to lunch with the Chairman of Express Newspapers, Lord Matthews, who raised yet again the issue of 'lay off' clauses. I told him bluntly I would not change my mind – least of all to give Fleet Street managers a right to lay off staff during industrial action. 'Fleet Street's incompetent, frightened, divided employers would only sell it to the unions in some miserable deal to buy off a strike,' I told him, adding that until he had broken the closed shop I did not think it was me who should be criticised for timidity. We parted on strained terms but the discussion proved to have been useful!

During a long talk the next day Cecil said he was puzzled why I wanted to stir up trouble, as he saw it, over the political levy. I explained it was part of my proposed 'grand strategy'. Essentially that was to break up the Alliance, leaving the Liberals once again a dustbin for wasted votes; and to encourage a split in the TUC which could bring social democrats and right-wing Labour people together with backing from the sane trade unions. I hoped that if the ballots for political funds were accompanied by a real national debate led by the media it might precipitate a questioning of why the funds were wasted on the support of an unelectable muddled semi-Marxist party. The idea of creating an electable rival to the Conservative Party I agreed sounded crazy but it could set the scene for a long-lasting consensus on Thatcherite terms with no risk of a regression into Socialism. What was more, I told him, it would ensure victories for us in 1987/88 and 91/92 giving time for our reforms to become deeply established. I am not sure that Cecil was convinced but in 1988 as I look at the Labour Party, the broken Alliance and the splintering TUC I still wonder if there is any other way in which a sensible alternative government could be born.

My pre-election talk of the post-election consensus in which unions would find it possible to talk to the Government and my discussion with Len Murray seemed to have borne fruit. In late July I had discussions with the TUC employment committee and got indications of what sort of letter from me would receive a positive response. By the end of the month the TUC had formally voted (fourteen to eleven) to talk to me about my proposed legislation. This way of going forward had its dangers of sliding into the bad old beer-and-sandwiches routine but it seemed worth the risk if we could establish the idea that the unions' opposition to my legislation had been overcome.

Things generally seemed to be taking a turn for the better. Almost by chance, though perhaps more by my wife's mixture of instinct and determination, we discovered an almost ideal house in Devon and began negotiations to purchase it. We managed to get away to the Mediterranean for an early August break and on our return William heard that his A levels had turned out well enough to justify having a shot at the Oxbridge examinations in November.

My meetings with the TUC on YTS allowances (a touchy subject for them) and on my proposed repeal of the Truck Acts went pretty well, and, rather unexpectedly, the unemployment figures on 2 September showed the first underlying fall after forty-five months on the upward trend.

A few days later I saw Cecil who told me that he and his wife Ann were determined to stay together. Miss Keays, it seemed, was furious, and the whole story was about to break in the press. In despair, Cecil told me he had no option but to resign: 'I will be gone by the morning.' I implored him not to do so. More politicians than him had had affairs outside their marriages. A good number had deserted their wives, married their mistresses and continued in office; why should he resign because his marriage had outlasted his mistress? He said it was better to resign than be hounded out of office. 'No,' I said, 'and not just for your sake. If they get you, they'll want to go on and drag someone else down. They're like wolves behind the sledge – if they drag one of us off, the blood-lust will be worse and they'll be after the rest. You've got to stay.'

I had to see the Prime Minister later in the day and I told her of Cecil's mood, offering my opinion that she should ask him to stay as Secretary of State but stand down as Party Chairman, to avoid difficulties at the Party Conference. She had arranged to see him following our meeting and by mutual consent I stayed on. Margaret was wonderfully supportive and Cecil left, still as Secretary of State.

Over the next two days the Prime Minister's group on the prospects for employment met at Chequers. We were perhaps too large a group but it was deliberately broadly based – from Peter Walker to Professor Alan Walters. I was well pleased with the conclusions, particularly on the emphasis on training for the unemployed.

The Parkinson story had still not broken in the press when the next evening (the 7th) the Chief Whip, John Wakeham, telephoned from Chequers to sound me out on who should succeed Cecil as Chairman of the Party. I suggested we needed someone who would not be compared with Cecil – perhaps a good peer or businessman who would concentrate on organisation and not the political role. The problem, however, was who?

Despite protracted telephone conversations with Margaret we were unable to identify a candidate for the chairmanship who answered this specification, and with more and more risk of the Parkinson story breaking she decided that John Gummer's presentational skills and his youthfulness made him the best candidate for the job. I had my reservations as I thought he would be unfairly criticised for being too young and too junior, perpetually suffering by contrast with Cecil. However it was arranged that John would go to see the Prime Minister at two o'clock on Tuesday to be told his fate. I asked him to come and see me when he returned, to tell him I thought he had a very difficult time ahead and to offer him some advice.

Later that month, having got their conference out of the way, the TUC executive came to see me to deliver their views on my proposed Bill. Although there were twenty of them only Bill Keys and Len Murray spoke and they were pretty predictable but quite good humoured. Once they had gone I headed for the airport and off to Athens for an informal council of EEC Employment Ministers. I was concerned at the number of crazy Socialist schemes being proposed by the Commission and on my arrival I asked how the discussions between officials had gone. 'Very well indeed,' came the answer, 'we have made no progress at all.' The meeting was a complete waste of time – simply blocking one nonsense after another – and I was relieved to get back home for the weekend.

October started well with the election of Kinnock to replace Foot as leader of the Labour Party. Despite the early talk of his 'charisma', I had never rated Kinnock as anything but a windbag whose incoherent speech springs from an incoherent mind and I was sure he would pose the Prime Minister few problems. Within days, however, the Parkinson story broke in the press, posing more than enough problems for us. The

Sunday papers were pretty hard on Cecil, the most damaging article was a human and perceptive piece by Simon Hoggart in the *Observer* because it focused on his apparent changes of mind. It was a bad start to our conference but my part at least went well. With the theme, 'We are a party of trades unionists now,' I proclaimed our intention to give by law to trade unionists the rights they had been denied by their own leaders. Industrial relations reform used to be seen as a minefield but Jim Prior and I had gone through the minefield step by step without treading on a mine. 'Indeed the only casualties so far have been on the TUC side. They have been left hanging on the barbed wire of their own defences', I said. My reforms, I claimed, would lead to better industrial relations and thereby more jobs. It was a mixture of toughness, humour and a determinedly cautious approach that went down very well indeed. I returned to the platform to hear and support Cecil Parkinson who made a good speech although he was clearly very tense. That night I believed he could survive the Keays affair.

We were up early next morning and on the road to London soon after 8 a.m. I had decided to miss the Prime Minister's speech as it was Lord Mayor's Prizegiving Day at the City of London School in which our son William as Head Boy played a major part, including his first public speech, and we had promised William we would be there. By 10 a.m. we heard on the car radio that Cecil Parkinson had resigned. Not long after returning from William's prizegiving I received a call from a television producer telling me that the *Sun* newspaper was publishing a story that Cecil had spoken bitterly of the failure of his colleagues to support him, and quoting him as saying, 'but my worst enemy in the Cabinet over these weeks has been Norman Tebbit.' It was supposed to have been said to the editor of the *Daily Express*, but the Express carried no such story. I was deeply upset and phoned several friends for advice, then suddenly I made up my mind – I would go to see Cecil. It was already 10.30 p.m. and my Margaret said she wanted to come – I said no but agreed to take William with me for company. Cecil's home was surrounded by press men so I drove past, parked a little way away and sent William armed with a note to Cecil and a copy of the next day's *Sun* which we had bought in Fleet Street. William returned to say Cecil would of course be pleased to see me, and the pair of us walked quickly through the photographers and into the house. Cecil was pretty miserable. He did feel he had been badly let down, but assured me he had not only not said I had been an enemy but knew I had been a friend. We talked about his future, whether he would stay in politics or not. He was preparing to go abroad for a holiday and we agreed to meet on his return – before he made any irrevocable decisions. Well after midnight William and I pushed through the press men outside and headed for home.

Late next day, Saturday the 13th, the Prime Minister rang from Chequers to ask me to replace Cecil at the Department of Trade and Industry. Tom King was to succeed me and Nick Ridley was to go to Transport. As I was on TV the next day in the lunchtime programme *Weekend World* the announcement would be held back for about three hours after that. Within an hour of the announcement Sir Brian Hayes, one of the permanent secretaries at DTI, arrived at our flat to brief me and leave some important papers. I had gained the job I had wanted but in a way that I hated – at Cecil's expense.

10

Trade and Industry

I soon realised what a huge job I had inherited. Indeed when I handed over to Lord Young two years later he was given an additional Cabinet Minister to assist him. With a vast Department spanning many interests there were normally three or four dozen issues being dealt with at any one time in the Secretary of State's office – not counting those being brewed up all over the Department. Unlike the relatively simple pattern of matters I had dealt with at the Department of Employment, I realised that I now faced a huge patchwork of often rather unrelated issues, all clamouring for attention. At the time I took over, the requests of British Aerospace for launch aid to enable the company to participate in the A320 European 150-seat airliner and the Rolls-Royce request for similar aid for the V2500 aero-engine (an Anglo-American-German-Japanese venture) were coming toward a decision. British Leyland remained in difficulties, the negotiations on the completion of the deal with Nissan to establish a factory in Britain, the denationalisation of British Telecom, the shaping of the new legal structure in the City, the House of Fraser affair; and competition policy – these were all demanding decisions.

Fortunately, among those I inherited from Cecil was Callum McCarthy, my Principal Private Secretary, a man of immense ability who brought in two excellent assistants Ruth Thompson and Andrew Lansley. Together with Edward Blades who organised my diary and a team of other assistants they formed an office of unusually high quality. The merger of the Departments of Trade and Industry had however left me with the embarrassment of two Permanent Secretaries of great ability, Sir Brian Hayes and Sir Anthony Rawlinson, and I realised that the first requirement for integration of the Department was to have only one.

Whilst the most senior official in a Government Department is the Permanent Secretary, the tone and success of its work depends above all on the quality of the next rank down, the deputy Secretaries. Whilst I had had two at the Department of Employment I now had thirteen at DTI. I soon began to find my way through the Department, by meetings with all of my Ministers – six in all – and the key officials. I asked Jeffrey Sterling, the Chairman of P&O who had been first Keith Joseph's industrial adviser, then Cecil's, to stay on and I asked Michael Dobbs to continue as my special adviser and Iain Mills as my Parliamentary Private Secretary.

Cecil had all but settled the Department's 1984/5 expenditure with the Chief Secretary to the Treasury and I soon finalised the deal. That left me clear to become a member of the 'Star Chamber' under Willie Whitelaw's chairmanship to resolve the differences between other departments and the Treasury. It was a time-consuming task but to watch Willie at work again was worth every bit of it. He is so subtle a master of his craft that really to appreciate his skill one has to be in his confidence and know in advance his objectives and tactics. Despite his reputation as an old waffler, Willie has one of the sharpest political brains in Westminster – and I learned a great deal from him.

In between the Star Chamber meetings I began to clear a whole mass of policy decisions. Cecil had bravely stopped the legal action by the Office of Fair Trading against the Stock Exchange on the latter's undertaking to abolish fixed commissions on share dealings. Had he not done so our City markets would have been bogged down in fruitless court hearings whilst their rivals were winning business away from London. His decision opened the way for 'Big Bang' – the new dealing systems – but it left me with the task of creating a new regulatory structure for the City at a time of unprecedented change. In October 1983 the City could not agree on any aspect of the new regulatory system – except that it should be voluntary, not statutory. It took me over a year of patient discussions to build on the excellent report from Professor Gower to create a consensus on which to base my White Paper in 1985 and the subsequent legislation.

I found my days were all too well filled with briefing sessions although fortunately I was reasonably familiar with most of the issues, either from my earlier days as a Junior Minister or from Cabinet committees. Now I had to dig deeper into the details and initiate either policy or administrative action across a vast number of activities.

The Bill to denationalise British Telecom had been well on its way through Parliament before the election but we now had to start all over again. At the same time I had to make sure that each step of the flotation process was taken in due order and on time. Kenneth Baker was my Junior Minister looking after this but I found it necessary to have a weekly progress meeting to satisfy myself that everything was on schedule. In addition I had constantly to arbitrate between the claims of Mercury and British Telecom – no easy task itself.

I found my problem children, from my days as Keith Joseph's Junior Minister, were mostly still around although gradually they were being reformed. British Leyland remained a real problem but Rolls-Royce, under the chairmanship of Bill Duncan, and British Steel, under Bob Haslam, were progressing well. However Robert Atkinson had proved a great disappointment at British Shipbuilders and I was relieved to find Graham Day, a tough Canadian, in charge.

I was also busy redesigning regional policy, the structure of which had remained unchanged for over thirty years whatever the party in power, giving huge subsidies to rich companies to make investments they would have made anyway and attracting some scarcely viable businesses prone to collapse in any recession. I refined further the areas which qualified for help, and allowed potentially mobile service industries as well as manufacturing businesses to qualify, relying less on automatic grants for capital investment and more on the job-creating potential of projects in targetted areas of highest unemployment.

Competition issues, take-over bids and mergers are always a potential political hazard. I was determined to defuse and de-politicise as many as possible by applying a consistent policy based on the principle that unless there are compelling reasons of public policy to the contrary, then the owners of an asset should be left free to dispose of it, or retain it without political interference. Competition, then, became the key consideration in this policy area. The most usual cause to restrain a disposal or purchase of a business is the threat of a significant distortion of the market and restriction of competition by monopoly or market dominance. I let it be clearly known that that philosophy would guide my decisions and although I preserved the option of acting to block a proposed merger on grounds of the national interest it was a power I never had to exercise. As a result, by matching actions to words, my policy came to be seen as consistent and predictable.

My resolve was soon tested by the bid from the German Allianz insurance company to purchase Eagle Star Insurance which, despite political pressures, I refused to block or refer to the Monopolies and Mergers Commission. It was also reinforced later by my examination of the battle between Lonrho and the House of Fraser for control of Harrods.

Perhaps in retrospect I should have made more obvious my belief that in many spheres of business, markets have become either global or – with 1992 in view – European-Community-wide, and that the traditional British view of the relevant market being the British market alone is outdated. That is why in British markets where foreign-owned business can achieve market entry and potential significant market share (air travel for example) I have seen no reason to fragment our industry in a quixotic attempt to promote competition between British minnow companies in a world of international whales – if not sharks.

In illustration of this, on 31 October 1983 I privately advised Adam Thomson of British Caledonian Airways that once British Airways was in the private sector I could see no reason for perpetually weakening two flag carriers and that the only question was whether he and his financial backers, or the privatised British Airways, would initiate a take-over or reverse take-over bid. Five years later British Caledonian's financial difficulties precipitated a successful bid from British Airways but if Adam Thomson and his backers had found enough courage early enough it could have been the other way around.

In many ways the DTI acts as a merchant bank, most often for clients (like nationalised industries) who can go nowhere else and with only one – usually unwilling – source of funds, the Treasury. Negotiating between businesses like British Shipbuilders, the Post Office, British Leyland and British Steel, to clear their corporate plans, agree financing with the Treasury and often with the EEC Commission too if public subsidy was involved, was the staple diet of work, sometimes more difficult, sometimes less. However in 1983 I had two exceptional major applications for funds, one from Rolls-Royce – then still nationalised – the other from British Aerospace asking for launch aid to help finance major new projects. The British Aerospace request was in respect of their share of the Airbus A320 150-seat airliner which has come into service and now has 319 firm orders from 20 customers in its order book. It was not easy to make the business case to compete headlong with Boeing and McDonnell Douglas but I had no doubt that if Europe was to maintain a civil aircraft industry it had to be done. Nor was it made easier by having to double-guess BAe's negotiating stance and having the Treasury double-guessing mine. Fortunately I had very good relationships with both Austin Pearce and Ray Lygo, the Chairman and Chief Executive of the company. Those relationships were preserved from misunderstandings by my habit of producing an aide-mémoire of decisions, or differences reached in our meetings before we parted after a meeting. Indeed sometimes over a drink whilst the aide-mémoire was being typed a difference could be overcome and the note rewritten. Perhaps if my successor had followed the same technique the Westland affair might not have been his undoing.

It all took time, but bit by bit I was able to close the gap between the Treasury and the company, and as things have worked out the Treasury will gain a far better return on their investment than it expected. However, it was not until March 1984 that I finally closed that deal.

The Rolls-Royce V2500 engine, designed to suit, amongst other aircraft, the Airbus 320, was an easier project to sell to the Treasury. The participation of the American engine-maker Pratt and Whitney gave a commercial substance which impressed even that Department and that of the Germans and Japanese. This was also a good promise of sales in those countries. So I had only to bargain on the amount of money involved. Such arguments with the Treasury have a *Catch-22* air – if the project cannot be entirely financed by the private sector it cannot be viable, and should not be supported; but if one puts up a good business project then the Treasury says private money should be available and it does not need to be government supported!

Life at the DTI often took an unexpected turn. It was in November 1983 that Sam Toy the chairman of Ford UK first came to talk to me about the company's problems in the commercial vehicle market, which had collapsed to only about half of its peak volume of a few years earlier. The talk led to serious consideration of a merger of the commercial vehicle businesses of Ford and BL which proved abortive and was overtaken by the almost successful attempt to secure a similar deal with General Motors. It also led to the talks on a take-over of the BL cars business which were similarly aborted in early 1986. It was interesting to see how Ford's view of BL changed as the American company realised that in some aspects of industrial relations and labour productivity BL was already ahead of Ford and technical respect grew to the stage of serious discussion of a Ford proposal for the two companies to buy engines from each other, and eventually in 1986 to an interest in a purchase of the whole BL cars business.

By the turn of the year I had good reason to be satisfied with the progress I had made. The negotiations on the A320 and V2500 were going well. I had published my White Paper on the new regional aid policy, re-established my relationships with all the nationalised industries for which I was responsible and had given a new impetus to the privatisation programmes of British Telecom, British Shipbuilders and Jaguar. I also published, for the first time, a statement of the Department's aims, setting them out in a detail and clarity that I believe has acted as a model for other Ministers.

I had also insisted that all my Junior Ministers worked out with their officials work programmes for the next six and twelve months, setting objectives where appropriate and dates by which they would be achieved. Later in 1984 the programmes were agreed and we began to see whether objectives were being achieved on time or not – a useful discipline.

Together with the successful use of my trades union legislation by Mr Eddie Shah, the newspaper proprietor, against brutal mass picketing by print unions, and by Mercury against the Post Office Engineering Union for unlawfully refusing to interconnect Mercury circuits with those of British Telecom, the year seemed to be ending on a good note.

At home my Margaret had survived all the pressures. We had become grandparents in November, John had announced his engagement, and we enjoyed an extremely happy family Christmas. Fortunately we did not know that it was to be the last of its kind and that never again would Margaret stand in her kitchen at Christmas or wrap presents for her family.

I was conscious of the fact that because of my heavy workload, mainly on industrial affairs, I had been able to do little foreign travel as a trade Minister, although I had made a brief visit to Saudi Arabia in December. Determined to put that right I left for India on 7th January. Although it was expensive (the taxpayer rarely pays for wives to accompany Ministers), I took my Margaret with me. I felt she deserved a break and the chance to see something of India. It was a successful trip and we carried out our engagements in grand style. I had a long and friendly meeting with Mrs Gandhi and a most interesting private lunch with Rajiv Gandhi and his wife. Mrs Gandhi I found most impressive, and, unlike most people, I found her easy to talk to and surprisingly pragmatic. I also liked Rajiv and on my return expressed the view that he would succeed his mother when the time came and probably cope reasonably well with that most difficult job, little realising how soon that would be.

In early February I was in Washington bluntly warning the Americans of the dangers to the economy of the free world and even to NATO of protectionism, extraterritoriality (the attempt to impose US law over transactions outside America), unitary taxation (a similar practice in relation to company taxation) and agricultural subsidy. At the annual Davos conference, I followed the same theme. That event is attended by a very wide range of business people and politicians, including many ministers, heads of governments and indeed leaders of the oppositions. I found that these personal contacts were a valuable investment of time which often helped to build bridges in formal negotiations, perhaps even years later.

At home most things were moving on well although I seemed to be in near constant negotiations with the EEC Commission to clear the funding of British Steel, the Airbus, Rolls-Royce V2500 and Nissan arrangements and many smaller issues. (Having since seen the muddle over the 1988 takeover of the Rover Group by British Aerospace I am sure that I was right to clear the ground in Brussels before publicly committing Government or companies to the terms of a deal, however attractive the instant action announcements before deals are really done may look at the time.)

After months of very hard negotiating (mostly by my officials) I announced to Parliament on 1 February that, stemming from the earlier agreement of January 1981, I had signed an agreement with the Nissan motor company to establish an assembly plant in Britain which both sides expected to lead to full manufacturing in due course – as it indeed has. It was a great coup to have convinced a Japanese car maker that Britain was the best place within the EEC in which to build cars, marking a complete change of perception about Britain's future. Then a month later on 1 March I made a statement in Parliament on the British aerospace industry including the commitment to the new Anglo-Italian EH 101 helicopter, funding for the Airbus A320, BAe's decision to go ahead with its ATP prop jet airliner, funding for the Rolls-Royce V2500 engine in partnership with Pratt and Whitney, and the collaborative agreement of Rolls with GEC, Pratt and Whitney's main commercial rival. It was an impressive package, although the Rolls/GEC collaboration was later ended when Rolls found themselves strong enough to go it alone in developing very large engines, and it set the pattern for the industry for a decade.

I was finding myself in too many difficult battles with the Treasury so Nigel Lawson and I began to meet informally to try to head off some of our clashes. As the Prime Minister had said to me earlier, 'You and I and Nigel must stick together': it was unhelpful if our Departments were constantly at war. Some of our differences were over arcane (but vital) matters concerning the control of public expenditure, particularly how we could sensibly avoid EEC spending rising, often in the very areas where we wished to reduce public expenditure. Others were irritating pieces of Whitehall politics in which junior Treasury officials delayed decisions whilst second-guessing my judgement on quite minor matters. At one stage I almost lost Professor Carsberg, whom I wanted to appoint as Director General of OFTEL (the regulatory body for telecommunications), because approval of his contract was delayed. One incident was resolved only when I told the Chief Secretary, Peter Rees, that I would announce a decision that day whether he had agreed or not.

Fortunately Nigel and I have a great deal in common. We are both pretty well 'leak proof', both liberal Thatcherites and we can both recognise when a disagreement is best settled. We soon found we could resolve many problems between us without involving other Ministers, and Nigel generously gave me plenty of opportunity to contribute to his thinking on budget policies at their earliest stages.

The Department of Trade and Industry was involved in many commercial matters, not least a huge and complex privatisation programme and I found the interventions of some colleagues irritating beyond measure. One issue on which we always had a Cabinet of experts without experience was BL. I proposed to achieve privatisation by separating the operating companies – Jaguar, Land Rover etc. – into discrete companies each initially wholly owned by a holding company, then selling 75 per cent of each company leaving 25 per cent in the holding company. In that way, when only the hard core business of volume car making (what became the Rover Group) was left in 100-per-cent ownership, the BL group would still have a market value because of its holdings in Jaguar and other businesses and we would not have to pay someone to take it away. To my regret I was unable to convince my colleagues and it was decided to sell the whole of each business separately, starting with Jaguar. I had had approaches from General Motors (and another was to come from BMW) to buy Jaguar; but I preferred the flotation route both to avoid foreign ownership which would have been unpopular and because it gave a fairer valuation of Jaguar. However it was clear to me that flotation followed by an early take-over bid by a foreign manufacturer would have looked very untidy and I fought for a very long term 'Golden Share' arrangement to frustrate such bids. Unhappily I could secure agreement only to a golden share lasting until the end of 1990, which may raise a touchy issue of take-over battles in the run up to a general election.

I returned to my office on the day of the decision in a most unhappy mood. 'I hate losing – especially when I am right,' I observed to my officials who very kindly observed that fortunately I seldom lost!

Fortunately only the Treasury and the Prime Minister were privy to

the various expressions of interest in Inmos, the silicon chip manufacturers. I had strongly resisted putting the company into liquidation
despite its losses and voracious appetite for investment cash, and I
rejected several near derisory offers, mostly from America. No deal was
easy because the founders of the firm had built themselves into a very
secure position although the taxpayer had put almost all the investment
into the firm. Eventually, however, I completed a sale to Thorn EMI
for £95 million, a better return than had seemed possible for our £65-
million investment. Peter Shore, for the Labour Party, foolishly claimed
I had sold the company as it was 'moving into strong and growing
profitability', a move which had still not been completed even four years
later.

I also fought a long-standing battle to achieve clarification of one key
aspect of the long and successful Whitehall battle to reduce the costs of
Government. At first the inefficiencies were so great that cutting manpower was the priority, leading automatically to reduced costs.
However, reducing staff could lead to a sacrifice of revenue or poorer cost
effectiveness, making priorities less easy to be distinguished. Sometimes
manpower limits could be met by hiving off – simply turning civil
servants into employees of quangoes or private sector business – which
might be a genuine cut in government numbers or simply a clever dodge.

The task of getting clarity into this area of policy particularly affected
the Companies Registration Office which keeps the returns of about a
million companies. Its manpower had been squeezed, its workload had
increased and a huge backlog of defaulting companies which had not
filed returns had built up. I could not allow that to continue and insisting
that privatisation was not appropriate and that hiving off as a quango
was a poor managerial way of concealing the reality of the situation, I
obtained agreement to increase the staff and improve the service. No
doubt such practical attitudes led to a *Times* article headed 'Is Norman
Tebbit Growing Soggy?' 'Soggy,' or 'Abrasive', according to *The Times*
political correspondent shortly afterwards, 'Tebbit is Top Choice as
Thatcher's Successor'!

Amongst the long-running issues beyond my Departmental responsibilities were the complex negotiations with China over the future of
Hong Kong, the row over union membership at GCHQ (the intelligence
services communication centre), and the threat of extreme left-wing
local authorities to defy the law by incurring illegal expenditure or
making illegal rate demands which threatened a city like Liverpool
with bankruptcy and administrative breakdown. Cool heads and steady
nerves were needed week after week – indeed month after month in the

face of sensational press comment, unrelieved misconceptions from the BBC and outbreaks of cold feet and hot-heads in the parliamentary party.

By far the biggest issue however was the coal strike which had been gradually spreading. Scargill knew he could not obtain a majority for a national coal strike and sought to bring the miners out region by region, which under the rules of the Mineworkers' Union, did not require balloting. Unfortunately the provisions of the 1984 Act which withdrew immunity from strikes not endorsed by ballots were not yet in effect or the coal strike could have been defeated almost before it began. The Cabinet committee dealing with the strike soon became a major commitment and as the dispute grew it increasingly affected British Steel.

I had my good and bad days. 4 April, when I spoke at a press gallery lunch was a bad one. My speech about the failure of nationalisation and our privatisation programme was dull and not well prepared. Unwisely I added an off-the-cuff remark commenting on how different the coal industry might have looked had it gone back to private enterprise twenty years earlier and compounded my error by adding, 'Ah, there's a thought.' I knew it was a mistake as soon as I had said it and the next day's papers were full of nonsense talk of Tebbit revealing secret privatisation plans for NCB. Rather than let the issue hang over that morning's Cabinet I intervened before Peter Walker's report on the coal disputes to express my regrets at having made such an unhelpful remark. My apology was accepted and the matter was never raised again.

On the other hand the following weekend's *Mail on Sunday* ran a full-page article on the inevitability and rightness of me succeeding Margaret as Prime Minister!

Later that month we made our move from Berkhamsted to our new home in Devon. We were delighted with the house and began the long programme of turning a neglected wood into a garden. On each visit it became more of a wrench to return to London and the heavy load of the office again! However, once back at work, the excitement took over and I was ready for work again. Within days of returning from our first long stay in Devon I had rebuffed Opposition demands for me to interfere with Lonrho's management of the *Observer* newspaper – seen in some quarters as favouritism towards Mr Rowland, it was simply playing the issue straight down the line – a policy which I found usually paid. Then with agreement reached on most of the major issues, on 2 May I made a Commons statement on the privatisation of British Telecom including the unprecedented requirement that it should cut its prices (after allowing for inflation) by 3 per cent a year for the first four years in the private sector. That price cut formula has now been tightened to RPI − $4\frac{1}{2}$%. This achievement on its own justifies privatisation.

Three weeks later I made a statement confirming the privatisation of Jaguar. Together with the announcement of the sale of Inmos in July and the beginnings of denationalisation of British Shipbuilders' yards I was, I thought, hustling things along.

My second trip to America as Secretary of State in May came as something of a relief from Whitehall and Westminster. This time I went to the West Coast − carrying my usual messages about protectionism, extra territoriality and unitary taxation − to see Boeing and McDonnell Douglas in search of opportunities for transatlantic co-operation which might help BAe and Airbus in the American market. It was a useful trip, especially on the problem of unitary taxation and I returned to London in a good mood only to be saddened by the news that my mother, whose health had been failing, had died earlier that morning. The sadness of her funeral a few days later was lightened by the happiness of our elder son John's wedding the next day. Both he and William were at their best. John stood, typically casually, at the gate of the Church, calmly directing reporters who wanted interviews with him to the chief usher, William, who with the authority of a fit young man of six feet four and sixteen stone told them they were unwelcome!

By the summer the coal dispute was at a critical stage. Leon Brittan at the Home Office had a most delicate task. He had to avoid exceeding his powers although there was a clear need to encourage the various police forces to co-operate more closely than they had ever done before to overcome violence of the flying pickets. There were instances of near riot − involving extreme violence, notably at the Orgreave coke works − but there was no backdown as at Saltley in the 1973–4 strike. However the pace of the courts in convicting and sentencing offenders was all too slow, and for a while it looked to the public as though violence would pay. Gradually the appointment of more stipendiary magistrates eased the backlog of cases but the equivocal attitude of the Opposition made life very difficult for local magistrates who lived and worked in the mining communities. Fortunately the refusal of Scargill to allow a ballot undermined the legitimacy of the dispute sufficiently to prevent the spread of sympathy strikes. Although the railways were affected and there were attempts to bring out the dockers, Scargill found no real solidarity in the union movement and faced bitter opposition from the steelworkers who were kept on side quite brilliantly by Bob Haslam and Bob Scholey of British Steel.

Before the House rose for the summer recess I was involved in a messy row with the Select Committee on Trade and Industry and its Chairman, Ken Warren, an old friend and supporter. The Committee had asked for confidential papers concerning alternative draft corporate plans from British Shipbuilders. The information in the papers was not particularly important but releasing them would set a new precedent which would allow Select Committees to obtain highly confidential commercial papers in a world where leaks could prejudice vital deals being patiently negotiated over many months. Even worse, if leaked, the EEC Commission might well gain information entirely unhelpful to our negotiations on a wide range of issues – a stupid mistake other EEC governments would be unlikely to make. Having consulted other colleagues it was agreed that as it affected all Departments, I should refuse to allow the papers to be supplied as an act of principle. When the chips went down, however, the Chief Whip advised that he could not win a vote in the House on the issue and I had to give in. The incident left a nasty taste in my mouth. Not since my early days in BOAC had I been put out on a limb and then seen it sawn off in that way.

There was no point in grumbling, if a misjudgement had been made I had to carry the can and that was that, and I simply developed ways of handling commercially sensitive information within nationalised industries which kept it out of the reach of the Select Committees.

Although Parliament takes a long break through August and September, Whitehall's break – certainly under this Prime Minister – is much shorter. After a blissful but all too short time enjoying glorious weather at our home in Devon I was back at work by the end of August. It was after a Chequers lunch and ministerial meeting on 2 September that I stayed on to tell the Prime Minister that I felt I must resolve the issue of my two Permanent Secretaries. I told Margaret that I had cut down my deputy secretaries from thirteen to eleven, I could give up one of my Junior Ministers, but it all looked pretty odd if we were 100 per cent overmanned at the top. The talk of my ministerial team took us on to the reshuffle expected in about a week's time and I bid for the people I wanted in my Department. She, however, broadened the conversation saying, with an intent look at me, that she had her best communicator in the least political department. I told her that people thought it a rather unpolitical department because the awkward issues had been managed without letting them become political issues. We could not of course foresee just how political the Department would become with the Westland crisis and the Land Rover/General Motors row. I said I wanted to stay at DTI for another year, by which time British Telecom, British Steel, the new city regulations, British Shipbuilders (notably the decision to privatise the warship-building yards, a process completed only twenty months later) and even British Leyland should be set firmly on course and I could hand over a Department with few difficult issues to resolve. After that I would do anything, although I made it clear that despite the rumours already running I would prefer to have another Department rather than become Party Chairman.

September continued busy but with few major public initiatives from me although I was able to approve the purchase of ICL by STC subject to ITT of America reducing its holding in the latter to 25 per cent. That was a quiet triumph for Michael Edwardes who in a year as Chairman of ICL accomplished our aim of finding a good British owner for the company capable of funding its investment programme. After that my main Departmental concern was to manage our annual negotiations with the Treasury and to prepare for the Party Conference.

11

Brighton and After

Unusually I had arrived at Brighton for the Conference with both my Departmental speech and one on wider aspects of Conservative policy almost complete. Everything seemed to be well under control. I was entirely relaxed and both speeches went well.

On Thursday the 12th Frank Johnson's column in *The Times* put it as wittily as ever, under the headline, 'Tebbit Succeeds to Darling Title.' 'Mr Norman Tebbit,' he wrote, 'was yesterday appointed Darling of the Conservative Conference in succession to Mr Michael Heseltine, who had held the title for eight years ... Mr Tebbit became Darling at a simple ceremony involving his receiving a longer standing ovation than Mr Heseltine the previous day.' I chuckled as I read Frank Johnson but I was looking forward to getting down to Devon for a long weekend. We were very much in love with our home there and had wanted to get away from the Conference on Thursday without waiting for the Prime Minister's speech which we could have seen on television. However, I had missed her speech in 1983 when we had attended William's school prize-giving, and I decided that rather than give some mischievous columnist a story if my absence was noticed we would stay on.

There was the usual round of too many parties and receptions to attend but skipping most of them we went to the Party Treasurer, Alistair McAlpine's soirée, as it was always known. Alistair is an excellent host offering exceptionally good food and drink, and company too – provided one was selective about all three. There were always journalists aplenty (as Alistair's relations with the 'hacks' were excellent), a good number of parliamentary and Government colleagues and most of the Party establishment. I have never discovered at what time Alistair's parties ended but my wife and I drew stumps around midnight and, walking down to our room, encountered the BBC political correspondent, John Cole, on his way upstairs. As John and I chatted, Margaret excused herself saying she was tired and would head for bed. We gossiped on for a while before I said, 'John, if I wake my wife just as she's gone to sleep I'll be in terrible trouble so I'd best be off to bed,' and we retired to our rooms.

It seldom takes me long to go to sleep and that night was no exception and we were both sleeping soundly when the bomb exploded.

We were woken by the blast which I recognised at once for what it was. There was just time for Margaret to call out in alarm and for me to reply, 'It's a bomb!' before the ceiling came crashing down on us and then, in a hail of debris, the floor collapsed, catapulting us down under an avalanche of bricks, timber and plaster. The force of the impact was indescribable – blow after blow as the debris smashed on to my left side. Something tore into my abdomen with a terrible blow and I heard my very guts sloshing inside me. There was a colossal impact tearing a great hole in my side, then I stopped falling – with no idea where, nor even which way up I was, as the debris cascaded down. The hammer blows eventually stopped and the sounds of falling masonry died away. It was pitch black and, at first, silent, then came screams and groans – some rattling and choking into silence. I called for Margaret and miraculously she replied from somewhere quite close. I found I could move my left arm and reaching out, our fingers touched and we grasped each other. Like me she was trapped, but bent almost double under a great weight of debris that had fallen on to her shoulders and neck. My head was trapped as in a vice. I could neither move nor feel my right arm which I feared I might have lost. Nor could my left hand reach my face which was half wrapped in bedding forming a trap for dust and grit threatening to fill up and cover my mouth. As I reached down my hand encountered a great sticky bleeding mess, in the gaping hole in my side.

I found Margaret's hand again. At first we assured each other we were all right, each lying to comfort the other. Then Margaret began to shout for help. 'Don't shout yet, wait until you hear them digging, or you'll exhaust yourself – it may be a long time yet.'

My mind had already constructed a picture of the scene. I assumed the whole hotel had collapsed like the American building that had been bombed in Beirut and that it might take days to reach us. I could hear water cascading down through the wreckage and hoped that we would neither be drowned, nor burned to death if fire broke out.

We had no sense of time. Gradually the cries of other victims fell silent as they died, and we comforted each other. I wondered how bad it was. How many other survivors there were. What was to be done if the Prime Minister and other members, perhaps even most of the Cabinet, were dead? We listened waiting for the rescuers without any sense of time. Great waves of pain came and went and I could feel my life ebbing away as I bled. With each new fall of debris I feared that the crushing weight on my skull might simply crush it like an eggshell. I had begun to fear that I would not last until we were rescued when suddenly my whole body was galvanised with searing pain. So this is death – how strange, what a waste, I thought – then it stopped and I was still alive. Again the pain rose to a crescendo then suddenly stopped. I realised that it had been caused by massive electric shocks but only afterwards did I discover that the rescue workers had inadvertently cut through the live main. Somehow we lost our grip on each other's hands. It may have been another fall of debris which moved Margaret or, although she did not tell me, it may have been the paralysis which was creeping through her body. Nor did I mention what I thought was the cold dead limb of a corpse I found near me in the debris. In fact it was my right arm which I thought I had lost but was merely crushed. At times I felt myself losing consciousness in the great waves of pain, and as we continued to comfort each other, I gave Margaret a message for our children if I died before rescue came.

Then suddenly there were voices. We shouted – or croaked as loud as we could. They called back, 'Who are you?' We told them. 'Can you move?' they asked. We exchanged names and told them how we were trapped. They reached Margaret first. I could see their lights and then I felt a rough hand touch mine. I grabbed it – holding on foolishly like a child begging its owner not to let go. It was Fred. He found that I was under my mattress which had probably saved my life as the masonry fell down on me, and they began to dig me out. A doctor came and tried to see what injuries I had. Then as they dug they found what they too thought was the arm of a corpse until Fred realised it was mine. Painfully, carefully, brick by brick, they cleared the debris – but I was still trapped by a great timber which they dared not cut for fear of bringing down a whole mass of wreckage precariously balanced above us. 'Can you struggle free?' they asked me. With the pain deadened I tried to lift myself over the timber. Fred leaned over to help. My shout of, 'Get off my bloody foot!' seemed to break the tension. We laughed and with another great heave they had hold of me – in minutes I was strapped on to a stretcher and swung clear of the wreckage, into the light of the blazing arc lamps and the cold air of the seafront.

Once out of the wreckage I knew that I would survive but the effort of struggling free had been too much. As the cold bit into me, I began to shiver – great convulsive shivers.

Every movement of the stretcher and bump of the ambulance struck another chord in a crescendo of pain. I asked if my wife was all right and whether the Prime Minister had survived. 'Your wife is all right,' they assured me. 'And the Prime Minister and the Cabinet are safe too.' Pain, exhaustion, relief washed over me until I lost consciousness.

I came to again at the hospital as they lifted me from the ambulance on to a trolley. I seemed to be surrounded by people talking to each other in controlled urgency. Someone noticed I was awake.

'We are taking you to the operating theatre to clean you up. Are you allergic to anything?'

I said the first thing that came into my mind.

'No – well, only bombs.'

They laughed – I think I did too but it was the laughter of the relief from death. Then suddenly I could no longer speak, or hardly nod or move a hand, drifting half-conscious with pain as they lifted me on to another trolley. The lights blurred – I was in an operating theatre and then, oblivion.

When consciousness returned I was in a hospital room. A nurse was sitting by my bed. I tried to move and found tubes and pipes through my nose and throat, tugging on my arm against the sticky plaster attachments. I orientated myself slowly, guessing by the light that it was morning. I was in hospital all right, but where and why? Then the nightmare of the bomb, the hours buried in the debris and the rescue seeped back into my mind. The nurse realised I was awake, using some words of comfort. As my mind refocused the questions spilled out again. I asked about my wife. 'She's alright – she's here in hospital too.' The Prime Minister, I was reassured, was quite safe, she had been to see me, and of the Government only John Wakeham, the Chief Whip, and I, were injured.

Spells of drugged exhausted sleep alternated with periods of awareness. People came and went with a dreamlike quality – sometimes there, sometimes gone. Bottles of blood and clear liquids hung over me dripping life back into my veins, and tubes in my throat sucked drily at my lungs. As awareness returned more fully so the pain came back in ever-growing waves until a great symphony of pain filled my mind. It seemed to come from every part of my body. I could not distinguish the pain of a leg or arm – my whole being was filled with pain, yet I seemed half detached from it. They gave me painkillers and I drifted away again. Gradually other people materialised. My children were there as

I woke and then gone again whilst I slept – or were they there in a dream, disappearing as I woke? Somehow young Winston Churchill materialised with tooth brushes, soap and flannels – happily they remained substantial even after he had de-materialised.

I became more coherent and with coherence came reorientation and awareness. My old friend Tony Trafford, the former Member of Parliament for The Wrekin, came and sat by my bed. I had forgotten he was a doctor but he reminded me that he was a senior consultant at the hospital. He told me that the Prime Minister had come to see Margaret and me but we had both been still unconscious. I asked him about the bomb and the other casualties. He explained that a great section of the Grand Hotel had collapsed after the explosion. The Prime Minister herself had narrowly escaped but several people, including Tony Berry, the MP for Southgate, had died and many others were injured, some critically ill, including John Wakeham whose wife was dead. Although he reassured me about my own wife I had a great gnawing anxiety that I was not being told the truth, though I lacked the will to press my question.

Even on that first day the machinery of Government was able to react. By the evening Callum McArthy had set up a temporary ministerial private office at the hospital and the Government Whips had established themselves too. A telephone appeared beside my bed and I was able to put Paul Channon, my Minister for Trade, in temporary charge of the DTI.

In those first dark days, especially once I knew that Margaret was totally paralysed from her neck down, Callum, Ruth Thompson, Andrew Lansley and Edward Blades from my DTI office, my PPS Iain Mills and the Government Whips were my lifeline and support. Civil servants are famed or notorious for protecting Ministers – but I think no Minister has ever been protected and supported in the way that Callum and his colleagues looked after me – and indeed my wife.

I soon became restive, asking to sit up and get rid of all the pipe-work. Few things have tasted better than the first sips of water that I was allowed, and before long tea and solids followed. Gradually I became aware of my injuries. My left side had taken the brunt of it and I had little skin intact between shoulder and ankle, oozing blood as though I had been sandpapered. Bruised all over, I gradually changed colours through a rainbow of black, blue, red, yellow and green, but clearly the worst problem was a gaping wound over my left hip and lower abdomen. Several inches of muscle and flesh had been simply torn away and part of the top of my pelvis had been sliced down too. A main nerve was severed leaving me without sensation in part of my leg but fortunately neither my internal plumbing nor the main artery to my leg had been damaged. I soon got used to watching and then helping with the dressing of the wound and became quite fascinated to see my own pelvic bone! Before long I was sitting up and I spent hours looking out along the seafront watching the waves breaking on to the beach.

Within a few days I was struggling to be out of bed and walking again. Struggle it was, but leaning heavily on a stick I could get to the wash basin and managed to brush my own teeth and wash my hair. Somehow, my mind seemed easier and the nightmare of being buried alive washed away with the dirt and the debris from my hair.

It was not long before I was able to get down from my room to the Intensive Care unit to see my wife. She was flat on her back under traction, unable to move even her head which was in calipers. Although she seemed amazingly resilient and as usual protective and concerned about me, no-one could offer an opinion on what the future would hold for her. I think I reassured her about myself although, in retrospect, when I recall what I looked like, I wonder!

Through those early days Tony Trafford spent many hours sitting by my bed quietly giving me support as delayed shock took its toll. He told me of his concern for John Wakeham whose life was threatened by the injuries to his crushed legs. The easy option would have been amputation and Tony took a considerable risk in setting out to save John's legs. I remember him sitting with me as together we tried to think who might have the most experience in dealing with similar injuries. The American military and the Israelis were both consulted but in the end it was Tony's professional courage and John Wakeham's grit which saved his legs.

Whilst the hospital was well able to cope with most patients it was clear that Margaret's spinal injury required specialist care. It was agreed that she should go to Stoke Mandeville and I should go with her. An ambulance would have been restricted to ten miles per hour or so, making the journey impossibly long, so in conditions of great secrecy to frustrate the inquisitive press, at least as much as the psychopathic IRA, an RAF Puma helicopter was arranged for the journey. The RAF people were led by a formidable lady Wing Commander doctor with whom I fell out rather badly over how I would be transported. She began to tell me about the special stretcher and I told her very firmly that I proposed to walk to the ambulance and on to the helicopter. She was equally firm. I created a scene from which I was rescued only by a look from Callum signalling that I was well over the top, prompting me to agree sulkily that as it was her helicopter I had no choice but to comply with orders. She was of course quite right but I had already become sensitive to newspaper stories that my injuries were far more severe than had been admitted and that I might never return to my office at all.

The RAF operation was completely successful. Whilst an ambulance was being ostentatiously prepared at the main entrance to the hospital, Margaret and I left through the kitchens with me strapped to a casualty evacuation stretcher and Margaret clamped into a most extraordinary bed mounted on a pivoting frame. We arrived at a nearby boys' school a few minutes before the big Puma helicopter, flying low to avoid being seen, appeared over the houses and landed on the school playing-field. The headmaster, having welcomed us to his school, allowed his pupils to witness this unusual event and we were loaded aboard to the accompaniment of a lusty cheer from the boys. Less than an hour later, before the press knew we had left Brighton, we were safely installed in the spinal injuries unit at Stoke Mandeville.

They were difficult times for me, let alone for Margaret, but the darkness and depression of pain and emotion were lit by the kindness and humour of so many people around us. My civil service office was soon established in the hospital, and with fears that the IRA might try to show they could finish off the job – as well as to repel the media – a police post was also set up and I was allocated two personal protection officers, Doug and Dave, who, like all their successors soon became friends to both Margaret and me.

I could not have fallen into better hands than those of Mr Bruce Bailey, a man representative of the very best in the NHS, totally devoted to his work and his patients, always unhurried despite being overworked, whose professionalism was lightened by humanity and humour. To my relief and delight he prescribed daily baths to help clean and heal my wounds, a little red wine for my appetite (I had lost over 30 lbs) and a little whisky to help me sleep, which, with our mutual dislike of tobacco, promised a good doctor-patient relationship. Initially I had to face an operation which included removing part of my hip to prepare for the skin grafting which was necessary to allow my abdominal wound to heal. The aftermath was pretty painful and it took a while before I was fit for the skin-grafting operation. The initial grafts did not take well and had to be repeated. Each grafting session was followed by three or four days of immobility, flat on my back, unable to be moved even to change the sheets under me. The slowness of it all, the delayed shock and accumulated effects of anaesthetics left me rather depressed at times and I was grateful for the support of my family and friends, my nurses and civil servants and police. They were all amazingly kind.

Friends brought me tempting food and bottles, indeed crates of Champagne. Stalwart Sisters were patient with me, and policemen made tea at three in the morning when I could not sleep. Callum McArthy and his colleagues kept me in touch with the world outside, and Iain Mills, my PPS, took care of my constituency correspondence.

Support came in many ways but none more practical than the suggestion of Jonathan Aitken, MP for Thanet. He came to ask my permission to set up a trust fund to help care for Margaret, telling me that he knew a number of generous people who would like to contribute. It was a most generous and practical thought that eased one problem in our minds and it has done much to help my wife.

We had many distinguished visitors: Prince Philip, the Prime Minister, and a number of colleagues from both sides of the Commons. I was very touched that despite all our differences Ted Heath came to see me, as did my Labour shadow John Smith, and David Owen. Jimmy Savile was an almost permanent feature of the hospital and I came to realise there was a lot more to him than the showbiz personality.

Once the operations were over the physios began to teach me to walk properly again and to manage steps and stairs. It was quite late on before it was discovered that some of my pain stemmed from another broken vertebra, next to those crushed in my Meteor accident years before, and that apart from my broken shoulder blade and ribs I had broken a leg too – happily the bone was not displaced and was well on the way to mending itself!

Every day one of the civil servants from my office at the DTI came in to keep me in touch with the Deparment and to deal with the sacks full of mail that came to Margaret and me from all over the world. The television pictures of our rescue had gone around the world evoking a wave of sympathy, and thousands of letters from heads of state and ordinary people alike – not least from the Republic of Ireland – and from incredible numbers of children. Callum and his colleagues also came as friends, often helping to feed Margaret or reading to her late at night when she could not sleep – I doubt if many other Private Secretaries have helped their Minister put on his shoes and socks, fed his wife and read poetry to her late at night.

I have always believed in work therapy and I soon resumed meetings of officials and Ministers to carry on the work of the Department. We were approaching the flotation of British Telecom – a £4 billion flotation. This was not only the biggest ever, but according to a good many people too big to be achieved. By late October the only key decisions left were over the pricing of the shares, and subsequently their allotment. These decisions were finally taken in hospital with, appropriately enough, a telephone line open between me and Geoffrey Pattie, the responsible Junior-Minister, and our professional advisers gathered in London. I had also decided that I could no longer allow the problem of two Permanent Secretaries within one Department to continue. Although I had the Prime Minister's agreement and the reluctant acquiescence of the head of the civil service, Robert Armstrong, nothing had been done to resolve the issue. I wrote to let Robert know that I intended to ask Anthony Rawlinson to take early retirement when both Brian Hayes and Anthony came to the next routine meeting in hospital. At the end of the meeting I asked Anthony to stay on. I started awkwardly.

'Anthony, this is very difficult for both of us, but I take it you have some idea of what I have to say.'

'No,' said Anthony clearly puzzled.

I realised that Robert Armstrong had not given him any advance warning. It was the most difficult interview I have ever had. Anthony was heartbroken. I assured him that I had no criticism of him, and would have happily had him as my Permanent Secretary but I could not ask others to rationalise within the Department, or lecture businessmen on the need for efficiency, whilst I had two men sharing a job that would be better done by either.

He was silent for a moment, and I said, 'Anthony, you'll be no worse off financially – indeed I am sure you will find other interests and be better off.'

His response encapsulated the ethos of many of his colleagues: 'I love my job, Secretary of State – and I'd rather have that than be better off.'

We were both pretty miserable as we parted but it was a mark of Anthony's generosity that when we met in the summer of 1985 during the speculation that I was to become Chairman of the Party, he told me he hoped it was not true. I hedged, unwilling to tell him a lie, and he said, 'I'm sure you would do the job well but I never worked for a better Secretary of State and I hope you stay at DTI.' Sadly Anthony, who was a considerable mountaineer – he had been first reserve for Hilary's party to Everest – was killed in a fall on Snowdon soon after.

During late November I received the draft of my White Paper on the financial services industry and investor protection. Whilst the policy was generally correctly set out it looked what it was – a paper drafted by a committee. Over the next couple of weeks Callum and I completely re-wrote the early chapters with a welcome improvement in style. All this added to my appetite for work and, although my wounds still had to be dressed daily and I walked with a stick, I felt I had to get out of hospital.

The Prime Minister had been exceptionally kind and concerned about both Margaret and me and, although a room was ready for me at RAF Halton, she insisted that I should at first stay over Christmas at Chequers from where it was an easy drive to Stoke Mandeville both to visit Margaret and for my own treatment.

It was a week before Christmas and bitterly cold with light snow when I left hospital. As ever Chequers was warm and inviting but it has no lift and I found it a struggle to manage the stairs. The Prime Minister had made Churchill's favourite suite ready for me and I was given a light supper in the sitting room before preparing for bed. One of the staff came to ask at what time I would like my tea – what luxury after hospital routine – but as she took my tray and the door closed behind her I realised that I was alone for the first time since the bomb. I wondered if I had been unwise to insist on leaving hospital. I was not even certain that I could get undressed without help. Eventually I struggled out of my clothes, tidied up the dressings and climbed into bed.

It was Churchill's bed – a great oak four-poster – with a great soft feather mattress. I tried it – but it was hopeless. I needed a very firm bed not least for my crushed vertebrae. There was only one thing to do. I dragged some blankets off the bed and lay on the floor. As I fell asleep I was wondering whether Churchill's ghost, if he haunted the place, would be more displeased to find me on the floor than in his bed.

Just before Christmas I made an unannounced trip into London. The journey was agonising and I must have looked awful as I got out of my car at DTI. To my surprise a queue of people at the nearby bus stop burst into applause and I hurried indoors as quickly as I could. Callum had not told anyone I was coming and I walked into the staff Christmas party being held in my office. I could still neither stand nor sit without a good deal of pain, but wedging my backside on the edge of a table I managed a couple of drinks before having lunch. Although I did almost no work, the trip was worthwhile. My officials now knew I was coming back and so did I.

It was even harder for my Margaret once I had left hospital, leaving her without the support of my civil servants and protection officers. Although there had been early optimism when she found she could move her left toes there had been little more recovery. She suffered the agonies of illusory sensations common to those with spinal injuries, and awful disorientation as she first began to be sat up in bed. Her spirits sagged and Christmas, with all its memories of better times, made it worse. I had been half surprised to realise that I was not consumed by bitterness, but Christmas was very hard to bear. Somehow it was the decorated Christmas trees in the lighted windows of other people's homes which turned a knife in my wounds as I thought of our house, dark, lonely and silent. I was glad my mother had died a few months earlier – it would all have been too much for her to bear.

Everyone did their best to support us. Both Denis and Margaret Thatcher were at Chequers with lots of guests – most of whom I knew – on Christmas Day itself. I went back to Stoke Mandeville for lunch where the consultants on the spinal unit (ironically two Jews and one Palestinian!) officiated at the Christmas feast, carving the turkeys with great style in traditional British hospital fashion. Upstairs, on St. Patrick's Ward where I had been, Sister Brennan had decreed fancy dress for nurses with the theme of St. Trinians. So my Christmas Day dressing was done by a nurse in gymslip and school blouse!

When Chequers closed down after Christmas I stayed for a few days with friends in Bedfordshire and then moved to RAF Halton where the officers' mess made me very welcome. The Wing Commander Admin was a WRAF officer, Daphne Veitch-Wilson, who lived in the mess and made sure I was well looked after. She was a delight, obviously efficient, full of humour and good sense, and she terrorised young pilot officers in great style. I was comforted by the comradeship of the mess and the years seemed to slip away as I attended dining-in nights, though as the oldest present I slipped away rather earlier than in the North Weald days.

In the New Year the Queen herself, who had come to visit Dick Herne (her horse-racing trainer) in hospital, spent some time with my wife.

Gradually, I became stronger and keen to be back at work. I do not think there was any precedent for a Secretary of State remaining in office during such a lengthy period of hospital or convalescence and I was very aware that stories were being spread that I would never fully recover. One problem was that I had nowhere to live. My security advisers were strongly opposed to me staying in our Barbican flat. Quite rightly they felt they could not control access to the block and I agreed to leave. Finding somewhere else was more of a problem. Through the kindness of the Duke of Westminster I was able to look for a property suitable for Margaret on the Grosvenor Estates, on terms far more favourable to me than to him, but that was a long-term project. Finally, under the urging of the Prime Minister, a long-unoccupied garret flat in Admiralty House was identified and offered to me.

It was scruffy and the access up what had clearly been the servants' stairs – a stone spiral staircase of 180 steps – was awful. Michael Havers, who had a flat there since his home was blown up, kindly allowed me to use the lift into his apartment which helped as I then had only one more flight to go. The flat was, however, all that was available and with a lick of paint it was habitable, if austere, with just a living room, bedroom, bathroom and kitchen. I collected my clothes and a few personal belongings from the Barbican and with the help of my old BOAC friends, Roy and Sally Hutchings, packed up and sent the rest into store. I was glad to leave it mostly to them. I found it hard to look at Margaret's shoes and clothes or to be in our room. Even photographs of her standing, running or laughing were too painful to see and for many weeks I just sank into misery whenever I was alone.

Realising it was best not to contemplate Margaret's future or how we would cope if she remained severely disabled, I immersed myself in work as a prophylactic against bouts of misery and self-pity.

I had been disappointed that my recovery was slower than John Wakeham's although he had been so near to death and savagely injured. I became all the more determined to get back to my office. Having returned to London I had to part with Doug and Dave, my Thames Valley Police protection officers. They were replaced by Jim (who had looked after my security before Brighton) and Frank. Not only did they provide protection but friendship and support, too, during a very difficult time as I made the transition back to work. Indeed I cannot speak too highly of the protection officers who have looked after me. Sadly, I have to respect their anonymity, although they would justify a book in their own right.

On 10 January I attended my first Cabinet since Brighton, and after lunch I made my return to the House of Commons during questions on Northern Ireland, sliding into my seat on the front bench having entered the Chamber from behind the Speaker's Chair shortly before the Prime Minister arrived to take her Questions. Everyone was exceptionally kind – an unnatural state of affairs, which I knew could not last long! And I did not stay long – it was still painful either to sit down or indeed stand up for very long at a time – but I felt a great sense of achievement. I had come back and looked forward to being back at the despatch box to take on the Labour Party again.

My opportunity was not long delayed. Our hope for flotation of British Airways still remained bogged down in legal actions brought by Laker in the United States, leaving a gap in our privatisation programme. My suggestion that we should sell the Government's remaining forty-nine-per-cent holding in British Aerospace was accepted and on 15 January I returned to the despatch box to announce the decision. It was an ideal return for my purpose, as my statement was politically controversial and firmly Thatcherite. I was determined to demonstrate that I was the same old Tebbit and certainly not looking for sympathy or a soft ride.

I hoped it did not show but I was inwardly shaking with nerves. It was six months since I had last spoken in the House and I could not be certain that I had retained my touch. I need not have worried. I was all but physically lifted to my feet by the growl of support from the Government benches – and to be fair a sympathetic murmur from the other side of the House, and one after another Labour MPs offered me the sort of partisan questions I loved to hit back for six. It was all over in just twenty-five minutes and I knew that I was back in control.

My next major policy initiative was the unveiling of my White Paper on the shape of the new regulatory system in the City. It was generally well received and for a while the pressure of Departmental work was more on filling in details of existing policies and drafting legislation than on more new initiatives. I decided therefore that subject to my Margaret continuing to make progress I would make my much delayed trip to Japan in April. Before then however I had given my ruling on the House of Fraser affair which I had inherited. Essentially as I saw it the company was not of great significance to the economy, that there was no threat to competition whether either Lonrho or the Al Fayeds owned it. Under my policy the original Lonrho bid would never have been held up at all. The company had suffered too long from ownership battles. I had to assure myself that both parties, Lonrho and the Al Fayeds, whose bid was supported by Professor Smith, the Chairman of the House of Fraser, were in a position to honour their obligations of their bids. I saw no reason to doubt the assurances given to me by Kleinwort Benson, a leading merchant bank, although I pressed both them and the Al Fayeds for assurance that the money they would use for their purchase was theirs and unencumbered. I listened carefully to Mr Rowland's criticism of the Al Fayeds but I had to judge it against the fact that Mr Al Fayed had been his co-director on the Lonrho Board, and that Rowland had sold very recently to Al Fayed Lonrho's commanding stake of 29.9 per cent of the Fraser shares, presumably believing the Al Fayeds were men of substance suitable to own such a powerful holding in the company. The Al Fayed bid was supported by the Chairman of the House of Fraser, Professor Smith.

In my view it was not for me to take sides in a personal quarrel at the expense of many more months of uncertainty if I referred the bid to the Monopolies and Mergers Commission. There was no competition issue, no national interest, Lonrho had sold to the Al Fayeds so why at that company's behest should I prevent others from selling their shares to the Al Fayeds too? It was to widespread approval that I stood back to let the owners of the House of Fraser decide if they wished to sell the firm and to whom.

One problem which began to cause me serious concern was the difficulties of Westland, the helicopter manufacturer. The firm had been on the Department's cause-for-concern list for some time. Despite the optimism of the Board we could see that the WG 30 civil helicopter programme was in trouble. Although the concept was sound the recession had delayed the development of the market and the WG 30's rather old-fashioned rotor system was becoming less and less competitive. Despite great efforts by the Government even the prospective sale of twenty aircraft to India was in doubt. The Anglo/Italian EH 101 held great promise but it was too far in the future to provide much needed production work and I approached Michael Heseltine to see if the Ministry of Defence could help with any orders to fill the gap. I met not only a flat refusal – in view of the tight defence budget, that was understandable – but a complete indifference as to whether Westland survived. With helicopters available from America, France and Germany the survival of Westland was a matter of industrial not defence policy I was told by MoD.

Somehow – partly buoyed up by an unsuccessful bid by the helicopter operator Alan Bristow but most significantly by the appointment of John Cuckney as Chairman, which gave institutional shareholders confidence to support the company for some months – the company survived through the summer. By the winter, however, it was a fused bomb waiting to explode.

By then of course the great coal strike had finally ended in defeat for Scargill. It is a pity that the Government made almost no political gain from one of the most important political events of my time in politics. Governments had walked in fear of a coal strike for decades. Ted Heath had destroyed his own Government, but it was the miners who delivered the *coup de grâce* in 1974. Margaret Thatcher's Government had broken not just a strike but a spell. Parliament had regained its sovereignty. To make so little of it was poor thanks to the lorry drivers who had risked their lives to carry coal and iron ore, the steelworkers who rejected for the first time the miners' brotherly invitation to suicide-pact strikes, the dockers who hesitated and followed the steelworkers, not the mineworkers, the police who endured long hours of great discomfort and physical danger, and above all it was poor thanks to the brave and decent miners who worked to save their jobs and their industry and in doing so save their country, too. For had the Thatcher Government been broken and the craven Mr Kinnock installed in office by Scargill's thugs Britain would have been a grim place indeed.

I do not think anyone has properly assessed the skill with which the dispute was foreseen and then managed by the Government. Few of us who were members of the committee on the coal strike had much of a summer break in 1985. Even my short escape to Devon was interrupted all too often by phone calls or trips back to London. The action of British Steel in breaking the miners' blockades, bringing in coal and ore by road, was critical in preventing sympathy strikes elsewhere. Our decision not to over-ride British Steel's wish to dock and unload the ore carrier 'Ostia', without registered labour, was a key decision in the strike. The ore was needed to keep the Ravenscraig steel works open and we realised the risk of precipitating a dock strike. A dock strike did indeed follow but it was a strike with no popular backing. Once it had flopped the striking miners knew that they had played their last card and that even if they stayed out another year they could not win the dispute. I doubt if any other Prime Minister would have had the courage to win a coal strike, yet within weeks of that victory we suffered heavy losses in the local elections and the polls showed us in third place. No wonder the Government's friends bemoaned our poor communications. In a leader headed 'Send for Mr Tebbit' *The Times* said that the next election would not be a 1983-style walkover: 'it has all the makings of a genuine contest.' The Government needed 'a new face'. 'The Conservative Party can give it one. The sooner Mr Tebbit takes the chair the better.'

Before that moment came I still had a good deal to do and the Government had some even worse days. Much was going right. For example, my trade union reforms forced strike ballots in the civil service dispute in March, the London Transport dispute in May and the railway dispute in August. In each case the strike call was defeated. In April a Post Office strike petered out when the union declared it to be unofficial under the threat of a High Court injunction. Yet we seemed to step on one banana skin after another.

The teachers' strike did not yield so easily and caused much public concern. Throughout the first half of the year the handling of the Bill to abolish the Greater London Council did the Government a great deal of damage and our efforts to deal with the extreme-left councils were all too often in trouble rather than triumph.

In contrast most of my work was going well and, after considerable discussion and argument, I even secured approval of the 1985 BL corporate plan involving closer collaboration with Honda, including the manufacture of Honda badged cars in BL plants and the production of a new small engine which for some time had been in doubt. Had I failed to assure BL's future I have little doubt that as Chairman of the Party I would have failed to carry the West Midlands at the 1987 election.

My life had been hectic through the spring and early summer and the strain of almost daily journeys to Stoke Mandeville to see my wife was considerable. That was eased by her move to the spinal injuries unit at the Royal National Orthopaedic Hospital at Stanmore and it was from there that she made her first public appearance at Wimbledon. It was an emotional occasion which she managed well. However the progress we had hoped for had not materialised and it became clear that she would be terribly disabled for the rest of her life. A hint of how difficult that would be came when we determined to go to Portugal to seek some sunshine and rest. A seven-seat private aeroplane was laden to the gunwales with medical equipment and of course not only Margaret and me but a nurse and the inevitable Special Branch minders – happily on this trip with their wives as we had rented a large villa and it seemed a shame for their wives not to enjoy some sunshine too. The holiday rubbed in that no longer would we be able to wander across France casually booking into hotels each evening. Nothing would ever be the same. Nonetheless the holiday was a success and I returned to London waiting for the September shuffle which I had known since July would take me to Central Office.

I was very sad to leave the DTI. I had had two good years there (Brighton excepted) and had achieved a great deal. Perhaps I had been foolish not to expect it but I was totally unready for the whispering campaign which I realised was going on against me. It had begun with the suggestion that I would never recover from my injuries, then that I had either lost my drive – or that I had been consumed by ambition. A selective piece of leaking from a letter by Robin Ibbs of the Prime Minister's efficiency unit was used to promote a piece in *The Times* suggesting that I had failed to manage the DTI – a story strongly rebutted by Robin Ibbs himself, but regularly regurgitated, and my prospective switch to Central Office was talked about as a move to a less demanding job. Would that that had been true!

Having taken the decision to privatise the naval shipyards, I was anxious to carry that through and take the BL group towards the private sector too. I was worried about Westland and about the future of GEC and Plessey. I had set my heart on bringing these two companies to realise that their continued obstinate rivalry in the production of main telephone exchanges, sharing the British market between them and gaining almost no business elsewhere in the world, would end with the loss of the British business too and that rationalisation would have to come. However winning the election would now have to come first.

I was very pleased that when I was appointed Chairman of the Party the Prime Minister also made me Chancellor of the Duchy of Lancaster, a post whose history goes back to 1399. Many of its holders were forgettable and have been forgotten. Four of them met untimely ends. Thomas More was martyred by Henry VIII, another died on the scaffold, a third awaited trial in the Tower, a fourth was assassinated. On the other hand four became Prime Minister including both Churchill and Spencer Perceval – who was the one assassinated. The Chancellor's duties cover the appointment and discipline of the magistracy in the County Palatine of Lancaster, and, separately, he has the role of non-executive chairman of what is in effect a property and investment company managing the estates of the Duchy which are personal to the Queen and separate from the Crown Estates. Those matters are dealt with by a highly professional staff under the direction of the Council of the Duchy, in effect a non-executive board.

My work as a non-departmental Minister was managed from a delightful office overlooking the Horse Guards parade ground only minutes away from my attic flat. To my delight, Andrew Lansley, one of my private office team from the DTI, volunteered to come and organise my staff there and provide a link to the Duchy but principally to brief me on the tremendous range of Government matters in which I had an interest. I had a role in the Cabinet and its committees which, like that of Willie Whitelaw, extended very widely at times, and often put us in the position of non-executive directors or a court of appeal for unhappy colleagues.

12

Chairman of the Party

I arrived at Central Office as Party Chairman to meet my staff there in a sea of goodwill. I had always been on good terms with the professional staff at Smith Square, and those who had served Cecil Parkinson and had been loyal to him knew how close I had been to him during his difficulties in 1983. It is only fair to say that the appointment of Jeffrey Archer as my deputy raised quite a few eyebrows. Jeffrey's immense energy and brash confidence did not initially overcome the caution of the old hands but both his barnstorming trips around the country and his very good staffwork, improving the organisation in the key vulnerable constituencies, soon won him many friends.

Once the dust had settled over my appointment I began to set my priorities and plan for the election. My first task was to improve morale among our grassroots supporters. Quite stupidly many people who either have not practised politics or who have practised but failed do not understand that a party which cannot enthuse its own supporters will never enthuse the doubtful, so my efforts were aimed at encouraging our hard core of supporters, not towards influencing waverers.

My early analysis of the reasons for our unpopularity was that the unremitting campaign of vilification against the Prime Minister was doing her great damage. Our opponents had been skilful in creating a self-perpetuating myth that 'everyone' was against her. The flavour ran right through programmes like the *Today* show on Radio Four, where even the spokesman for the Conservative view was likely to be a 'wet', critical of the 'harsh' Government. Even worse, poor presentation of policies, the muddling of rhetoric and action, had given the impression of an embattled government, unsure of itself. My first duty, as I saw it, was to take some of the fire off the Prime Minister. If by the vigour of my attacks on Labour I could force them to turn their fire on me it would give the Prime Minister more chance to stay clear of the rougher brawls of politics and to play her strength as a great national leader. My high-minded critics fell into the same trap into which they had stumbled in 1981 when I was appointed Secretary for Employment. They assumed I used these tactics because I knew no others, instead of wondering why I deliberately chose tactics which made life more uncomfortable for me than it need have been.

Clearly I had no more influence over the general course of government than I had as a Secretary of State. My job was in that respect to persuade colleagues to think of the political impact of what they were doing, to present it more skilfully and above all to use the resources of Central Office to plan that political impact – not as a fire-fighting team to dampen down fires of resentment after a political explosion.

However I could do something to harmonise and focus the presentation of policies. I was ready to try new ideas and to experiment, not least through Party Political Broadcasts (six ten-minute peak-viewing-time slots each year) and constituency campaigns; I could also involve our activists more closely in our national campaign, and set about bringing resources of cash, equipment and personnel into the key constituencies to build up support ready for the general election.

Within weeks I had categorised every constituency in Britain, distinguishing between those where only a political earthquake would unseat the party holding the seat, the Conservative seats at risk in a tightly fought election and the Labour and Liberal seats we might expect to win if things went reasonably well. Our 1983 majority of 144 was unlikely to be repeated unless the split of Labour and Alliance votes was to be so near perfect for us again. My first priority was to achieve a good working majority. That meant identifying and putting our efforts into the key seats which we had to hold.

In the past that had been a simple matter of looking for those held by small majorities, but three-party politics – or in Scotland and Wales, four-party politics – complicated the issue. I also looked at the qualitative factors – how good was the sitting Member and how good were his agent and association?

Jeffrey Archer loved his barnstorming role visiting the constituencies and enthusing our workers and, finding that he was coming back with some shrewd assessments to supplement those of my area officials and elected officers, I involved him in what became known as the critical seats campaign. Together with a retired agent, Stuart Newman, who came back to work on the project, he completed the catalogue of assets and deficiencies in the local organisation of the key constituencies and helped to raise a considerable sum of money to finance extra staff and equipment where it was needed. Sir Anthony Garner, as chief agent, and his staff also stepped up the training and briefing of the agents and elected officers, and well before the election of 1987 I had achieved a substantial shift of effort from constituencies which we would win or lose anyway to those where local organisation could make a vital difference in tightly fought elections.

Of course such low-profile reorganisation was not what the press wanted to see. They had convinced themselves that Central Office was a bureaucratic nightmare and I should 'sort the place out'. Like many people who talk or write about politics they failed to understand that the Conservative Party has only a few hundred paid employees (about 200 directly employed by Central Office) and tens of thousands of volunteers. It is the latter who *are* the Party, not Central Office, and it was on them and their motivation I concentrated. With less than two years before the election I decided that there was no time to assess the organisation properly, make any desirable changes and heal the wounds of what might be painful reorganisation. The organisation had won the elections of 1979 and 1983 and I decided to build on it, eliminating weakness where I could, and recommend my successor to make any major changes in the year after an election, not the year before one.

The Party Conference was only five weeks away as I settled into my new office and I knew in that time there was little that I could do about it except to assure myself that the administrative arrangements had been well made. I could only put my gloss on it. I knew that my own popularity with the grass-roots party workers would carry me through so long as I launched a vigorous attack on our opponents, a vigorous defence of the Government's policies and listened and responded to their calls for 'better presentation' – often a coded way of saying would Ministers please think about politics and explain why on earth they do such unpopular things. Above all, we had to demonstrate unity and confidence in ourselves and our policies.

Reading the weekend papers on my return from the Blackpool Conference, I thought we had got a better press than we perhaps deserved. The conference had no consistent theme, it was a series of rather unrelated debates and speeches, the media had received little help or guidance to enable them to sift wheat from chaff and the public impact was all too swiftly dissipated. It had been a huge investment of time, money and effort for very little, if any, gain.

From then on as each conference or similar annual event came around

I insisted that we asked ourselves these three questions. Why are we holding this event? What do we want to get out of it? How will we go about it?

Before the end of the year I had to ride out a most unpleasant incident in the House of Commons which confirmed my belief that the yobbish tendency had taken control of the Labour Party. I was winding up a debate on the inner cities engendered in part by the Church of England tract 'Faith in the City', a political plea to return to the Butskellite policies which had created the desolate council estates. I started in a deliberately rumbustious style but I had progressed no more than a few paragraphs into my speech before the Labour Party began a clearly planned and concerted attempt to shout me down. I had plenty of experience of noisy debates but never before had I experienced a screaming mob of MPs determined to refuse me a hearing at all. With the arrival of Mr Kinnock, who was excited and aggressive, the noise grew even worse and the House of Commons began to look like an extreme-left town hall. The debate was a fiasco – as no doubt Labour planned – and, delighted with their success, they later tried to scream down Nigel Lawson. Fortunately the Speaker was slightly more ready to restore order and the attempt failed. At least, I thought, my strategy of redirecting the flood of personal abuse away from the Prime Minister was working – even if too well for my comfort.

In early November my Margaret and I attended the Lord Mayor's Banquet at the Guildhall as the guest of her friend Pam Davies, the wife of the Lord Mayor. Pam had invited her whilst she was still totally bed-bound and Margaret, now able to sit in a wheelchair, was determined to go. It was a painful, exhausting and emotional evening for her. Next day almost every paper published a photograph of me wiping a tear from Margaret's eye with touching captions about her tears of emotion at the welcome she had received. 'If only they knew,' she commented, 'I'd just said, blast these intensive TV lights – they make my eyes water!'

The work had begun during the summer on the rebuilding of the house which was to become our London home and on an extension to our house in Devon to provide suitable accommodation for my wife. Although the London house was not completed until June 1986 the work on our Devon home was finished in time for Margaret to leave hospital for a few days over Christmas and the New Year. It was exceptionally difficult for her to sit in a wheelchair in her own home, in pain, unable to help prepare a meal, wrap presents or decorate the house. The cruel process of coming to terms with the prospect of a life sentence of imprisonment within her own paralysed body was hard to bear, and I think it was a relief for her when Christmas was over.

I soon realised that the workload on the chairman's office was too heavy to be carried just by me and Shirley and Alex, the two stalwart and dedicated chairman's secretaries, and I persuaded Michael Dobbs to return to Central Office as my Chief of Staff on leave of absence from Saatchis. I had no worry about any conflict of interest as I saw no reason to change the winning combination of the Conservative Party and Saatchis in political advertising. Saatchis were devoted to helping us win again, their reputation was at stake, and they had priceless years of experience which no other agency could acquire in time; so I asked them to stay with us for the next campaign.

I was concerned that our critics were too easily able to characterise us as a Party and Government solely concerned with a narrow short-term economic policy. My Selsdon speech of October 1984 – on British Society in the nineties – had been over-shadowed by the Brighton bomb and in November 1985 I initiated the annual Disraeli lecture with a speech linking political and economic liberty to the wider condition of society, putting the blame for many of its ills not on economic conditions but on a moral climate of permissiveness which had degenerated into a society without values. It attracted a good deal of attention and angered the left who believed social concern was their monopoly.

Our reputation on the so-called 'caring' issues was appalling even amongst our own supporters. Taking advantage of our rhetoric about cutting public expenditure (which, in any case, we never achieved), our opponents had convinced the great majority of the electors that we had 'cut' the National Health Service, and most other things beside, when in fact never had so much been spent on the social services. We were getting neither the bun, nor the halfpenny, let alone both, in this controversy.

To begin a campaign to change such a widely and deeply held misconception we had to persuade our own supporters first and then give them the arguments to convince others too. To do that by talking at them in the traditional way simply would not work so I decided to involve them in a campaign ostensibly to convince the uncommitted. In reality I was intent on re-committing our supporters to believe in our own case. The campaign was quite simply a massive distribution of some two and a quarter million leaflets in five hundred constituencies, backed with a thousand poster campaign, all to be completed within forty-eight hours of a party political broadcast. The PPB, leaflets and posters all followed the same theme, pleading guilty to a great list of cuts – in inflation, strikes, hospital waiting lists, income tax and even cutting Scargill down to size. The list was balanced by one of what had not been cut – hospitals, nurses and doctors, home ownership, productivity and pay.

The costs and effort required to co-ordinate a PPB, ministerial speeches and leaflet campaigns were too high to use the technique regularly but it had certainly demonstrated the effectiveness of concentrated communication techniques.

The direct mail campaigning which had been started by Cecil Parkinson had lapsed after his departure. I saw it both as a communication exercise and a fund-raising system and soon restarted the work. The problem of political direct mailing is that many letters (at about 30 pence a shot) go to hostile voters, many friendly voters may not read what looks like junk advertising mail, and few who do will send their cheques. The heavy costs would normally take years to recover, but the privatisation programme gave us a great opportunity. The million-plus British Telecom shareholders, whose names and addresses are easily taken from the share register, were our first target.

The programme shot straight into substantial cash surpluses, recruiting thousands of new members and becoming the most successful direct mail campaign in British politics.

The Westland helicopter affair had been left rumbling over Christmas, but as we returned to work in January it looked as though Michael Heseltine was digging himself into an impossible hole. I have often asked myself why the future of a company to which he had been so indifferent became a matter of such importance to him. I think that Michael's thinking is sometimes dominated by a single issue, making him somewhat myopic. I had experienced this during a long-fought argument over which yards should receive orders for frigates, when it seemed to most of us that Michael was determined to place orders with Cammell Laird on Merseyside rather than Swan Hunter on Tyneside. In the Westland case I thought Michael was still sore because the Cabinet had refused to allow the dilution of the specification of the proposed European fighter aircraft to keep the French, who wanted a less capable aircraft, in the consortium. This had damaged his sensible policy of securing common arms system procurement by the European nations and I think he badly wanted to restore his credentials by forging a European helicopter company, keeping the Americans out of the market. I never thought that was possible and wanted to ensure that Michael himself would be forced to realise that his scheme simply would not work. Before that happened Michael's stance of negotiating in public against the rest of the Cabinet progressively forfeited the sympathy of his colleagues. As Party Chairman I was well aware of the damage that his resignation would do to the Government's standing and I did all I could to avoid it. In the end Westland – a small affair – had so dominated Michael's world that it became to him an issue of principle on which to resign. In so doing he escaped from the looming problems of the overstretched defence budget.

Michael walked out of a Cabinet in which he had made himself a minority of one and although it was a huge media event I was reasonably confident that the damage could be limited. I had earlier arranged to return to hospital the following day for an operation to strengthen the torn muscles of my abdomen by a graft of tissue from my leg, which I hoped would diminish the nagging pain I had suffered since Brighton, and I hoped that the worst of the affair would blow over whilst I was there. That was not to be and the resignation of Leon Brittan was fuel to the fire for the mad conspiracy peddlers. It was all a sad story.

As so often in life, troubles then followed one upon the other. I had encouraged confidential talks between General Motor Corporation and BL, aimed at merging the commercial vehicles business of the two firms, for well over a year. The deal that began to emerge would have made Britain the centre of all GM's European commercial business, but to make sense it had to include the Freight Rover vans business and that began to drag in the Land Rover/Range Rover businesses. I was not unduly anxious to include those as there was a good prospect of a better price through a separate sale or flotation and I realised that there would be some political problems; but I certainly did not rule it out. The talks continued under Leon Brittan and, following his resignation, Paul Channon, reaching a stage where collective discussion between a wider circle of Ministers became necessary. At that stage the whole issue became complicated by two factors – a leak about the GM talks and an approach by Ford to open talks on the sale of the whole or some part of the BL business. Whether that initiative would have led to a deal, or whether it was just a 'spoiler' to frustrate the GM talks, I do not know. However, once a possible takeover became public, unless the issue was resolved within weeks, BL's business would have suffered permanent, serious damage as the uncertainty drove the firm's best dealers to look for other franchises and fleet customers to seek other suppliers. The Ford proposal could be resolved quickly in only one way – by ruling it out. The GM bid was much more difficult. Continuing the negotiations under a blaze of publicity amidst enormous volumes of political claptrap was exceedingly difficult, and the hostility shown to GM and the anti-American hysteria of the Labour Party began to cause doubts in Detroit about the wisdom of increased investment in, and reliance on, the United Kingdom. The press was given briefing or leaks that I had opposed the deal and fallen out with the Prime Minister over it. In fact the deal was my idea on which I had worked for over a year. Certainly I was well aware of the emotive West Midlands politics but the whole thing only collapsed when John Wakeham, the Government Chief Whip, advised that he could not promise a majority for any deal involving the sale of Land Rover to GM. The American company was unwilling to proceed without Land Rover in the deal and withdrew on 24 March.

The scars of that encounter were hardly healed before the Chief Whip had another nasty shock when the Sunday Trading Bill – of which I was a keen supporter – was defeated on the night of 14 April. The media were naturally delighted with a 'shock defeat' story, but even whilst their stories were being written the next shock was on the way with the US raids on Libyan terrorist bases.

Following so soon after the wave of crude anti-Americanism whipped up over the BL–GM affair, the decision to allow American F1-11s to use bases in Britain to make their strike on Libya stirred up an absolute hornet's nest of protesters ranging from cowards afraid of Libyan terrorist reprisals, through Labour's anti-Americanism, to little Englander nationalists. I was concerned that because the decision was made in some haste, the political implications were not fully considered. The Prime Minister was made to look vulnerable to the charge of being too eager to please the Americans at our potential expense.

Even many reasonable minded people were uneasy, especially as they watched the misleading and unbalanced BBC coverage of the affair. I have no doubt that if, instead of allowing the American F1-11 bombers to use bases in Britain in an all-American operation against the Libyan terrorists, we had used our Tornado bombers alongside the American carrier-borne aircraft the public reaction would have been totally different; but so far as I know that option was never discussed.

These events coming so soon one upon the other sent the ratings of the Government and the Prime Minister sliding down. Just before the Libyan raids we had lost the Fulham by-election and in early May we did poorly in the local elections and in the two more by-elections which were held on the same day to avoid two days of bad news rather than one. I was far too busy defending the Government and the Prime Minister on radio and television, in speeches at by-elections, lectures in churches and articles in the press to have time to join in the back-biting and destructive criticism of colleagues endemic in any party in such political disarray as we experienced in early 1986. At their most ridiculous the stories told of Geoffrey Howe and me plotting to overthrow the Prime Minister. Who was to succeed her if the 'plot' had been successful was never clear! All such stories did was to foment an air of crisis.

For some time I ignored the renewed bouts of stories about my health, and then those saying that I had quarrelled with the Prime Minister, accepting that if governments lose by-elections it is naturally the Chairman of the Party who carries the can. I simply got on with rallying the Party faithful and the planning of the election campaign.

After the difficult weeks in the spring I was planning the campaign to put the Government back into the lead in the opinion polls during the autumn conference season. It needed careful planning too; if it failed the prospects of a third election win would be very far from good. By the late summer however the papers began to carry stories of my resignation and looking back I realised that many of the stories must have resulted from regular press briefings by someone whose position gave him credibility with the lobby. Whoever it was also had a fair amount of inside knowledge. For example my anxiety that we should avoid repeating the error of 1983 when the writing of the manifesto was left very late, appeared in the press as my alleged plan to monopolise its production. I had not bothered the Prime Minister with what I regarded as trivia as I knew she was well enough burdened with more substantial matters and that she almost never reads the papers, relying on briefings instead. However at one of our regular meetings she produced a typical newspaper article on the theme of the Thatcher/Tebbit split and expressed her surprise and anger. I brushed the matter aside but she persisted and I said I saw no reason to make an issue of one article – typical of dozens at the time – and closed the conversation promising to send her a file of similar stories. I realised that if Margaret had been previously unaware of the stories she would not have briefed Bernard Ingham, the No. 10 press spokesman, to refute them; and his lack of comment must have added credibility to them. Her response next day was swift and the briefing coming out of No. 10 was that the stream of stories was baseless and the Chairman and Prime Minister were at one. It is however never easy to get the toothpaste back in the tube. The stories continued to be written whenever political journalists had nothing better to write about, or when over-ambitious colleagues had nothing better to talk about. There was no doubt, however, that someone was actively trying to undermine the confidence of the Prime Minister in Central Office, Saatchis and me.

I had more to do than follow every unpleasant story in the newspapers.

At last in early June our London home had been completed, I had moved in and made sure all was ready for Margaret's homecoming after twenty-one months in hospital.

The readjustments presented many problems but we were profoundly grateful to leave hospital life behind us and begin to construct a new life at home.

Not that I had too much time at home. My Cabinet workload seemed to get heavier as I found myself on more and more Cabinet committees – particularly those set up to deal with the knottiest problems. Such groups were usually chaired by Willie Whitelaw. I remember once, as we discussed tactics, I said to him I thought that perhaps I was too abrasive to put a particular point. 'No,' said Willie. 'Your image may be abrasive but I have not found you so. It's like me – my image is emollient – and so I am but only when I'm getting my own way.'

Happily my load was eased in September by the appointment of Peter Morrison as a second Deputy Chairman. Peter had been my junior Minister and although he is not a good public speaker he is an excellent manager, a tireless worker checking every detail, questioning every assumption to ensure that plans are practical and are carried through. He was – and is – an old friend and he had the Prime Minister's confidence too.

I was busy, out listening to what voters were saying and commissioning opinion surveys to check my own findings and test some of our ideas of how to drag the party back from a poor second, and, from time to time, third, in the polls.

The surveys confirmed earlier findings. The voters believed the Government had lost its way. Given a clear sense of direction the Government's actions looked decisive and realistic. Without that sense of direction, however, they looked just mean and uncaring. The Prime Minister's toughness and her leadership were in danger of being seen as harshness and bossiness. Clearly the Labour Party had made similar findings and their attacks were successfully exploiting them. I decided that the 1986 conference at Bournemouth had to change that public perception and the loss of confidence creating that missing sense of direction. The Saatchi team, Michael Dobbs, the party's Director of Research, Robin Harris, and I set about planning the conference and devised the theme, 'The Next Move Forward'. For the first time ever we ran pre-conference advertising to give notice that 1986 would be a conference of a different kind. 'The Next Move Forward' was not just a slogan and I persuaded the Prime Minister that Ministers should include in their speeches statements of objectives they would achieve within the next three years. Their speeches should imply an assumption that the Government was already planning the execution of plans stretching beyond the election. Most important of all, Ministers should let me have their lists of achievements to come, so that Saatchis could design posters, leaflets and brochures ready to go up, or be handed out, as each Minister was finishing his speech. My aim was that in 1986 the media should reflect the image I wanted – of a Government confident, united, clear in where it was going – and determined to get there.

We knew that voters saw the Labour Party as old-fashioned and mistrusted its ability to deliver. So my main speech attacked Socialism as 'a creed that has had its day', and Mr Hattersley's policies as simply 'not adding up'. Moreover, both the Prime Minister and I emphasised the wide differences between us and the other parties. We wanted no fudging or smearing over the divisions between our proposals and theirs.

It was more successful than I had dared to hope. The purposefulness and coherence were unmistakable. The message was clear and unambiguous and the opinion polls which had us 7% behind in June and still 5% down in September now put us back into first place – a position we never relinquished from then right through the election campaign. The Prime Minister's ratings were immediately restored. Once people knew that she knew where her Government was going they saw her as a tough purposeful leader again. After months of planning, in just four days of the conference the Party's support was revitalised.

My opinion of Mr Kinnock has never been flattering and I was sure that his intellectual incoherence would show in the Labour campaign. However I saw a danger if he was simply portrayed as 'nice', caring about caring issues, avoiding policy, and capitalising on any weakness or divisions on our side.

This view was confirmed by the groups within Central Office which acted as shadow Labour campaign advisers. We also had an Alliance shadow group – which, I might add, would not have advised the Liberals and SDP to fight the campaign which they did! To outwit Labour we had to ensure that Kinnock was firmly linked to his left wing, with the so-called 'loony-left' councils being given prominence; that the party's policy commitments, with all their contradictions and the influence of the trade union leaders, were shown up; and that issues of taxation, inflation and defence were played very strongly.

One of our difficult tactical problems was to decide whether potentially disenchanted Tory voters of 1983 would be more likely to defect to the Labour Party or the Alliance. As I saw it Labour was our national

opponent. Labour constituted the only alternative government although
it was more likely to be put in office by our losing votes to the Alliance
than direct to Labour. Our main campaign had to be directed against
Labour with the Alliance depicted as an indirect route to Labour government. At constituency level, however, in some seats our candidates,
hoping to split the non-Conservative votes more evenly, faced a greater
threat from Labour, while in others it was from the Alliance. We at
Central Office had to supply ammunition to fight on either front.

Our polls showed that the electors were still in a mood for change
and a Labour campaign based on a theme of 'It's time for a change'
might be appealing. I believed this could be countered by showing we
were not only a party of change but the best party to manage change.
Moreover, as I was to emphasise to the Prime Minister, it was vital to
leave clear water between ourselves and both opposition parties. I
believed that the starker the choice between Labour and Conservative
the more difficult it would be for the Alliance to bridge the gap by being
all things to all men.

As I saw it the first priority was to fight a positive campaign based
on our record and our proposals.

The second was to argue that if we were defeated the result would
be a Labour not an Alliance Government.

Third, we should depict the Alliance call for a coalition (which was
popular) as a call for the uncertainty and confusion of a hung parliament
(which was not).

Fourth, we should hammer the far-left policies and record of Labour
in Government and in the Labour town halls.

Fifth, we should expose the differences between the Liberals and the
SDP, concentrating our attacks on the Liberals and Mr Steel, not the
SDP and Dr Owen, as he was too well liked by wavering Tory voters.

Sixth, we should target our campaign on the traditional Labour voters
in the C1 and C2 groups without whose support Labour could not win.

These formed the background to the election campaign which I had
promised the Prime Minister by the end of the year. Like Cecil's 1983
election plan it was highly secret. Contained in a large blue book, it was
known as the War Book. Just for fun, I had the Prime Minister's copy
delivered to Chequers wrapped as a Christmas present a week ahead of
our deadline.

The plan was comprehensive. In its order of battle it listed each job
to be done at Central Office and who would be drafted to do it.

It began with an assessment of the strengths and weaknesses of each
party, recommended the tactics and style we should adopt, including

alternative plans according to whether the Alliance challenge developed or failed. Our assessment of Labour's campaign strategy proved absolutely correct – a tribute to the planners as well as to us. In the words of the War Book,

> Specific policy commitments have been generally avoided [by Labour] for fear of exacerbating internal splits. Almost every firm commitment which has been made has subsequently been altered and watered down! Labour will concentrate on destroying the Government rather than presenting themselves as a credible alternative ... and on the key 'caring' issues of pensions, health and education with a constant reference to inner city 'blight'.

The tone of our campaign was planned to be positive – the emphasis more on our record and our proposals than on knocking copy. Assuming we started as expected with a lead in the polls, it proposed as short a campaign as possible. The less time for electors to get bored, or to be turned off by partisan bickering, and the less time for some unexpected adverse factor to pop up, the better. Only if we were lagging in the polls should we run a long campaign giving Kinnock more time to make a serious error.

The detailed planning extended even to a provisional schedule of the main subjects of our daily press conferences, which was in effect our game plan for the ideal order in which issues should come to the fore. Broadly, we aimed to get the negative issues such as unemployment out of the way early and to finish on our strong subjects – the economy, taxation and defence.

One of our strongest assets was the Prime Minister – particularly when contrasted with Mr Kinnock or the split leadership of the Alliance – and the plan was that she should travel the country whilst I kept control from Central Office making only short forays by car or helicopter and always remaining in touch with Central Office and her by phone. By early May we had designed and built a coach protected against terrorist attack and equipped with the most up-to-date communications equipment to ensure that both Margaret and her staff could be briefed at any time. The need to guard against terrorist attacks was an extra complication in planning the Prime Minister's personal campaign schedule. Although Margaret would want to decide the details herself we planned her tours on the theme of national renewal. The idea was for her to be seen in places where Britain was clearly moving forward – the campaign theme – with visits chosen to link with the issues which we were intent on raising on the particular day.

With the advantage of our 1983 experience I built on Cecil Parkinson's campaign plan a 1987 plan which proved to be absolutely sound. Our problems were to come in the one area where the plan was not carried through.

Early in the New Year the Prime Minister agreed the plan and we stepped up the preparation of the material that would be needed. Saatchis worked with us on outlines for the election broadcasts, producing draft scripts, poster and press advertisement designs. Those we liked were refined, prepared and then 'put in the freezer' – our bank of material. Much was never used simply because we had prepared for any turn the campaign might take. In the event the Alliance never became a serious threat and our best material with which to attack them never saw the light of day. Nor did our 'high-risk, hard-hitting' material appear, as we were comfortably ahead throughout the campaign. With no need to take risks, we could afford to play safe.

Shortly after the Party Conference the arrogance and what our supporters saw as the bias of the BBC became a major issue. The BBC had a well-known record in committing libel and then trying to brazen its way out, knowing that few victims would dare risk bankruptcy in legal battles where the costs might run to many hundreds of thousands of pounds. Just such a case was that of the *Panorama* libel of two Conservative MPs, Gerald Howarth and Neil Hamilton, which despite its own legal advice the BBC had steadfastly refused to settle, presumably believing that the two MPs would simply run out of money to pay legal fees and have to give up. They were made of braver stuff and, fortunately, shortly after his appointment as Deputy Chairman, ex-Labour Minister Joel Barnett asked to see the BBC's legal advice on the case. Soon after that the BBC settled, paying substantial damages to both MPs.

Complaints from the public to the BBC about political bias met the same arrogance and willingness simply to brazen things out. Generalised complaints were easily brushed aside and whilst particular undeniable examples of lack of balance might be admitted, it was always claimed that they had been, or would be, redressed in other programmes or at other times to achieve 'over-all balance'. The Labour Party also maintained a barrage of complaints which enabled the BBC falsely to claim that criticism from both sides proved its impartiality. I decided that if our complaints were to be effective we would have to choose an example where the 'we'll redress it next time' response would be clearly invalid. In order to do this we had to assemble and analyse the evidence with care in a professional manner.

The BBC's notorious TV news coverage of the American raids on

Libya was an ideal case. All the material was contained in a relatively few broadcasts which could be analysed word by word and picture by picture and contrasted with that of ITN. The work was done to the highest standard by a professional who regrettably had to remain anonymous for fear that his career might be blighted. Later when both my case against the BBC and the Corporation's reply were submitted to a leading academic lawyer, who overwhelmingly upheld my case, he too, sadly, asked to remain anonymous for the same reason. I was anxious neither to make accusations which I could not substantiate nor to put the BBC in a position where it could not accept my criticisms. I therefore made no charge of political prejudice and the dossier concluded that:

> The BBC did not offer objective evidence so much as a highly flavoured editorial view. It prompts charges of professional incompetence or, even worse, prejudice. This could be held to have arisen either through bias or incompetence. Given the pressures under which the broadcasters operated a serious shortfall in professional and editorial standards is much the easier alternative to accept.

Despite the furious reaction of the BBC and its usual total rejection of my conclusions I have little doubt that they struck home and that members of the editorial staff began to look more critically at their own work.

I was of course subject to as much abuse for suggesting that the BBC was falling short of the standards properly to be expected of it as, earlier, I had been for criticising the conduct of trade union leaders. Significantly my critics, both without and within the Tory Party, were the same people on both issues. So too were some of my supporters, not least *The Times* whose leader of 31 October was headlined 'Mr Tebbit Makes His Case' and which continued its editorial support in a long and considered piece on 7 November.

Some of my critics on the Conservative side felt that the timing of my blast would make it more difficult for the incoming BBC Chairman Marmaduke ('Duke') Hussey to make the changes he might think necessary. Naturally it was a a point considered before the Prime Minister agreed I should publish my dossier. I would have thought that the reverse was true. Indeed it was not to be long before both the Director General, Mr Milne, and his Assistant Director General, Mr Protheroe, left. Some months earlier I had accepted an invitation to lunch at the BBC with Mr Milne on 5 November. The BBC chose that day to release their considered reply to my complaint (it had been the subject of near instant kneejerk rejection on receipt) and I had to push my way through reporters who had been tipped off that I would be coming to a private lunch. During the lunch Mr Milne was adamant that as our lunch was private I should not comment on it to the press and naturally I agreed. Mr Milne later published his version of what took place but despite that I would say only that the meeting underlined to me that Mr Milne was a very weak man unlikely to be capable of imposing decent standards within the Corporation. Eventually the affair blew over but I have every reason to believe that my complaint had the desired effect of focusing attention within the BBC on its falling standards. Despite a continuing fixation with South African politics I think the Corporation's news coverage has improved. The lack of balance in the drama department and parts of current affairs remains a challenge however.

I also had my internal problems at Central Office. One highly public row was caused by the progressive takeover of the national organisation of the Federation of Conservative Students by a coalition of people some of whose views and actions were incompatible with Conservatism. Some, the so-called libertarian wing, were more nearly anarchist, others practised highly dubious election tactics to gain influence in the organisation. During the summer I had taken legal action to prevent distribution of an FCS magazine bearing the imprint of the Party which contained an actionable article about the Earl of Stockton (Harold Macmillan), and later in the year began moves to wind up the FCS and replace it with a broader-based organisation, less open to takeover bids.

I had less success in another internal problem. With the detachment of Harvey Thomas to support the Prime Minister's team I had no director of communication to co-ordinate our press, radio and television advertising, direct mail and other communication programmes, nor did I have a managing director or director of finance responsible for routine management and expenditure at Central Office. Even worse, I was unable to persuade the Prime Minister that I really needed either. Had I been able to appoint a good director of communications I believe we could have avoided some problems which arose at the general election. I was lucky to have persuaded John Desborough, the *Daily Mirror*'s political correspondent (but lifelong Tory) to join my press team and later I recruited Christine Wall from the press office at No. 10 but I still lacked that over-all director. At one time I hoped I could persuade Gordon Reece, who had played the role for Lord Thornycroft in 1979 to come back for the 1987 election but that was not to be. As a result for two years I carried at Central Office the responsibilities shared in the Labour Party by Larry Whitty and Peter Mandelson as well as my Cabinet work – and during the general election, as the Government's second spokesman, I played the role performed in the Labour Party by Bryan Gould too.

I was glad to take a break from the office for Christmas and on Christmas Day our whole family sat down to lunch together for the first time since the Brighton bomb. It was a real family Christmas again and although Margaret was still cruelly frustrated by her injuries she was back in charge, directing operations in her own home. I was desperately tired but heartened by all that had been achieved in 1986. We were together in our own home and learning how to cope with Margaret's injuries. At work I knew that we had hauled the Government back from the black pit of unpopularity of the spring and we were clearly ahead in the polls, and favourites to win a third time in 1987. With that victory I had decided that I would have honoured my then current political commitment and be free to honour a promise I had made to my wife that I would step back from front-line politics to give me time to secure her future. Despite the fund set up by my colleague Jonathan Aitken to benefit my wife it was clear our financial needs greatly outweighed our resources. If my Margaret's future was to be assured I would have to earn a great deal more and I wanted to spend more time with her now that her life had been so tragically narrowed. My promise however was a secret between the two of us and Michael Dobbs. It was to remain so until I told the other Margaret in April at the beginning of the local election campaign that I could not serve in her new administration.

Election fever had been rife throughout the late months of 1986 and it promised to be a pretty dirty campaign. On 6 January, in an article which I thought was over-full with personal animosity towards both the Prime Minister and myself, the *Guardian*'s columnist Mr Hugo Young set a style later followed by the Labour Party. It was mostly a nastier version of a piece he had written in the previous March, just as unimportant and unlikely to influence prospective Conservative voters, but in one respect Mr Young had gone too far. Placing the words between inverted commas Mr Young accused me of saying, 'Nobody with a conscience votes Conservative anyway.' I had, of course, never said any such thing. Clearly it was untrue and grossly insulting to the very voters whose support I wanted. From my assessment of Labour's likely election campaign such a 'quotation' was exactly what they wanted to substantiate their theme of uncaring Conservatism. My Chief of Staff, Michael Dobbs, immediately wrote a letter for publication in the *Guardian* reminding readers of Mr Young's evident dislike of myself and the Prime Minister, saying, 'Perhaps this explains the invention of the quotation he [Mr Young] attributed to Mr Tebbit.' Before it was published the words 'the invention of' had been removed, thus removing the repudiation of Mr Young's allegation. Even worse, despite agreeing to publish a letter from me the *Guardian* repeated Mr Young's libel and Mr Young himself claimed in a further libellous letter to *The Spectator* that the quotation was not a fabrication 'as several witnesses know'.

It was clear to me that, if no action was taken, invented quotations would become a major part of the Labour election campaign and Margaret Thatcher authorised me to demand a retraction and apology under the threat of legal action. She had never before given a Minister authority to sue for libel and it was a mark of her concern.

In their defence Mr Young and the *Guardian* never sought to claim or prove that I had ever used the words Mr Young attributed to me but it was almost eighteen months before I had, in an out of court settlement with substantial damages, the satisfaction of a public withdrawal and apology which should have been given at once. I can only hope that the *Guardian* has learned, along with the BBC, that libel, even of political opponents, is a serious matter.

Apart from my brush with the *Guardian*, of which my detractors within the Party made plenty, I had to manage two difficult by-elections – that in Truro, where we were unable to dent the majority of the late Liberal Member, and at Greenwich which the SDP won from Labour. On the surface they were both poor performances for us and, although I have never set too much store by parliamentary by-election results, as general election pointers they demonstrated that I was right to be concerned that the Alliance might take enough Conservative votes to put Labour into office.

At the Party's Central Council meeting (a mini party conference) at Torquay in March I directed my fire on the Alliance – or, as the sharper political minds noticed, the Liberal half of the Alliance. The effect was all the greater as my attack was matched by the Prime Minister the next day. As had often happened, we had not had time to co-ordinate our speeches but had instinctively made speeches which interlocked one with the other. As Margaret pointed out, we had never made discordant speeches so we hardly needed to consult.

In the run-up to the local elections I then gave a press party at Central Office to mark the tenth anniversary of the Lib–Lab pact in which Mr Steel had supported the Callaghan Labour government. Again I was criticised as being abrasive or going too far, but as usual my critics never grasped that the event was not just an anti-Alliance event but part of a strategy to sow dissension between the Liberals and SDP and give our people ammunition with which to fight off any Alliance challenge.

At about the same time my tough tactics with the BBC scored a notable success. Some months earlier I had initiated discussion with the BBC on the use of subtitles for the deaf on party political broadcasts. Having got nowhere, I produced a PPB with subtitles which the BBC initially refused to carry, saying that the proposal needed the agreement of the other parties. The BBC gave in only after the Director General was told that the film would be delivered for transmission with subtitles and they could either transmit it or explain why they had refused. It was an incident which underlined the arrogance of the BBC and did little to improve my opinion of the Corporation.

As we approached the local elections the Prime Minister at last began to force the pace of policy clearance to prepare the election manifesto. Remembering the scramble to finish the 1983 document I had asked for the work to be done much earlier but for months it had drifted. At first a series of policy groups was formed, each chaired by a Cabinet Minister and a mixture of other Ministers, back-bench MPs and outsiders. I saw these as a waste of time and eventually as we discussed the reports in the so-called 'A' team meetings so did the Prime Minister. The 'A' team meetings in themselves were not terribly productive. The group was founded mainly to defuse awkward political issues – or to avoid banana skins which the Government at one stage seemed always to be stepping upon. Fears that it might be seen as an 'inner cabinet' turned it into little more than a talking shop and it could do little constructively with the party policy group reports. Finally it fell to Ministers to put forward their proposals which were then cleared through the normal machinery of Government for inclusion in the Queen's Speech for 1987 or later years. The rush at the end was horrendous and a small group of us had some hard work to do to put the proposals into manifesto form, whilst David Young was deputed to deal with the style and printing of the manifesto and its companion booklet listing our achievements in Government.

By the time of the local elections on 7 May the momentum for an election was almost irresistible. Indeed Margaret herself seemed to make no effort to cool the election fever. As in 1983 Keith Britto and his team at Central Office had prepared a computer programme to analyse the local election results and offer a range of forecasts for a general election on various assumptions about the possible movement of opinion during the election. These were more elaborate than in 1983, even calculating a factor to correct the mismatch between the opinion poll measurement of support for the parties and the support actually given at the general election of 1983 and at the local elections of 1987. Our statistics were not only more detailed and comprehensive but more quickly fed into a more sophisticated computer programme than those of any other party or the TV companies. Results, ward by ward, across the country were telephoned, faxed or rushed by road to be fed into the computer. From the central computer they were even fed to me through my own personal terminal as I sat in the television studio commenting on the local election results that night. When we met at Chequers on the Sunday morning I had already supplied Margaret with our findings and unlike 1983 there was no drama as I presented my conclusions. June it was to be, and 11 June the date.

Although our analysis pointed to a majority of 98 I told the others that my central forecast was for one of 50 to 60. The over-all arithmetic had always been pretty clear. If we could achieve 40 per cent or more of the votes and lead Labour by 3 per cent then we would achieve another victory. If our share fell below 38 per cent than at best it would be a hung parliament.

The Prime Minister's decision was welcomed by the Cabinet next morning and I outlined the strategy of the campaign to those who had not yet seen the War Book. The need to clear up parliamentary business dictated a longer campaign than I would have ideally preferred, but it gave us some leeway to complete our preparations. The 'Campaign Guide', our compendium of political facts (published for sale and used by all political parties and journalists) was already printed and available. The printing of the manifesto, however, was badly delayed and we missed the peak demand, although David Young assured the Cabinet that we would have enough to satisfy the press, if not the public, by publication day.

I told the Cabinet that I had planned a delayed start to our main campaign, concentrating on a steady build-up to a strong finish on our ground, having pushed the less favourable issues early to let the media become bored with them well before polling day. Everyone was happy and the campaign was launched just as I had planned. A little later the Prime Minister, confident and optimistic, began to talk to me about the new Cabinet she would form after the election. We were on our own and I interrupted her saying, 'Margaret, if you are thinking about your next Cabinet, I have to tell you again that I have decided that I cannot be part of it.' I explained that I owed it to my wife to secure her future – which I certainly could not do on a Minister's salary – and I needed time to be with her too. Margaret seemed reluctant to accept that my mind was made up, and changed the subject. Not until the afternoon of polling day did we discuss the matter again.

It had been clear to me in the latter part of 1986 that whoever had been making trouble between Margaret and me were still active. Part of the problem was the activities of Saatchi's commercial rivals, some of whom had traded on political acquaintanceship to sell their wares. Not surprisingly, when the Government's standing was at its lowest some of those around Margaret advised her that she should listen to what they had to offer. Naturally enough the various salesmen had made their pitches to me, too, but I was disinclined to buy what I thought were inferior, more expensive ideas than those we had already developed and tested and I told Margaret I had no use for the gimmicks being offered. I later discovered they had been funded without my knowledge. I thought it a terrible waste of money but, fortunately, it did no great harm although it caused the Prime Minister a great deal of unnecessary alarm and me considerable irritation.

Without a director of communications I knew I would be overworked during the campaign and I looked around for extra help. David Young, as a peer, had no constituency commitments. We had worked closely together in the past and had met regularly to discuss the coming campaign. What is more, Margaret Thatcher liked and trusted him. So I invited David into Central Office to help in the election campaign. He knew very little about elections having never stood for one; nor had he worked for the Party in a local association. However, he has always been a persuasive, indeed compulsive, talker to the press, and I asked him to take on the top-level Fleet Street briefings for editors, as well as the organisation and management of the Prime Minister's own pro-gramme of country-wide tours. These were both tasks that would have been undertaken by a director of communications if I had had one. A number of political friends told me I was mad to give any colleague positions of such influence. I simply shrugged, saying we were all in the same team and that I trusted David. But it may be that it was the knowledge that I was leaving the team and had no need to fight for my position that left me so relaxed. Perhaps if a few more colleagues had known I would be leaving the Cabinet and represented no threat to their ambitions, things might have gone more smoothly; but I could not afford the risk of a leak. Fortunately, David proved to be very good at talking to editors, as the Prime Minister's tours became a near disaster that threatened the campaign. The themes I had set out were abandoned and day after day the press corps who accompanied her were left wondering whether there was a plan, quite unable to see how the Prime Minister's personal campaign was supposed to lock into the master-plan for the whole campaign. Industrial visits were made to areas on holiday for Wakes Weeks, to factories empty of workers. Hasty re-planning led to frantic travelling which confused the media and exhaus-ted the Prime Minister. Central Office, 'naturally', took the blame for events over which I had no control! The result was an extraordinary contrast between the Central Office view of the campaign, based on opinion polling and reports from the key constituencies – that all was going according to plan, and the reports from the press corps following the Prime Minister (and for a while her own perception) of things going badly wrong.

In fact things were going very well indeed, mainly because we had the best Party leader, the best programme and the best record, and for a while I did not realise what was worrying her. As the polls showed, support for the Government remained rock steady throughout the cam-paign. The extraordinarily badly conceived and ineptly executed Alliance campaign was fatally handicapped by the dual leadership. That helped Labour, whose campaign, as I had predicted in the War Book, was far more professional than ever before. We had foreseen that Labour's campaign would be 'presidential', avoiding discussion of their policies and concentrating on Kinnock's personal image. However, we had concluded that, 'presentation cannot be sustained on its own without a firm foundation in politics and policies,' and that such a campaign would run out of steam. It proved to be an entirely accurate prediction. Their first party election broadcast, nicknamed the 'Kinnock coronation theme' was both very clever and effective – but to repeat it was a cardinal error. The Labour strategists were absolutely right to display Kinnock on film, carefully rehearsed, with no risk of his intel-lectual fragility or his macho aggressiveness showing through the misty sentimental camera shots, keeping him as far away from shrewd in-depth questioning as possible. But to repeat the film, as they did, drew attention to its lack of substance. It was a frustrating period waiting for Kinnock's first major mistake but it came eventually on the defence issue with his half-baked talk of surrender to a nuclear threat to be followed by guerilla resistance to the foreign army of occupation. The Saatchi poster, 'Labour's Policy On Arms', depicting a British soldier, arms raised in surrender, was the most powerful of the campaign, hitting straight at Labour's weakest point amongst its own traditional working class – C1 and C2 supporters.

Quite mistakenly, because many media people admired the slickness and professionalism of the Labour campaign, they thought it was effect-ive. It was not. Soft pink muzzy camera shots and red roses do not carry many votes amongst car workers in Birmingham. They were effective only amongst Labour's small but vociferous middle-class media-based trendies.

We had our mishaps apart from the muddles of the Prime Minister's tours. John Wakeham had been asked to 'whip in' Ministers selected for radio and for broadcasts, and early on fielded himself to fill a gap. As Chief Whip he was out of practice at broadcasting and it was a disaster. Subsequently by far the heaviest load fell on myself, as, apart from the Prime Minister and Willie, I was better briefed on policy across the board than anyone else. Then, by an excessively cautious reply to a question on education, the Prime Minister opened herself to misrepresentation. Those apart, our main problems were caused by the continuing muddles over the Prime Minister's itinerary, and the confusion caused by a lack of consistency between my briefings and those of David Young. No doubt this arose because David was also being briefed by Saatchi's commercial rivals whose reports on public opinion did not tally with ours. Not only was all this bad for our public relations but it undermined the Prime Minister's confidence. Her unease was compounded by an abscess on a tooth which was at its most painful on the Thursday before polling day when an aberrant Gallup poll wrongly put Labour within two points of us. Her anxieties were played upon by messages from Saatchi's competitors claiming that their research showed the election was all but lost. It was perhaps not surprising that David should have been alarmed – even though no reputable poll ever suggested there was a scrap of evidence to justify that view – as he had not been through 1983's 'wobbly Thursday'.

The campaign was in fact going well. Both Central Office and the Party in the country were confident and we simply got on with the job in hand. Unfortunately I had been given legal advice that my scheme for a mail drop of an election newspaper to virtually every household in Britain over the last weekend of the campaign would conflict with election law, so I decided instead on a very heavy press advertising campaign over the last days of the campaign. The Saatchi advertisements followed closely our 60/40 formula for a majority of positive rather than negative advertising, but clearly echoed the 'Don't Let Labour Spoil' theme which had been effective in earlier elections. It has been claimed in one account that a former Saatchi employee – a very able copywriter who had established his own business – had designed the advertisements used in the press. They were not his; although it is only fair to say that he had a part in the designs used in 1979 and 1983 and had submitted, through David Young, some work which also reflected his earlier ideas and was not wildly different from the Saatchi advertisements which were actually used.

The flurry of excitement over our 'wobbly Thursday' annoyed me – but did not divert us from the campaign plan, although I regard the way in which highly coloured accounts of a difficult meeting were hawked up and down Fleet Street as absolutely unforgivable and in great contrast to the way in which the similar 'wobble' was dealt with in 1983. We finished exactly as planned on the ground where Labour was weak and we were strong – defence, taxation, and the economy. At first it was not easy to get the economic issue going. The press had been diverted by the stories of divisions in our camp but Nigel Lawson, by sheer persistence and strength of his personality, finally focused attention on the economy just as our heavy advertising campaign did the same. Labour were in a mess as Hattersley's figures clearly did not add up and in the last few days – unlike 1983, when we lost several points – our support remained rock solid.

It is always a relief to arrive at polling day. The die was cast and I was confident and glad it was all over. I saw Margaret at Number 10 to give her the latest reports and found her rather tense and still concerned about the result. I now realise that she was being fed with even more misleading panicky stories that things were going wrong, right to the end of the campaign. However, I reassured her – except on the subject of my future. I was adamant that there was no post within the Government that I would accept although I would be happy to stay on as Chairman until after the Party Conference.

I was in Chingford to hear my own result declared – a majority up from 12,000 to 18,000 – and even more significantly we had won Walthamstow, which before Margaret became leader of the Party was a Labour seat with a safe majority of over 10,000. As I drove back to Central Office listening to the results it was clear to me that we had won a great victory. The BBC was still deluding itself into believing what it wanted to believe, that we were sliding to defeat, only conceding our victory as its best political journalists telephoned their editors, telling them the unwelcome truth and imploring the Corporation to stop making a fool of itself.

It was after three o'clock when my wife arrived at Central Office to join the party. It was a night of great happiness – perhaps the greatest for us. I had done my part. I had honoured my commitment to Margaret Thatcher and now I could honour my commitment to my own Margaret, by stepping back from government.

Friday passed in something of a haze, but at least it was clear that we had won a third victory on a magnificent scale. Without Foot or the

Falklands Factor and against the best organised Labour Party for many years we had held our over-all share of votes to within a fraction of one per cent of the 1983 result. Indeed in England we had increased our share. Only Scotland had saved the Labour Party from total humiliation. The plan conceived a year earlier had brought the Government the success its record deserved – a majority of 101. So much for the 'wobblers'! On Saturday I took part in my last meeting as a Minister when a small group of us was invited to offer our advice on the formation of the new Cabinet. The others were as surprised as Margaret had been to be told that I would be standing down from Cabinet, and it was not until I had convinced both them and the Prime Minister that there was no prospect of me changing my mind that we got on with the discussion.

As I left No. 10 I had a deep sense of relief at setting down a heavy load, but it was tinged with sadness. After eight years as a Minister I had gone whilst still on top. It's better, I thought, to go when they are asking you to stay, than to stay when they're wanting you to go!

I stayed on for a while as Chairman for three reasons. First I wanted to give Margaret time to find a successor, second to give me time to put to her my recommendations for the changes needed at Central Office, and third because I wanted to report formally our victory to the Party Conference in October and to help set the tone for the third Thatcher administration. The search for a successor caused some problems and eventually delayed my resignation but, in Peter Brooke, the Prime Minister made a wise choice for a post-election victory chairman. My report on the changes needed in the Party organisation was not difficult to write. Central Office had stood the test far better than its extreme critics would have allowed. It has an accumulated fund of knowledge and experience that should be carefully nurtured and built on. With the approval of the Prime Minister I formed a small group including Willie Whitelaw and Cecil Parkinson (both ex-chairmen who had fought general elections), my deputy, Peter Morrison, and the Party Treasurer, Lord McAlpine, and with their help I was able to leave my successor a unanimous report. I was not the only member of the Prime Minister's team to leave after the General Election. Stephen Sherbourne, her most able and trustworthy political private secretary at No. 10, left to join the advertising firm run by the ex-employee of Saatchi's. He was a loss to the Prime Minister and those of us who had over several years found him a man of ability, and integrity.

Now a year later I look back not just on the election campaign but almost twenty years in Parliament, eight of them as a Minister. There is very little in those years which I regret. I played my part in turning the sick country of Europe into one of the most successful and respected in the world. The talk of the 'English disease' has been replaced by wonder at the 'Thatcher miracle'. Britain the laggard has become Britain the leader. Our policies have become the standard against which others are measured. There has been a revolution whose chief casualties have been Socialism and the weak complacent Conservatism of the sixties and early seventies. Much privilege has been abolished simply by extending it far more widely than ever before – undoubtedly right, but bringing with it problems. Like the extension of affluence, the weakening of paternalist bonds and the old social restraints has exacerbated many problems. The development of responsibility which should go with the enjoyment of what was once privilege has lagged and anti-social behaviour has been on the increase.

The Thatcher revolution has come a long way but most of its work has been devoted to the destruction of the restraints which had brought our economy to its knees. None of those gains must be lost – indeed there is more to do – but the task for the next stage must be the rebuilding of the social restraints which have been greatly weakened by the doctrines of the permissive society. I would not want a return to a stuffy, prudish society; but, to be stable, a liberal society must be one in which individuals accept prime responsibility for their own actions.

The church – particularly the Church of England, once a pillar of society – seems to have lost certainty and authority on moral issues as it has gained certainty on political and economic issues. Having thrown out the baby of the authority of the scriptures it seems now to ask its dwindling followers to worship nothing more than the bathwater of ephemeral sociological theories. Until some other moral authority outside the State develops, I fear that the less sophisticated and less comprehensive structure of law, punishment and reward will have to fill the gap left by the loss of moral, as opposed to State, authority.

That is why education reform is necessary and will have to go further. So too must economic reform and the reform of personal subsidies, with the State returning to each individual more and more responsibility and capability to solve his own problems and seek his personal successes. The growth of state services and extensive public dependence upon them frequently seems to me both to undercut personal responsibility and impose economic demands which cannot sensibly be met. Even worse, by imposing dependence it has progressively limited the ability of many citizens to achieve responsibility, leaving them as a sullen sub-class whose children are born into a society with few if any moral guidelines.

The test for any political party in the closing years of the century will be to maintain the Thatcherite liberal economy whilst building a liberal yet structured and orderly society upon it. It is impossible to see who might carry forward that task other than the Conservative Party. It would be tragic if Mrs Thatcher proved to be an isolated phenomenon and that a yearning for the quiet life and soft consensus might let post-Thatcher Britain drift, economically modestly successful, but failing to tackle the problems of crime, unruly behaviour and vandalism. But I do not think that this will happen as long as able and radical Conservative politicians offer the leadership necessary to carry out the policies which we are now developing.

Although in the past year or so I have stepped back from government the quiet life has eluded me! Indeed, freedom from the collective responsibility of ministerial life has opened up wider fields of political debate – and action. I hardly hoped when I left the Government that, in partnership with Michael Heseltine, I would achieve within eight months a prize that I failed to win in eight years of government – the abolition of the Inner London Education Authority. The freedom to differ from my friends still in the Government is one that I shall use very sparingly, but it is there to be used if needs be. I hope also to be able to encourage those friends to keep up the pace of reform, most notably of education and the health service; and to begin to question more boldly some of the assumptions which underlie our attitudes to social deprivation, crime and law enforcement.

Parliament is the base for any politician, but freedom from office gives greater freedom to promote debate more widely than is possible in the Chamber of the House of Commons. The foundation of the Radical Society earlier this year, in which I played a leading role with Stephen Haseler and Neville Sandelson, in company with friends outside the Conservative Party – some of them former Labour supporters – should begin to widen a new, and much better, consensus – one which accepts almost all that has been achieved by the Thatcher Government since 1979 and seeks to explore the new policies for the 1990s in which Socialism is rejected.

Since the general election I have been able to spend more time with my wife and, through my business interests, have been able to provide more adequately for her future. Things have gone as I had hoped – indeed even better; and, although I thought I had exchanged political life for family life, I find now that I may have discovered how both to have my cake and eat it.

'Fain would I climb, yet fear I to fall.'
'If thy heart fails thee, climb not at all.'

Index

Abbreviations used: NT = Norman Tebbit, M = Margaret Tebbit,
CP = Conservative Party

ACAS (Advisory Conciliation and Arbitration
    Service) 199, 200
'activists' 68
Adamson, Campbell 133
Admiralty House flat 235
Aitken, Jonathan 232, 258
Al Fayed 238
Aldington, Lord 123
Alexander, Andrew 104
Allason, James 63, 88, 92, 95, 96, 98
Alliance Party 203, 207, 252, 253, 254, 255, 259
Allianz (insurance company) 214
Allied Steel and Wire Company 179
Amalgamated Union of Engineering Workers
    (AUEW) 137
America see USA
Amery, Julian 114–16, 140
Amin, Idi 124
Andriessen, Franz 179
Archer, Jeffrey 242, 243–4
Argentina and Falklands War 194–6
Arlott, John 47, 87
Armstrong, Robert 181, 233
Armstrong, Sir William 106, 130
Atkins, Humphrey 194
AUEW (Amalgamated Union of Engineering
    Workers) 137
aviation politics
    navigation aids 97
    nationalised and private-sector airlines 98,
        104–5, 167
    hijacking 99–100, 112, 124, 128
    RB211 103

Civil Aviation Bill 104, 168
Roskill Report 108
aircraft noise/baggage handlers 116–17
Maplin Development Bill 128, 170
NT consulted by Jim Callaghan 155
Laker Skytrain and Denning 167–8
chairmanship of BA 168
air services with Far East 169
airport policies 169–70
Eurocontrol 169
A320 Airbus 212, 215–16, 218
B Airways/B Caledonian 215
RR V2500 engine 216, 218
aerospace industry ('83) 218

Bahrain, landing at ('56) 50
Bailey, Bruce 231
Baker, Kenneth 174, 214
BALPA, NT active in 54, 58, 60–62
Barber, Anthony 99, 101–2, 103, 128
Barbican flat rented 120, 127
Barnes, Denis 182
Barnett, Joel 257
Batt, Don 19
BBC see British Broadcasting Corporation
BEA and women pilots 108
Beith, Alan 129
Bell, Ronnie 96–7
Bell, Tim 199
Benn, Tony 112
Berkeley, Humphrey 98
Berkhamsted, NT and M move to 53
Berry, Tony 229

Berwick-on-Tweed by-election ('73) 129
Betchworth (Surrey), The Red Lion at 46, 49
Biffen, John 173, 203
Biggs-Davison, John 118–19, 120
Bishop, Johnnie 48
Blackpool Conferences 186–7, 244
Blades, Edward 212, 229
BOAC
    NT joins 38, 44
    navigation training 45
    dismissal threatened 51
    Technical Liaison Committee with BALPA
      54, 60
    trans-Pacific services 56
    promotion prospects – and strikes 66–7
    command course 86–7
    severance and pension 92, 93–4
    and private-sector airlines 104
Boardman, Tom 130
Botnar, Mr (Nissan-Datsun in GB) 174–5
Boundary Commission for England 75–6, 118
Boyd-Carpenter, John 122
Boyle, Edward 98
Boyson, Dr Rhodes 74
Brighton bomb 226–33
British Aerospace
    flotation 176–7, 237
    A320 Airbus 212, 215–16, 218
British Airways
    denationalisation 165, 167, 177
    appointing Chairman 168
    takeover plans 215
    flotation 236–7
British Broadcasting Corporation
    relationship post-Falklands 196
    '83 election 206
    Libyan bombing coverage 249, 255–7
    libel issues 255
    sub-titles for PPBs 260
    '87 election results 265–6
British Caledonian Airways 215
British European airways and women pilots 108
British Leyland (BL) 176, 200, 214. 216, 219
    Honda 174, 240
    and General Motor Corporation 248–9
British Rail 123
British Shipbuilders 214, 216, 222
British Steel (Corporation) 177–8, 179, 214, 218, 222
British Telecom 213–14, 216, 221, 232
Brittan, Leon 173, 222, 248
Britto, Keith 203, 260
Brooke, Peter 266
Brown, Eric, Captain (BOAC) 87
Brown, George 71

Brown, Ron 107
Browne, 'Buster' 48
Bryant, Bill (NFBTE) 158
budgets
    '70 101; '72 122; '75 138; '77–8 156; '81 180;
      '83 201
building industry 138
Bull, Mike 46
Bush Hill Park elementary school 8
Butler, 'Rab' 169–70
by-elections *see* elections, by-
Byrne, Flt Lt (RAF S. Cerney) 25–6

Cabinet
    NT appointed 181
    NT puts employment reform proposals
      187–8
    Falklands crisis 194, 195
    '83 election 201–2, 203, 204
    heavy workload 252
Callaghan, James
    Boundary Commission and Redcliffe-Maud
      75–6, 81
    mentioned 130, 151, 162, 205
    NT and 154–6
    'no autumn election' (1977) 158
Cardiff, wartime evacuation to 6–7
Carlisle, Mark 181
Carr, Robert 109–10
Carrington, Peter 194
Carsberg, Professor 219
Castle, Barbara 138
Cathay Pacific airline 169
Chamberlain, Neville 5
Chancellor of the Duchy of Lancaster, NT
    appointed 241
Channon, Paul 115, 229, 248
Chapple, Frank 193, 200
Chequers, Christmas at, post-bomb 234, 235
Chingford
    council house sales 97–8
    NT selected for 119–20
    re-elected 133, 138, 163, 205, 265
Church of England 267
Churchill, Winston (Sir Winston's grandson)
    115, 229
Cirencester, Black Horse Inn 23
City, the, new regulatory structure for 213, 237
Civil Aviation Bill *see under* aviation politics
Clark, Alan 206
Clark, Robin Chichester 108, 121–2, 131
closed shop 185–6, 190
coal industry
    '72 strike and Wilberforce settlement 117–
      18

coal industry—*cont*
  NUM and Heath/Gormley deal 130
  '74 strike, NUM and Foot settlement 131,
    132, 136
  '84 strike 221, 222, 238–9
Cockfield, Arthur 200–1
Cole, John 226
Community Programme (adult long-term
    unemployed) 191
Companies Registration Office 220
Concorde project 102–3
Confederation of British Industries (CBI) 110,
    122, 126, 133, 189–90
Confederation of Conservative Students 257
Conservative Party
  '70 Conference (E. Heath) 101–2
  reaching working-class supporters 136
  choice of leader 139–42
  chairmanship 180–1
  '82 Blackpool Conference 186–7
  chairmanship post-Parkinson 209
  '83 conference 210
  '84 Brighton Conference 225
  NT becomes Chairman 241
  NT at Central Office 242–4, 246–7, 250–5,
    257–66
  '85 Blackpool conference 244
  Confederation of Con. Students 257
Conservative Party Research Department 94–5
Conservative Trades Unionist Conference ('75),
    M Thatcher's speech at 142
constituencies
  boundaries 75–6, 118–19
  'critical seats' campaign 243–4
container-blocking dispute 122
Cooke, Robin 95–6
council house sales 97–8, 111
Craig, Wendy 28
Cree, Jimmy 62
'critical seats' campaign 243–4
Cropper, Peter 201
Cuba 58, 59
Cunningham, George 160
Cunningham, Grp Capt. John 'Cat's Eyes' 33

Daily Express, '83 industrial relations 207
Dalyell, Tam 160
Darlington by-election ('83) 201
Darrell, Jeanette 164, 166
Davies, John 101, 112
Davies, Pam 245
Davignon, Stevie 179
Dawson's Field affair (hijack) 99
Day, Graham 214
Deadman, 'Corpus' (BOAC captain) 49, 50

defence 80, 83
  Labour Party split 205
Dempster, Derek 34
denationalisation *see* privatisation
Denning, Lord 123
  Laker Skytrain case 167
Department of Employment, NT at 182–93
Department of the Environment 106
Department of Industry, NT Minister of State
    173–80
Department of Trade and Industry
  Heath government 106
  NT appointed ('83) 211
Department of Trade, NT at 164–72
Desborough, John 257
Devlin, Bernadette 99, 117
devolution of Wales and Scotland 138
Devon, NT and M's home in 221, 223, 225, 245
Deytrich, Andrew 33, 34
Digital Equipment Limited, NT joins 138, 158–
    9
direct mail campaigning 247
'dirty jobs' dispute 101, 102
Disraeli lecture, annual 246
Dobbs, Michael 199, 213, 246, 258
dockers dispute 101, 122–3
Donaldson, Sir John 122–3, 137
Douglas DC10 airliner grounded 172
Du Cann, Edward 140
Duffy, Terry 181–2, 193
Duncan, Bill 214

Eagle Star (insurance company) 214
economy
  post-war restrictions 13
  problems of immigration 54
  '68 Islington speech 70–1
  '70 manifesto 94
  Labour government's record 155–6
  see also employment; industrial relations;
    inflation; prices and incomes policies
Edmonton County Grammar School 4, 8–9, 10,
    12
Edmonton (N. London), childhood homes in
    2–3
Edwardes, Michael 174, 224
Egan, John 176
elections, by- 156, 201
  '73 129; '74 138; '86 249; '87 259
elections, general
  '45 11; '55 47; '64 94; '70 87–90, 91, 94;
  '74 (*Feb*) 131–4; '74 (*Oct*) 138–9; '79 163;
  '83 199, 200, 201, 202–4, 205; '87 253–5,
    258–66

elections, local
'72 124, 129; '83 200, 202, 203; '86 249;
'87 260–1
Ellison, Ian 174
employment
cheap labour and Macmillan government
54
skilled labour 79
Heath government 117
Labour government 156
unemployment rising 180, 183
training 183
'82 Employment Act 184–5, 186–7
'Lay off' 187, 188
Community Programmes/YTS 191
'claiming while working' 191–2
'paint the gates' 199
downturn in unemployment 208
see also economy; industrial relations;
inflation; prices and incomes policies
Enterprise Allowance Scheme 201
Epping
adoption and election 76–83, 83–4, 84–90
constituency boundary 118
Essex County Education Authority 93
European Economic Community 80
Heath government 94, 106, 117
Council of Ministers 168–9, 178–9, 209
Commission 178, 218
Evans, Moss (TGWU) 182, 188
Ewing, Bob 20, 23, 26
Eyre, Reginald 164

Fair Wages Resolution (1946) 192
Falklands War 193–6
Farley, Fl. Off. (RAF Middleton St George) 27
Ferrybridge Six affair 151–2
film industry 165–6
Finance Bills 204
financial services industry 233
Financial Times
NT works for 13–15
further job prospects 30–1
Finlay, Graeme 77
Fisher, Nigel 139, 140
fishing industry 171–2
Foot, Michael 136, 151–2, 196, 205
Ford UK 216
foreign policy 80
Rhodesia 123
Falklands 194–5
Fowler, Norman 191, 192, 193
Franklin, Olga (*Daily Mail*) 100
Fraser, Hugh 142
Freud, Clement 129

FT indices, NT's work on 13–14

Galpern, Meyer 104, 150
Gandhi, Mrs Indira 217
Gandhi, Rajiv 217
Gardiner, George 144
Gardiner, Lord 122
Garner, Sir Anthony 244
Gatwick airport 109, 169, 170
GEC 241
General Aviation Services Ltd at Heathrow
116–17
general elections *see* elections, general
General Motor Corporation and BL 220, 248–
9
Gilmour, Ian 181
GKN merge with BSC 179
Gormley, Joe 130
Government costs 220
Gow, Ian 144, 175, 199, 202, 203
Granville, Keith 93
Gray-Fisk, Miss 108
Greater London Council 204, 239
council house sales 97
Grunwick strike 152–3
Guardian, H. Young's article in 258–9
Gummer, John 206, 209

Haggett, Stanley 116–17
Hall, Joan 141
Halton, RAF, NT's convalescence at 235
Hamilton, Neil 255
Hammond, Eric 190
Harlow new town 84–5, 88, 95, 97
Haseler, Stephen 268
Haslam, Bob 214, 223
Hastings, Stephen 140
Havers, Michael 236
Hayes, Sir Brian 211, 212
Hayling Island, family rent house 124
Healey, Brian 127
Healey, Denis 137, 138
Heath, Edward
mentioned 54, 83, 140
'70 victory 94–5
Europe 94, 106, 117
'70 Conference 101
Scamp settlement 102
relinquishing Selsdon 105–6
U-turning 110
and miners 117–18
unemployment and N. Ireland troubles 117
industrial relations 122–3, 125
Ugandan Asians 125
talks with TUC and CBI/pay freeze 126

Heath, Edward—*cont*
  prices and incomes policies 128, 129
  Joe Gormley and miners' strike 130, 131
  election campaign and defeat (Feb '74) 133–4
  leadership election 141–2
  visits NT in hospital 232
Heffer, Eric 104
Hemel Hempstead Conservative Association 68
Hemel Hempstead, NT and M take flat 51
Herts and Essex Flying Club 39
Heseltine, Michael 141, 238, 247–8
hijacking 99–100, 112, 124, 128
Hoare Govett 177
Hoare, Joe 34
Hogg, Quinton 88
Hoggart, Simon (*Observer*), Cecil Parkinson 210
Holbrow, Alan 19, 28
home ownership 97–8
Honda (corporation) 240
Hong Kong 169
Honolulu, NT posted to 57
Hornchurch, RAF, aircrew selection at 17
House of Commons, NT in
  introduction 95
  maiden speech 103, 104
  debating 110–13, 116
  Heath freeze 126
  asking questions 143
  in Opposition 148, 149–51, 160–2
  v. Tom Swain 150
  industrial reform 188, 189, 190
  return after Brighton 236–7
  disorderly debates 245
House of Fraser affair 237–8
housing 79–80, 86, 95, 97–8, 111–12, 114
Housing Committee (House of Commons)
  Secretaryship 95–6
  Vice-Chairmanship 114
Howarth, Gerald 255
Howe, Geoffrey 105, 140, 200, 201, 202, 250
  '81 budget 180
  '83 budget 201
Howell, David 201
Hussein, King of Jordan 100
Hussey, Marmaduke ('Duke') 256
Hutchings, Roy and Sally 54, 58, 64, 236

Ibbs, Robin 240
immigration 54, 79, 82–3, 124–5, 137
incomes policies *see* prices and incomes policies
India visit ('84) 217
Industrial Development Executive created 122

industrial relations
  need for reform 79
  Heath government problems 117
  Heath government seeks wages/prices policy 122–3
  IR Act 123, 125, 137, 152
  improvements 193
  '83 Green paper 197–9, 201, 207
  'minefield' passed 210
  see also economy; employment; inflation; prices and incomes policies; trade unions
industrial training 183, 184, 188, 189
inflation 118, 129, 132, 156, 180, 193, 202, 206
  Denis Healey's calculations ('75) 138
  see also economy; employment; industrial relations; prices and incomes policies; trade unions
Ingham, Bernard 250
Inmos 220, 222
Inner London Education Authority 73–4, 268
Inside the Treasury (Joel Barnett) 158
International Marine Consultative Organisation (IMCO) 170
International Monetary Fund (IMF) 155–6
IRA 180
Irwin, Potter 32
Isle of Ely by-election ('73) 129
Islington, NT and M in 73, 92–3
Islington, South West, prospective candidature 69–75

Jaguar (motor manufacturers) 176, 217, 219, 222
Japanese companies in Great Britain 174–5, 218, 240
Jellicoe, Lord 88
Jenkin, Patrick 201
Jenkins, Clive 98
Jenkins, Roy 103
jobs *see* employment
Johnson, Frank 104, 189, 225
Jones, Jack 123
Jones, Pauline 109
Jones-Aldington report 123
Jopling, Michael 175, 203
Joseph, Keith 140, 153, 154, 184, 201
  at Department of Industry 173–79 *passim*
  TVEI 192–3

Keays, Sara 205, 208, 210
Kennedy, John (US President) 58–9
Keys, Bill (SOGAT) 188–9, 209
Keyser Ullmann and E. Du Cann 140
Khaled, Leila, affair 99, 100–1

King, John 168
King, Tom 211
Kinnock, Neil 209, 245, 252
Kirkpatrick, Chester 62
Kleinwort Benson 177
Knight, Sir Leslie 177

Labour Party
    NT's views on socialism 72, 82
    Housing finance bill 114, 115
    unemployment 117
    left-right splits ('72) 125
    local elections ('72) 129
    '74 election 133
    Wilson government 136–39
    Callaghan government 151, 154–8, 159–163
    union domination 197–8
    '83 election 203, 205
    disorderly debates 245
    BL/General Motors 248–9
    CP views of '87 campaign 252–4, 263
    complaints re BBC 255
labour see employment
Lake, Norman 68
Laker, Freddie 167–8
Laker Skytrain case 167–8
Lambsdorff, Count Otto 178–9
Land Rover/Ranger Rover 248–9
Lansley, Andrew 212, 229, 241
Latrobe, Lyn 46–7
law and order 80, 99
Lawson, Nigel 68, 201, 218–19, 245, 266
'lay off' (employers' rights of dismissal) 187,
    188, 197, 207
Le Marchant, Spencer 114, 115, 162
Leeson Hall (HQ, SW Islington constituency)
    70, 74
Legge-Bourke, Sir Harry 107
Lever, Harold 137
Liberal Party
    Rochdale/Sutton and Cheam 125
    Chingford 129, 133, 134
    coalition with Heath Govt.? 134
    Lib-Lab pact 156, 157
    mentioned 203, 207
Libyan bombing, BBC and 249, 255–7
Lilley, Tom 58
Lipton, Marcus 103–4
Little Bardfield cottage 121, 127
Liverpool, government assistance for 180
Llandaff, wartime evacuation to 6–7
local elections see elections, local
Locke, George 'Gussy' 8
Lofts, Keith 33
Lonrho 238

Lowry, Pat 199, 200
Luce, Richard 195
Lygo, Ray 215

McAlpine, Alistair 225
McCarthy, Callum 212, 229, 230, 232, 234
McFadzean, Sir Frank 168
MacGregor, Ian 173
Macleod, Iain 12, 74–5, 99
Macmillan government 55, 62
Macmillan, Maurice 130
McNair Wilson, Michael 118–19, 120
McWhirter, Ross 81
Malta, R Aux AF camp in 34–5
Manchester Exchange by-election (1973) 130
Manchester International airport 170
Manpower Services Commission (MSC),
    appointing a Chairman 183–4
Maplin project (Foulness) 116, 170
Matthews, Lord (Chairman, Express
    Newspapers) 207
Maudling, Reginald 109, 117, 125
Members of Parliament, pay of 207
Mercury (telecommunications) 214, 217
mergers 214–15
Mersey Docks and Harbour Board 110
Middleton St George, RAF 26–8
Midland Cold Storage 124
Miller, Ronnie 199
Mills, Iain 189, 213, 229
Milne, Alastair (Director-General, BBC) 256–7
miners see coal industry
Moncrieff, Chris 104
Montgomery, Fergus 140
Morgan, 'Bunny' 77, 84
Morrison, Peter 206, 251
motor industry
    Nissan/Datsun 174–6, 218
    BL 200–1, 214, 216, 219
    BL/Honda 240
    BL/GMC 248–9
Mount, Freddie 201
Murray, Len 184, 188, 190, 193, 206, 209

National Coal Board (NCB) see coal industry
National Economic Development Council
    (NEDC, 'Neddy') 193
National Enterprise Board 177
National Federation of Building Trades
    Employers, NT joins 158–9
National Health Service (NHS) 246
    disputes (1975) 137–8
National Industrial Relations Court 122–3
National Union of Mineworkers (NUM) see
    coal industry

National Union of Public Employees (NUPE) 102

nationalisation, Labour plans for 137, 138; *see also* privatisation

NATSOPA, NT joins 15

Neave, Airey 140, 141

Newell, John 81, 84, 89

Newens, Stan 78, 85, 87, 89, 90

Newham by-election (1974) 138

Newman, Stuart 243–4

Newton, Tony 193

Next Move Forward, The (theme for '86 conference) 251–2

92 Group (House of Commons) 96–7

Nissan in Great Britain 174–5, 218

Nixon, Gordon 83, 84

North Weald, RAF 35

Northern Ireland 117, 119, 122, 123–4

Nott, John 141, 164, 165, 169, 173, 195, 199

O'Brien, Sir Richard 183–4

Office of Fair Trading 213

Official Secrets Act 175

O'Flyn, Padraig 169

opinion polls 250
  CP surveys ('86) 251–2

Oppenheim, Sally 150, 164

Orgreave coke works picketing 222

Orme, Stan 175–6

Osborne, Miss 181

Ottaway, Bill 119, 139

Owen, David 180, 232

Padgate, RAF 16–17, 17–18

Paget, Reggie 92

Palmer, Arthur 107

Pardoe, John 151

Parker, Lord, security forces interrogation 122

Parkinson, Cecil
  mentioned 63, 68, 73, 92, 164, 242, 247, 255
  NT supports for Party chairmanship 181
  Falklands Cabinet 195–6
  '83 election campaign 199, 200, 201, 202, 203, 204–5
  Sara Keays 205, 208–9, 210–11
  DTI 206, 210–11
  NT's 'grand strategy' 207–8

party political broadcasts 243, 246

Patmore, Alec 49

Pattie, Geoffrey 233

pay policies *see* prices and incomes policies

Payne, Norman 170

Pearce, Andrew 81

Pearce, Austin 216

Pearce, Jack 12

Pearce Commission on Rhodesia 123

pensions, pensioners 79, 138

permissive society 80, 246

Perry Oaks sludge works 169

Peyton, John 121

Philip, Prince, Duke of Edinburgh 232

Phillips, Jimmy 34

Picken, John 31

Picton, Ian 187

Pike, Frank 74

Plessey 241

Pliatzky, Leo 165–6

police forces and picketing 222, 239

police protection officers (Thames Valley) 236

political levies 197–8, 207

pollution from supertankers 171, 172

Ponders End, childhood home at 1, 2, 7

Ponsford, Ian 34

population policy 107

Post Office Engineering Union 217

Potten End (Herts.), NT and M at 58

Powell, Enoch 74–5, 103, 126, 133, 143

press
  resignation stories re NT 250
  see also Daily Express; Guardian; Sun; Times

Prestwick, NT on flying course 86–7

Prices and Incomes Board abolished 102

prices and incomes policies
  mentioned 94
  Heath government 122, 126, 128, 129–30, 132
  Pay Board pay relativities and coal strike 136
  Wilson government 137
  Callaghan government 156–7
  Labour government sanctions against employers 160–2
  Price Commission 165
  economists call for 180
  see also economy; employment; industrial relations; inflation

Prior, James 152, 153, 154, 181, 183

privatisation
  mentioned 94
  British Airways 165, 167, 168, 177, 215
  Allied Steel and Wire 179
  British Telecom 213–14, 216–17, 221
  British Shipbuilders 216, 222
  Jaguar 217, 219, 222
  British Leyland 219
  NCB slip 221

Protection of Wages Bill, Green Paper 200

Pym, Francis 128, 173, 195

questions, asking, in House of Commons 143

Radical Society founded 268
Radice, Giles 207
RAF, national service in 16–30
Rawlinson, Sir Anthony 212, 233
RB211 jet engine 103
Reece, Gordon 199, 257
Reed, Brian 23
Rees, Peter 144, 219
regional policies (aid for trade and industry)
    214, 217
Rhodesian independence 123
Richards, Dick 19, 23, 26
Ridley, Adam 201
Ridley, Nicholas 105, 211
riots, rioting 180, 187
Rodgers, William 180
Rolls-Royce 102, 103
    V2500 engine 212, 216, 218
Roskill Report 108–9
Ross, Bob (Flt Lt) 20, 21, 22, 24
Ross, William 131
Rost, Peter 63
Routledge, Paul (*The Times*)
    industrial reform White Paper 188
    '83 Green Paper 198
Rowlands, 'Tiny' 237
Royal Air Force, national service in 16–30
Royal Auxiliary Air Force, 604
    Squadron 33–8, 40–3
Royal National Orthopaedic Hospital
    (Stanmore) 241
Rudwick, Miss (NT's history teacher) 9
Russell, Tom 34, 53

Saatchi & Saatchi 246, 250, 251, 255
St John Stevas, Norman 108, 173
Saltley coke-works 118
Sandelson, Neville 269
Savile, Jimmy 232
Scamp, Sir Jack 102
Scargill, Arthur 188, 190, 201, 222, 238
Scarman (Lord) Report 153
Scholey, Bob 222
Science and Technology, Select Committee on
    106–8
secretariat in government departments 213
Select Committees 106–8, 223
Sells, David 87
Selsdon 94, 105–6
Shah, Eddie 217
Shelton, Bill 140, 141
Sherbourne, Stephen 266
shipbuilding industry 214, 216

shipping 170–2
Shore, Peter 167, 220
Shrimsley, Tony 203
Sibald, Alan 65
Silk, Robert 31
Simpson, Crawford 20
Smith, Cyril 190
Smith, John 232
Soames, Christopher 140, 181
Social Contract (Harold Wilson) 137
Social Democratic Party (SDP) 180, 253, 259
social services, changing perceptions of, CP's
    attitude to 246–7
socialism *see under* Labour Party
Soper, Lord 99, 109
South Cerney, RAF (Glos.) 20–6
space, developments in 107–8
speeches
    '68 Islington South West 70–2
    '69 Epping 78–81, 82–3
    law and order 99
    Upper Clyde Shipbuilders and Tony Benn
        112
    aircraft noise 116
    '74 (Feb) election 132
    for M. Thatcher 142
    '75 Chingford anti-democratic forces, and
        'union-bashing' 153–4
    'on his bike' 186
    'party of trades unionists' 210
    '84 privatisation 221
Srivastava, Chandrika Prasad (Secretary
    General, IMCO) 170
Stacey, Admiral 170–1
Stagg, Sam (NT's grandfather) 2
Stainton, Ross 168
Stanmore, Royal National Orthopaedic
    Hospital at 241
Stansted airport 108, 169, 170
Staton, Bob 34
Steel, David 156, 157
steel industry 177–9, 214, 221, 238
Sterling, Jeffrey 213
Stock Exchange 213, 237
Stoke Mandeville hospital 230–2
Stradishall, RAF 29–30
strikes
    Heath government 102
    '72 miners 117–18
    Grunwick 152–3
    '79 Labour government 160–1
    '80 steel industry 177–8
    'political' 185–6
    '82 NHS, and private sector 193
    water industry 198–9, 200

strikes—*cont*
  criminal law 204
  '84 miners 221, 222, 238–9
  dockers 238
  teachers 239
Stuttaford, Tom, 121
Suez war 50–1
Sullom Voe (Shetland) 172
Sun, The, Sara Keays 210–11
Sunday Trading Bill 249
Sunningdale, NT and M take flat in 49, 51
supertankers and pollution 171, 172
Sutton, Bob 52–3, 65
Sutton, Pat 52
Swain, Ivor 119
Swain, Tom 118, 150
Sylvester, Fred 119
Sylvester, Michael 119
Szemery, John 92

take-over bids 214–15
Taverne, Dick 129
taxation 79
Tebbit, Alfred (uncle) 3
Tebbit, Alison (daughter) 74, 93, 120, 127, 135, 202
Tebbit, Arthur (brother) 3, 4, 5, 8, 16, 38, 39, 46
Tebbit, Arthur (uncle) 1–2, 7, 8
Tebitt, Edith (mother) 2, 3, 4, 16
Tebitt, John (son) 74, 89, 91, 92, 93, 120, 127, 135, 202
  engagement and wedding 217, 222
Tebbit, Leonard (father) 1, 2, 3, 7, 12, 16
Tebbit, Margaret
  marriage 48–9
  Hemel Hempstead/John born 52
  house at Berkhamsted 53
  and NT's BALPA commitments 54
  Alison born 54–5
  William born/illness 64
  Islington and Epping 69, 70, 73, 81–91
    passim
  part-time nursing 127
  '74 election, and illnesses 133, 135, 138, 139
  parents' death and sale of 'Gridiron' 158
  hospital and recovery 159
  press harassment 199
  plans move to West Country 201, 208
  grandparent/visit to India 217
  Brighton bomb 226–8, 229, 230
  Stoke Mandeville and Stanmore 230–1, 232, 234, 240
  Lord Mayor's Banquet 245
  home again 251, 258

Tebbit, Norman
  home, family, business
  childhood 1–5, 7–8
  wartime evacuee 5–7
  school 8–9
  wartime impressions 9, 10–11
  jobs in youth 10, 12, 13–15
  job-hunting 30–1, 31–2
  Margaret Daines and marriage 48–9
  early married life 51–3, 54–5, 58
  Honolulu 57–8
  William born/M's illness 64–5
  Islington 73–4
  Epping 92–3, 102
  Barbados 113
  London – and Little Bardfield 120–1, 127, 138, 158
  business 127, 138, 158–9
  M's illness and recovery 159
  grandparent/Devon home 217, 221, 223
  Brighton and after 226–32
  Portugal with M. 241
  national service (RAF)
  basic training 16–20
  flying 20–2, 24–6, 26–8, 29–30
  mess life 23–4
  Royal Auxiliary Air Force 33–7, 39–43
  BOAC
  joins 38, 40, 44–5
  navigator 45–6
  Tokyo run, and notice of dismissal 49–51
  Britannia co-pilot 53, 54
  BALPA 54, 58, 60–62, 66
  converting to Boeing 55, 65–6
  Honolulu posting 57
  promotion prospects 66–7
  transatlantic crossings 78
  command course 86–7
  farewell 92, 93–4
  political career
  youth 10, 11–12
  NATSOPA membership 15
  Home Counties North YC 46–7
  Macmillan, Kennedy era 54, 58–9
  CP and advice from Peter Walker 63
  prospects of candidature 68–9
  Islington – and principles 69–73, 74–5, 76
  Epping 76–86, 87–90, 91
  housing 95–8, 110–12
  hijacks and terrorism 99–101, 112
  industrial relations 101–2, 110, 112
  maiden speech 103–5
  RB211 103

select committees 106–8, 223
airports 108–9, 116–17
BEA sex discrimination 108
Pauline Jones 109
V-chairman of Housing Committee
    114–16
Chingford 118–20
PPS to Robin Chichester-Clark 121–2
misgivings re Heath administration
    122–7, 128–30
resignation as PPS 131
'74 Feb election 132–4
in Opposition 135–8, 142–58, 159–63
'74 re-election at Chingford 138
making M Thatcher leader 139–42
'79 re-election at Chingford 162–3
Department of Trade 164–72
Department of Industry 173–9
joins Cabinet 181–3
shaping Employment Act 184–94
Falklands 194–6
'83 Green Paper/union reform 197–9,
    201, 207–8
'83 election 199, 200, 201–4, 205–6
C Parkinson/S Keays 204–5, 208–9, 210–
    11
DTI 211, 212–23
India with M. 217
USA 217, 222
Brighton bomb and convalescence 226–
    32
keeps in touch 232–3, 235, 236
Chequers Christmas 234, 235
back in the House 236–40
Party Chairman 241–50, 257
BBC concerns 249, 255–7, 260, 266
'86–7 campaigns 250–5, 258, 260–5
stepping down 261, 265, 266–8
Chingford again 265
Tebbit, Peter (brother) 3, 10
Tebbit, Sydney (uncle) 3, 4
Tebbit, William (son) 73, 93, 120, 127, 138, 206,
    208, 210–11, 223
'Tebbits Law' 184–90
Technical and Vocational Educational
    Initiative, (TVEI) 192, 207
Temple-Morris, Peter 76, 77
terrorism 100–1, 119, 254
Thatcher, Denis 142
Thatcher, Margaret
    methods compared with E. Heath 106
    party leader 139, 140, 141–2
    British Leyland 176
    '83 election 200, 202–4
    '83 Cabinet appointments 206

Cecil Parkinson 208–9
    a move for NT? 223–4
    Brighton bomb 228, 229, 232, 234
    parrying criticism of 242–3
    NT resignation stories 250
    '87 campaign 254, 262, 265
    H. Young/Guardian 258–9
    NT standing down 261, 265, 266
Thomas, Harvey 257
Thompson, Adam 104
Thompson, Ruth 212, 229
Thomson, Adam (British Caledonian Airways)
    215
Thorn EMI 220
Thorpe, Jeremy 157
Times, The
    industrial law reform 187, 188
    '83 Green Paper 198
    Sara Keays 210
    NT 'soggy?' 220
    '85 'Send for Mr Tebbit' 239
    NT at the DTI 240
    NT and BBC 256
Tokyo run (BOAC) 49–50
Toy, Sam 216
trade unions
    reform 94
    Heath government 129
    Conservative TU Congress 142
    Ferrybridge Six affair 151–2
    Grunwick strike 152–3
    Callaghan government 159–62
    power of leaders 183
    closed shop 184–6, 189–90
    industrial training boards 188
    '83 reform measures 197–9, 201, 206
    Truck Acts 199–200
    see also economy; employment; industrial
        relations; Trades Union Congress
    'trades disputes' 185
Trades Union Congress (TUC)
    mentioned 101, 125
    Heath government 105, 110, 122
    industrial training boards 188
    Wilson government 137
    industrial reform bill 188–9, 190
    YTS 189
    political levies 204, 207
    talks with NT re '83 legislation 208, 209
    see also trade unions
Trafford, Tony 229, 230
training in industry 183, 184, 188, 189
Truck Acts 199, 208
Turnbull, Tom, 34
Turner, Colin 11, 31–2, 37

Ugandan Asians, immigration of 124–5
Ulster *see* Northern Ireland
unemployment *see under* employment
'union-bashing' 154, 186
Upper Clyde Shipbuilders 110, 112
USA
    BOAC Pacific routes 57
    Bay of Pigs 58, 59
    Vietnam war 58
    Cuban missiles crisis 59
    defence of West 80, 83
    Douglas DC10 airliner grounded 172
    NT visits ('83/'84) 217, 222
    General Motors and BL 248–9
    use of bases in GB in attacks on Libya 249

V-bombs on London 9
Varley, Eric 188, 190, 193
Vietnam war 58

Wakeham, John 209, 228, 229, 230, 236, 249
    '87 campaign broadcast 264
Walden, Brian 160
Walker, Peter 63, 68, 69, 97–8
Wall, Christine 257
Walters, Len 52, 91
Waltham Forest Borough Council 97–8
war, 1939–45, youthful impressions of 9, 10, 11
'War Book' (CP '87 election plan) 253–4

Ward, George (Grunwick) 152
Warren, Ken 223
water industry 198–9, 200
Watson, Stuart 30
wealth tax 138
Westland Helicopters 238, 241, 247–8
Whitelaw, William 124, 130, 142, 150, 160, 203, 251
    Chairman of 'Star Chamber' 213
Wilberforce (Lord) inquiry 118
Williams, Shirley 138, 164
Wilson, Harold 79, 87, 136, 155
Wittering, RAF, training at 18–20
'wobbly Thursday' ('87) 264–5
Wolfson, David 203
Wood, Sir Freddie 177
Woomera, fact finding at 107–8
working-class supporters of CP, reaching 136

Yates, Derek 19, 23, 25, 26, 32–3, 34
Young Conservatives
    NT joins 11–12, 15
    NT treasurer Home Counties North 46–7
Young, David 184, 191, 192, 260, 261, 262
Young, Hugo, in *Guardian* 6/1/87 258–9
Youth Training Scheme (YTS) 189, 191, 206

Zorab, Charlie 34